FLIGHT OF

THE RED BEAVER

A

YUKON ADVENTURE

BY

LARRY WHITESITT

For information or additional copies contact
your bookstore or write for an autographed copy to:

Larry L. Whitesitt
Box 887
Veradale, WA 99037-0887

Printed by Lawton Publishing Company, Spokane, WA
ISBN # 0-9629085-1-7

FORWARD

Front Cover Picture: The Red Beaver and I flying off the South Nahanni River in Deadman's Valley, Northwest Territories, September 1971. In the northern background are the mighty Mackenzie Mountains, the toughest and the most dangerous mountains I've ever flown in. I nearly lost my life while flying over a nearby ridge in bad weather, just a few miles downriver.

Back Cover Photo: The Red Beaver flying over Coal River, Yukon, returning to Watson Lake, after a flight into the fabled South Nahanni River.

This story is about my adventures as a Bush pilot in the Yukon, Northwest Territories and British Columbia, Canada, and the fulfillment of a boyhood dream.

Jim, my high school buddy and I were going to steal some horses north of Spokane, up near Colville, Wash., cross the border into Canada, build a log cabin, live off the land and become mountain men. We kept our dream alive and eventually immigrated to Canada.

Join me as I crank up the Red Beaver and fly into Deadman's Valley for the first time, meet a grizzly bear face to face, experience an airplane crash and meet these wonderful warmhearted people that live in the Bush. Meet Skook Davidson an old time packer and legend of the north as he sits on his horse drawn wagon, along the banks of the Kechika River, watching, as I unload the freight and mail off the Red Beaver, for his beloved, Diamond J Ranch, located in a vast northern wilderness.

Enjoy the flight and the magic of the Yukon.

"Happy Landings."

Larry L. Whitesitt

ACKNOWLEDGEMENTS

EDITING AND MANUSCRIPT PREPARATIONS:

Jackie McDaniel

Special thanks to the fishing and hunting outfitters and the many other warmhearted people of the north that helped to make this book become a reality.

The author is currently writing a sequel called
"Flight of Dreams"
a
Journey thru time

and a novel called "Yukon Bush Pilot."

TABLE OF CONTENTS

Prologue 1

1. Cabin On The Kispiox. 3

2. Flying Adventures in British Columbia 25

3. Learning To Fly Floatplanes! 41

4. Winter Flying On Skis 49

5. Fort Babine 55

6. Adventures In The Yukon 63

7. Water Bombing With The Beaver 83

8. Jim and Stan—Watson Lake Flying Service 93

9. Alligators To Grizzly Bears 105

10. Deadman's Valley 111

11. Wrangling Horses On The Nahanni With Scott 123

12. Almost Lake 135

13. Howards Pass White Knuckle Strip 151

14. The Yukon Season Ends 163

15. Return To The Yukon 193

16. Flight To The Arctic 215

17. Tuktoyaktuk 235

18. Old Crow 249

19. Yukon Skies 261

20. Spirits Of Telegraph Creek 278

Epilogue 289

TO MY SON SCOTT

Who shared many adventurous flights into the wilderness as my co-pilot, and some close calls. You were a cheerful uncomplaining companion in the air and on the trail and the joy of my life since the day you were born.

PROLOGUE

The lonely, haunting cry of a loon drifts through the night. It's been a long day and I'm tired as I step outside the cabin and gaze across the lake before going to sleep. The night that follows is too short, but the early fall morning is brisk and helps clear my head.

As I walk toward the dock, my favorite airplane, CF-IBP, a de Havilland Beaver, rocks gently on the lake like a giant red bird. After thousands of miles together over some of the most rugged and remote areas of North America without mishap, I have a special fondness for her and trust her with my life. We received a call from the Forest Service at Fort Liard in the Northwest Territories requesting the Beaver to fly men and freight into Headless Valley to fight a forest fire. Normally these remote fires are left to burn because of limited resources; however, they want to put this fire out as quickly as possible because it's in the proposed Nahanni National Park area.

It's a beautiful morning as I top the tanks, pump the floats, and do a thorough preflight check. Casting off into deeper water I prime the engine, turn the switches on and engage the starter; the engine coughs, sputters and catches, belching blue smoke, and then smoothes out to a steady roar. As I taxi to the south end of the lake, a couple of loons swim rapidly to one side, giving us a large berth.

The loon is a magnificent large black and white bird that comes early to Watson Lake here in the Yukon Territory. Once you've heard the lonely cry of a loon, you never forget. The loon and the far northern lakes blend together and are a part of each other. They like to be left alone and usually stay away from humans. The loons are my favorite birds, with Canada Geese a close second.

After warming up the engine until the oil temperature gauge indicates 40°C, I go thru my checklist, controls, instruments, gas, flaps, trim, prop and the runnup. As I turn into the wind I lift the water rudders and while holding the elevator control column hard back I push the throttle wide open. The powerful 9 cylinder radial engine deafens my world with a mighty roar, in a friendly, familiar, sort of way and the massive propeller pulls us quickly to the surface. Releasing the elevator back pressure we accelerate rapidly on the step in the cool thick morning air and within a few seconds fly off the water at an airspeed of about 55 mph. Once again I enter another world, in the clear blue, Yukon Sky. Reaching down with my right hand I grasp the hydraulic flap handle beside my seat and pump up the flaps to the climb position. Reaching forward to the top center of the panel I pull the throttle back to 30″ MP and bring back the propeller lever to 2,000 RPM. After trimming the airplane we make a lazy left climbing turn to our southerly heading at an airspeed of 95 mph.

PROLOGUE

After a flight to Scoop Lake in northern British Columbia, we head on a northeasterly course, crossing the Hyland River near Blind Lake. This is a new adventure for me as it's my first flight into Headless Valley, or as it's called on my Sectional Chart, Deadman's Valley. As a boy growing up in Spokane, Washington, I read an article called "Headless Valley" about today's destination. The story was about the McLeod brothers. Willie McLeod set off in 1905 for a gold prespecting trip to the South Nahanni River, taking his brother Frank and an engineer. On a previous trip, Willie had lost a large amount of gold when his canoe tipped over; he managed to save only a few ounces.

The party disappeared up the Nahanni, and after a year Charlie McLeod started a search for his brothers. He found their bones in a camp where Prairie Creek enters the South Nahanni River. It looked as if one brother was trying to reach a gun, and the other was killed in his bedding. The murderer took the gold and was never found, according to the story. The article went on to say the Indians avoided that place and that the wind blowing down the valley made an unearthly sound.

Charlie's son said at a later date that the bodies of his uncles were without their heads. Well, whatever happened, the valley is marked on my sectional map as Deadman's Valley and is also known as Headless Valley. Looking at my sectional chart, I notice that it's distinctly marked with black dots, giving it a dark appearance on the map. The mountains rising out of the valley to the west are called the Funeral Range--sounds like a desolate place, perhaps a place to stay away from.

The air is smooth, the 450 horsepower Pratt & Whitney radial engine roars reassuringly, and I trim the airplane level at about 7500 feet. There isn't a road or any sign of man as we head across the eastern part of the Yukon, and we'll soon be crossing into the Northwest Territories. It is a time for reflection as I marvel at the Creator's handiwork from this vantage point. We're a tiny speck in this vast expanse of sky and earth. After many long years of preparations, my dreams have been fullfilled. I'm finally doing exactly what I want to do--flying an airplane in the Yukon for a living. Each flight is a new and different adventure, the sky is constantly changing, and no two flights are alike.

Looking back to my early years, I recall my fascination with the North Country, Sergeant Preston of the Northwest Mounted Police and his dog King, stories by Jack London like *The Call of the Wild*, Dawson City and the Klondike. I remember when one of the cereal companies offered to sell you a square inch of land in the Yukon by Dawson City, and you could actually get a deed. These stories on the radio inspired many hours of creative daydreaming with me in the starring role in adventures in the Far North. As I so often do on these long flights, I think of the past that has brought me here, to the far north, and relive those years.

CHAPTER I
CABIN ON THE KISPIOX

Fighters streaking across the clear summer skies, their powerful engines deafening my world, caused me to look up in boyhood wonder as they passed overhead and quickly disappeared north of town.

My fascination with airplanes began during the war years, when I was only a few years old. The first toy I can remember playing with was a small metal airplane. My first flying model was a German Stuka divebomber, constructed of a light balsawood frame covered with paper and many coats of airplane dope and powered by a rubber-band-driven wooden propeller.

I often walked alone down a small hill just south of my grandfather's home to the nearby railroad tracks and watched in boyhood curiosity as the troop trains slowly rolled by. Servicemen waved and threw coins at my feet just before crossing the nearby trestle that spanned the Spokane River, as they headed west to fight in the Pacific war.

Across the river on another set of tracks, long freight trains laden with large cannons, jeeps, trucks, and tanks passed by in a seemingly endless line as they carried the instruments of war to the west coast ports. DC-3s, the new twin-engine airplanes, criss-crossed the skies overhead.

The river was a forbidden place, but I managed on several occasions to slip away alone and play on the banks of the fascinating waterway. A cable stretched across the river, and a large scoop shovel connected to the cable dipped into the river to scoop rocks off the river bottom and deposit them in a rock crusher. Many boyhood hours were spent watching this intriguing operation, just across the street west of my grandfather's house.

One day there was a great sadness; adults were crying. "President Roosevelt has died," I was told. Several months later there was a great rejoicing, and horns began honking all over town, celebrating the end of World War II.

The happiest and best times I remember as a boy were the summers I spent at my grandfather's cabin in northern Idaho on beautiful Lake Coeur d'Alene. For me the cabin, built shortly after the war ended, was an escape from the civilized world as I knew it, namely boring school and pesky adults always trying to tell me what to do and when to do it.

Grandfather wasn't like most adults. Born in Sweden in the late 1800's, William C. Rydblom was a tall, handsome man who drew his share of friendly looks from the ladies. Better yet, he was my pal and best friend and let me have the freedom to develop and be myself in that outdoor environment. He bought me a canvas-covered duckboat, powered by an old three-horsepower Johnson outboard, which gave me the freedom to explore the lake on my own. Trolling for cutthroat trout with my grandfather, exploring the surrounding forests with his dog Butch, and swimming in the lake, I developed a deep love and appreciation for nature.

One of my favorite places was a secret marsh across the lake south of Harrison, where I caught large bullfrogs. They were delicious; of course, you had to pull out the cords in their legs or they would start jumping around in the frying pan.

The summer following my freshman year in high school, several of us boys, all classmates, and our coach, whom we fondly called "Chops," and his wife drove from Spokane to Olympic National Park on the Washington coast. My best friend Jim Goerz and I camped together and were usually far ahead of the rest as we backpacked deep into the old growth rain forest, hiking into Enchanted Valley, where an old hunting lodge stood surrounded by waterfalls. We saw black bears and large, magnificent Roosevelt elk along the trail. We backpacked, netted smelt in the Pacific surf, dug clams, and spent time at a massive lodge overlooking the incredibly beautiful Lake Quinault; the seeds were planted that one day would take us to the far north and a different way of life.

That fall when we returned to school as sophomores, Jim and I began meeting secretly. Our guide was a book called *How to Live in the Woods on $10 a Week*, by Bradford Angier. We made plans to run away, steal some horses north of town, slip across the border into Canada, and live the lives of mountain men.

"Larry, wake up," an annoyed teacher yelled across the boring classroom as I stared out the window, watching a grand flight of Canada geese winging their way northward on a warm, lazy spring afternoon. I knew that my destiny was to go north one day and that school was a complete waste of my time and talents.

There were fun things to do outside the classroom. My job as a janitor after school enabled me to pay my tuition at this private school and buy my first car, a Model A coupe. Later I purchased my favorite, a 1941 green Chevy coupe with a good radio and heater which were necessary for those cold nights when I parked on a secluded road and learned about life with my girlfriend. Gary Johnson, a good friend, and I spent many happy week-ends skiing on nearby Mount Spokane and many hours during the week playing a variety of sports.

While I was a junior and Gary was a senior, we decided to join the U.S. Naval Reserve and voluntarily enlisted in a six-year program, with two of these years to be spent in active duty. After graduating from high school I went to boot camp at San Diego and began serving my active duty.

My only noteworthy attributes at the time were biceps measuring 16 5/8 inches. They did nothing to further my Naval career, but they provided hours of grunting and straining as another sailor and I tried to take each other's arms down in a three-day arm wrestling contest. I finally wore him down and for two weeks was the arm wrestling champ of our company and was on somewhat of an ego trip—that was, until a burly wrestler transferred in and promptly turned down my arm. I was the best rifle shot in the company; my vision was excellent and my hands steady.

Boot camp was a rather degrading form of physical and mental abuse, I thought at the time, but by the completion date our company was a close-knit team. We learned how to take orders and to work and live together in cramped quarters, things that would be necessary when we became shipmates.

Upon completion of boot camp I was assigned to the *USS Hassayampa*, AO145, a modern fleet tanker whose home port was Pearl Harbor, Hawaii. I caught a flight from California to Honolulu on a Constellation (Connie), a unique four-engine airplane with three tails. Upon arrival in Honolulu in the early morning darkness after a flight of some fourteen hours, I felt for the first time the wonderful South Pacific tropical breeze.

Hassayampa is the Indian name for a river in Arizona; the word means "upside down river," because most of it runs underground. Legend says that anyone who drinks its waters will never tell the truth again.

I walked up the gangplank of the *Hassayampa* for the first time, all my worldly possessions inside a duffle bag slung over my shoulder. I saluted the officer of the deck. "Request permission to come aboard, sir," I asked. "Permission granted," came the reply.

I borrowed a typing book from the supply department to teach myself the touch typing system and practiced until I reached the required minimum of thirty-five words per minute. Then I got a welcome transfer from the deck crew to the supply department and became a storekeeper in charge of managing the storerooms and selling clothes on payday. Being a storekeeper was probably one of the best and softest jobs aboard ship.

My good buddy Gary Johnson was stationed here on shore duty, and we often pulled liberty together. Occasionally another classmate, Gordon Smith, pulled liberty with us whenever his fleet tug came to Pearl Harbor. Gordon and I got together in Japan when our ships were in the same port.

We spent about six months operating out of Pearl Harbor in Hawaiian waters and the rest of the year patrolling the vast Pacific Ocean between Japan and the Philippine Islands. We occasionally pulled liberty in Hong Kong, and we once spent five days of R & R in New Zealand. The Philippines were always hot and sticky, but Japan was inordinately cold, as we were there in the winter. We went from one extreme to the other in a week or so. There were some beautiful girls overseas, and a lot of homesick sailors found their true loves—not once, but many times—as the waves washed away the memories of the previous port. While in the Philippines I read a book about a couple who owned their own airplane. I thought that owning a plane someday would be a worthwhile goal.

After my two-year hitch was completed, I was honorably discharged from active duty at Treasure Island, near San Francisco. I was a free man and promptly caught a bus to Spokane to visit my parents before heading north to Alaska, where I intended to live out my life. My worldly possessions consisted of a new 270 Winchester rifle, a new 12-gauge Winchester shotgun, navy clothes, pictures, and a map of Alaska.

After a short visit with my parents, I decided to meet the young lady who had written me a few letters while I was overseas. She had obtained my address from a high school girlfriend. After a thirty-minute drive to nearby Rathdrum, Idaho, I pulled into the Park Ranch. I stepped out of the car and saw a girl on horseback galloping across the meadow, her long black hair flowing in the breeze. By the time she dismounted in front of me, I was already a goner; I promptly fell in love with this young beauty, Kathryn Park, and my trek north was put on hold.

We shared a dream together of one day having a son and a log cabin in the far north. I became a logger, working at Burke, Idaho, in the summer where I set chokers on a high line off an Idaho jammer. In no time I was rid of my two years of Navy flab. I later set chokers behind a Cat north of Spokane during the winter months.

Kathryn and I were married February 18, 1959; we spent our honeymoon on Lake Coeur d'Alene at Grandpa's cabin. The following spring we camped out, working our way into Montana, where we got a job on a lookout station for the Hungry Horse Ranger District. The supervising ranger was Dick Baldwin, a super nice guy. As I gazed into the Canadian Rockies, I wondered how long it would be until we went north. Glacier Park was only a few miles north of our lookout. We spotted several fires from Desert Lookout and earned our keep that summer.

We had several encounters with black bears. One came walking up the steps to the top of the lookout around lunchtime, planning to help himself to our screened cooler just outside the door. We chased him off. Another bear and I went around and around in a circle--I had an axe, but the bear wasn't the least bit intimidated, although he finally left in disgust without getting his fill in our garbage pit.

Our son, William Scott Whitesitt, the joy of our lives, was born January 25, 1960. He gave us a twenty-five-mile race with the stork on a cold, blizzardy day in the heart of the Rocky Mountains and arrived a scant five minutes after we breathlessly arrived at the hospital. Kathy had kept pleading, "Pull over, I'm having the baby," and I had kept promising, "The hospital is just around the corner."

The following summer I began flight training at the Kalispel County Airport with Jack Archibald in his two-place fabric-covered taildragger (a plane with a tail wheel), a Taylor Craft N44286 equipped with a 65-horsepower Continental engine. We practiced stalls, emergency landings, turns, climbs, descents, landings, and take-offs for some ten hours.

Late one quiet afternoon on September 25, 1960, after we landed he said, "Stop and let me out. Take her up, Larry, and make three landings. She's all yours," and he stepped out the right side of the plane and walked away from the runway.

Full throttle without Jack's weight made a remarkable difference, and my craft responded quickly. Forward pressure on the elevator control lifted the tail wheel, and with slight back pressure on the elevators my craft quickly left the earth and climbed to the circuit altitude of one thousand feet. Looking over at the empty seat made me realize it was just the two of us, my craft and I, as we soared through the clear Montana skies in the heart of the Rockies.

Flying abreast of the end of the west runway, I cut the throttle to idle and began my descent, turning base when I was about forty-five degrees from the end of the runway and then another turn to final. Floating down in this high-lift, high-wing airplane, it soared as if I were in a glider. Rounding out above the numbers and continuing back pressure on the elevator control to the three-point landing attitude (stalling the airplane), my craft decided to float—and float for quite some distance—until it was ready to touch down. It did so very gently to a three-point landing. After two more landings I taxied back to the tiedowns, but it was quite some time before my head came out of the clouds. What could be more exciting and important than to pilot a plane alone? I made most landings in a tail dragger in the 3-point configurative (all three wheels touching at the same time); however, I occasionally made wheel landings on the main gear.

During that summer I fought forest fires and cleared trails, working again for the Hungry Horse Ranger District. Several of us backpacked eighteen miles into the Bob Marshall Wilderness Area and relieved a group of smoke jumpers who had already put a line around a fire. We worked twelve hours a day and spent about ten days on the fire. It was the dirtiest job I ever had. One day our supply plane, a twin-engine Beech 18, dropped a case of syrup by parachute. It landed in a tree above my paper sleeping bag (an experimental model), and when I finished up my twelve-hour shift that night I had one soggy mess covering my bedding.

Kathy, Scott and I left Montana in the fall of 1960 and moved to Spokane. We purchased a Piper J-3 Cub N42200, a taildragger, for nine hundred dollars when I had only fifteen hours total flying time in February, 1961. After building up additional time, I sold it for twelve hundred dollars and later obtained my private pilot license on October 10, 1961, in a Cessna 150 N6682T, which enabled me to take up passengers. Scott, Kathy and I flew the Cessna 150 to an airstrip near Radium Hot Springs in British Columbia and soaked in the hot mineral waters for a couple of days.

When Scott was two years old we manned Faucett Lookout in the Coeur d'Alene National Forest. Our perch overlooked Pend Oreille Lake. One day Scott disappeared. I called our faithful German shepherd, Smoky, and said, "Smoky, go find Scott." He cocked his head up at me for a moment, about-faced to the west, and led us in a direct line through thick brush to our son. Tears were streaming down Scott's dirty face, and, as he raised his arms, I reached down and picked him up for a mutual, grateful bear hug. The relief and joy of finding him safe was overwhelming.

That was a special summer for all of us; we lived together twenty-four hours a day and became very close. The morning after the first snowfall, deer came up to look at us through the window. That fresh snow ended our lookout days, and we boarded up the windows and headed down the mountain in our blue 1953 Chevy.

Three of us who had worked for the Forest Service bid successfully on a tree planting contract for the district. My family lived in a tent furnished with a wood stove; the other two men shared a tent nearby. We each planted about fifteen hundred trees a day until we finished the contract. The rain and sleet of late fall gave us all sore throats, but our nightly hot rums, purchased at a nearby bar in Prichard, Idaho, soothed our throats and helped us fall asleep.

We earned a good stake. Kathy, Scott, Smoky and I drove down the Oregon Coast into California. We took Scott to Knott's Berry Farm and Disneyland and then drove to Arizona and back to Spokane, where we rented a house.

All those years we kept in touch with my good friend Jim Goerz and his wife Mardella. We continued to plan and dream of going north.

In the spring of 1964, my family and I passed our physicals and were accepted as immigrants by the Canadian government. We departed Spokane with light hearts and high hopes and headed for Seattle to rendezvous with Jim and Mardella. We stopped to say goodbye to our friends Maria and Herb Bard, whose daughter had given Kathy my address in the Navy. Scott, my son, was four years old, and none of us have ever forgotten what he said: "Dad, let's hurry up or we'll be late for Canada!"

Pulling a fully loaded trailer behind our '53 Chevy, we arrived in Seattle, Washington, and met the Goerz family. Jim had a Jeep pickup and was pulling a larger, more heavily loaded trailer. We truly looked like immigrants.

We crossed the border at Blaine, Washington, and I remember kissing the ground--at last my dreams and goals of youth were at hand. I was in Canada and heading for the north to live my boyhood fantasies. The excitement built as we saw a huge, sparsely populated country with settlements getting farther and farther apart. Every bend in the road unfolded vast new forests, mountains and lakes; we saw game from the road. I was ecstatic.

We had researched the different areas and liked the Ootsa Lake country south of Burns Lake and the area west and north of there. Driving up the Frazer River canyon, we camped out in our tents along the way. We passed Hope, Lytton, Cache Creek, Clinton, 100 Mile House, Williams Lake, a ranching center with lots of cowboys, and Quesnel. At Prince George we headed west to Burns Lake, where we turned south.

When we arrived at Tchesinkut Lake, Jim's trailer broke down and required some welding. Ruth and Roy Lord's lodge was there, and they graciously invited us in for lake trout and stories; they were big game outfitters.

Omineca Air Service was down the lake a few hundred yards. I strolled over and talked to Bill Harrison, the owner, and asked what his requirements were for pilots. Bill said, "Oh, about two or three thousand hours." I had about sixty hours total at the time, but our paths would cross again in three years. I took pictures of his de Havilland Beaver landing and taking off.

We checked out the lake country and then drove through Houston and stopped at Smithers, B.C., founded by Dutch colonists. Mardella really liked this town set at the base of a glacier, and she and the children, Brent, age two, and Laury, age six, wanted to stay. Jim fixed up a farm chicken coop with some drywall, and they moved in. He eventually went to work for the railroad, and they bought a piece of land east of town where they built a comfortable log home.

Kathy, Scott and I left for Hazelton, B.C., about thirty miles away. The Bulkley River runs through this area, and the beautiful valley had a very quiet, peaceful effect on us. We were beginning to feel that our home was getting close.

We arrived in Hazelton and stayed overnight at a hotel there. We drove north, passing through Kispiox, an Indian village at the junction of the Kispiox and Skeena rivers. *Kispiox* means "place of hiding"; Indians from the Kitsan tribe came here to escape the Nass Indians, who were very warlike--the Nass would raid their villages and rape and carry away the women. The Kispiox village has one of the oldest original groups of totem poles.

Leaving Kispiox, we continued north, following the Kispiox River through a beautiful, quiet, sparsely settled valley. There were no power poles, the air was fresh, and the scenery was spectacular, with glaciers visible on Mount Thomlinson. It was a warm day, and the valley was a lush, lazy green. We saw a home, several cedar cabins, and a sign that said "Steelhead Fishing Camp" along the Kispiox. It looked like a good place for a base camp while we looked around to find a place that felt right for our new home.

Jim Walker, an Englishman, and his English schoolteacher wife were the owners and operators of this establishment. The Kispiox River produces a number of record steelhead, and a lot of Americans go there to try their luck. We soon met Marty Allen and his wife Dorothy, who owned a ranch up the valley a few miles. They were friendly and helpful, and Marty was a likable local character with a thousand stories to tell about his trap line days and days on the front lines during World War II. The coffeepot was always on, and there was always room for a few more at the dinner table. Like everyone else in the valley, they had a hand-cranked phone; few secrets were ever kept. South of Marty's we met a friendly couple, Wally and Marcella (whom we called Bunky) Love. Wally, his brother Bill, and their brother-in-law Jack Lee ran a successful guiding service near Stevens Lake for world record grizzly bear and around Tutade Lake in northern British Columbia for caribou, mountain goat, and moose.

The west side of the Kispiox was where the Wookey clan lived, and it was common knowledge that there was a Wookey behind every tree. Drew Wookey ran a competing fishing camp up the river a short distance. He had about a dozen kids and an airstrip that I would one day use. We often visited Drew and his wife to catch up on the local gossip and share a cup of coffee. They were warm, friendly people.

Farther up the river was the Campbell clan. They had a rustic ranch that reminded me of some of those places in the Catskill Hallers that I've seen depicted in *National Geographic*. They had a son, Bruce Campbell, who had a red beard and looked kind of like a mountain man. We went to visit Bruce at his place up the valley. He met us where the road ended. From there we canoed across the river and walked up a trail to his rustic, primitive cabin. His wife had fixed a sweet-smelling, plump roast that we proceeded to eat. I finally asked what kind of meat it was. "Oh, it's roast beaver," she said. Kathy and I looked at each other as we slowly finished chewing the meat.

Kathy, because of her skill with horses, good personality and terrific looks, soon made a hit with the local people. Scott was four years old, a stocky, good-natured boy. He took to country living like a native born.

The Huckstead family moved up the valley and planned to build a sawmill on Elizabeth Lake. I got a job helping to build the sawmill from scratch in the wilderness. After that job, I once again went to work on the green chain, my old trade in Montana. It wasn't any easier, but I was still young, in love with my wife, and now had a son to support. I was really quite happy to have my first job and the opportunity to earn a living in our new country.

The black flies, no-see-ums, and mosquitoes had a terrific appetite and were vicious critters. If you dove in the lake, the leaches sucked your blood, but when you're young and living out a dream, it doesn't really seem to matter--too much. Kathy's parents, Chet and Naomi Parks, came up for a vacation. Chet was bitten on the face by a black fly, and his face swelled up with just a slit for an eye on one side.

I was twenty-six years old, healthy, strong, and putting my back to the test as I piled lumber and timbers. I made arrangements with Marty Allen to put a cabin on some land he had leased from the government; I told him he could have it when I left. I soon built a small cabin with my own hands. It was the first thing bigger than a corner shelf that I'd built, and I was proud. It was to be our home for about two years and was on a knoll about one hundred feet from the Kispiox River.

My parents came up that summer and each following summer while we were in that area. They brought a gas washing machine, which we put alongside the river. There was no electricity in the valley, so we used a kerosene lamp and a Coleman lamp, wood cook stove and wood heater. I built an outhouse and carried water from the river for our drinking and domestic use.

Besides record steelhead, the river had other runs, including Coho (silver salmon) and Sockeye salmon. Coho were fairly easy to catch, and they helped us fill our larder. We purchased freshly netted Sockeye salmon from the Kispiox Indians for fifty to seventy-five cents a fish.

Scott caught one of his first fish there, on the banks of the Kispiox, at age four. He put his line in only a few inches of water close to the bank, and a two-pound Dolly Varden struck. Scott yanked it out with an instantaneous jerk; Miss Dolly V was on the bank before either Scott or that fish had time to figure out what happened. It was a treat to see the joy and wonder of Scott's catch radiate all over his face.

About this time our family expanded: the Hucksteads gave us a female German Shepherd pup named Gretchen, and we had a kitten named Mimi. The mill shut down in the fall, and I was out of work. Things like money and food were getting scarce. We determined that with the government allotment for every family's child, about fifteen dollars a month, we could make it. When you're not paying rent, electricity or water, it's amazing how cheaply you can live.

However, we needed to supplement our larder with game and fish. Late one night on the way home to the cabin, I shot a moose; it was about a year old and still with its mother. I dragged the carcass behind our Chevy over the snow to the cabin. Under the glare of a Coleman lamp, following the instructions in an *Outdoor Life* magazine on how to clean a deer, I began the gruesome job of gutting and pulling the insides out. Having cleaned nothing larger than a duck or fish, it was all new to me. I asked Kathy, "Is this the udder?" as I tried to figure out the different parts of the inside of a moose.

By about 4:00 in the morning, more than four hours since I had begun the gruesome job, it was finished. We put a couple of quarters in a snow bank and canned the rest in a neighbor's canner. Scott still remembers, with a sour look on his face, the canned moose and peas we ate for over a year. It was tender and quite tasty, I thought.

I obtained a goat permit and made arrangements to borrow Marty Allen's horses. I planned to go into the nearby mountains to try to bolster our larder with more meat. But one Saturday morning a fisherman knocked on our door and got us out of bed. Excitedly he asked if we had tame goats, and I told him we didn't. He said, "Well, there are two down by the river!"

I slipped on my pants, grabbed my .765 Mauser, a World War II vintage rifle, and a couple of shells as I bolted out the door. In what was probably the world's easiest wild goat hunt, I bagged my goat about 150 feet from the cabin and 20 feet from the river; the fisherman bagged the other one. He, being the expert, gutted both goats in just a matter of minutes. It was a young goat and delicious, certainly a welcome addition to our menu selection.

That was the last game I ever shot. We needed the meat, as I was out of work and about out of money. From then on, my pleasure was watching and taking photos of wildlife; I especially enjoyed seeing wolf packs in the winter when I was flying a ski-equipped plane. Occasionally I got some game meat from some of the hunting camps.

Fall comes quickly in the north, and soon winter was upon us. We were the last family up the valley on that side of the river, and the nearest neighbor was about eight miles down river. Bruce Campbell was the only one farther up the valley, but he was on the other (west) side of the river.

The stillness was complete as the snow fell day after day until it covered everything like a huge white blanket. Soon the river froze solid, and we had to cut a hole in the ice for water. We cooked on a wood stove and had a barrel heater. It was made out of a forty-five-gallon oil drum with welded link chains for legs. The snow piled deep, and the night temperatures dipped to thirty degrees below zero. After filling the barrel heater with wood, we snuggled in bed. We piled the blankets and sleeping bags on our bed on the cold nights, and Scott slept with us.

In the morning the fire was sometimes out, and the frost crystallized our bedroom walls. It was a cold trek across the room to the barrel stove and the task of lighting a morning fire before jumping back into bed. Kathy didn't complain and was a good pioneer wife and mother. We did things together as a family. Scott went with us on Saturday nights when we went to a movie or drove to town for groceries; he seldom stayed with a babysitter.

Daily chores—getting water from the ice bound river, getting firewood for the stove, heating water on the stove, and cooking with a wood stove—became a time-consuming part of each day. But my dream of living off the land was happening, not so much by choice, but by necessity. The wild game we obtained was like money in the bank.

When I thought the ice was thick enough to walk on, I cut a long pole and walked on the river ice. The pole was a safety device:if I fell in, it would catch on each side of the hole and I could use it to get back out of the river—or so I hoped.

Winter was long, cold and silent, but we were warm and had a good supply of food and, of course, free wood and water. We banked our cabin with snow, and it was quite comfortable. One winter I felled trees in the deep snow and worked in twenty-below weather in my shirt sleeves. The snow was about four feet deep. Before cutting a tree, I beat out an escape route in the snow. The snow tumbling from the falling tree would create a white-out that prevented my telling which way the tree was falling. It was a very hazardous occupation.

The winter slowly and reluctantly slipped away, and one day the ice started moving. Huge chunks crashed and leaped in the air like giant daggers. The ice jammed, and the river rose rapidly until the ice dam burst and allowed the water to roar down the valley.

The Forest Service was preparing to build a road that would connect to the Nass River to the west. I got a job clearing the road right-of-way up the valley. I bought a new chain saw and felled and cut up the trees to five-foot lengths. A Cat operator followed, clearing and piling the logs and building the road.

Early in the spring Jim Goerz and I hopped a freight and rode the rails from Smithers to Prince Rupert on the northern British Columbia coast, in hopes of finding work and making a good stake in one of the logging camps. We caught a ferry to Ketchikan, Alaska, but a flu epidemic in Alaska shut down the logging camps and chased us back to Rupert.

A phone call to the Queen Charlotte Islands (one hundred miles west of Rupert) resulted in a promised job, as I sold our services convincingly. We lasted about a month as salvage buckers (cutting up trees) on logged areas before the horizontally driven hail, rain and sleet drove us home. Jim taught me how to play chess. Those times gave us stories to tell our children in the years to come about the good old days when we made a fortune as big time loggers in the far north.

I went back to the States for a few months in the fall of 1965. My grandfather and fishing partner, William Rydblom, died shortly after we arrived.

In October I obtained an Aeronca Chief N86176, a tail dragger with a Continental 65-horsepower engine, for fifteen hundred dollars from a man at Deer Park Airport, just out of Spokane. Pete Anest, a well-known commercial pilot and instructor, checked me out, and we became longtime friends. The Chief was in excellent shape, and I brought it back to Canada with the idea of building up time and getting my commercial license. I got the plane licensed in July of 1966. The number on my plane was now CF-UVX. I initially kept it at Drew Wookey's airstrip downriver and later at the Smithers airport.

Sometimes while flying my ship I would point the nose skyward; and when it started to stall, I would kick the rudder and go into a spin. After about three spins it would really start to wrap up and seemed to increase greatly in speed—so three spins were about all I wanted to do.

In June 1966, I was falling timber for Colburn Ide in Terrace, British Columbia, when a tree limb fell on the top of my hard hat. I was working among large coastal timber; some of the cedars were over ten feet at the stump. The fateful limb put a dent in my hard hat, knocked me on the ground, and changed my life. While I was lying dazed on the ground, I saw a de Havilland float-equipped Beaver flying overhead. It was then I decided to get a float endorsement and work seriously toward a commercial license. Those Beavers flying overhead looked much safer and enjoyable than where I was felling and being felled by trees.

That month I began flying a float-equipped Champion two-place airplane with a 140-horsepower engine, CF-FWC. On June 12, 1966, after 2:45 hours of dual instruction with Gene Story, I had my license endorsement for seaplane flying. Landing seemed easy, and I thought flying floats was a piece of cake. I had much to learn. Ignorance is bliss. The flight physician told me I had eyes like an eagle and a good strong heart; as long as I pushed myself away from the table, I would probably live a long life.

Jim Woods, a supervisor for the B.C. Highway Department, owned the Champion, and we were to become well acquainted over the years. He once stopped at Iskut Village, in northern British Columbia, to take a nun who was teaching school at the native village for a ride. They ended up getting married. I met her and had dinner with them. She told me the diocese sent out a letter emphatically forbidding the nuns to go on any more airplane rides.

After two years on the Kispiox we moved to Lowell Davidson's ranch on an Indian reservation and looked after it for a time. It was located near Moricetown between Hazelton and Smithers. On Scott's first day of school, Kathy and I drove to Wookey's airstrip and flew the plane back to Davidson's ranch. We spotted a little boy walking away from the ranch back toward the highway. We landed in a field along the road, and there was Scott, tears streaming down his face. No one was at the ranch, and he felt we had deserted him. I left Kathy with Scott and flew off alone, as it was a very short field and I needed the plane to be as light as possible.

While we were on the Davidson Ranch, our faithful dog Gretchen was poisoned. Her condition worsened, and we put her out of her misery. We had kept one female pup from her litter. This was Gretchen II and would be Scott's and our family's close companion for many happy years.

I had mononucleosis, was laid up for a long time, and thought I would never get well enough to become a bush pilot. Bill Morrison had a sawmill nearby, where I worked for a few months until it shut down. Then we moved to Smithers and rented a house just east of town.

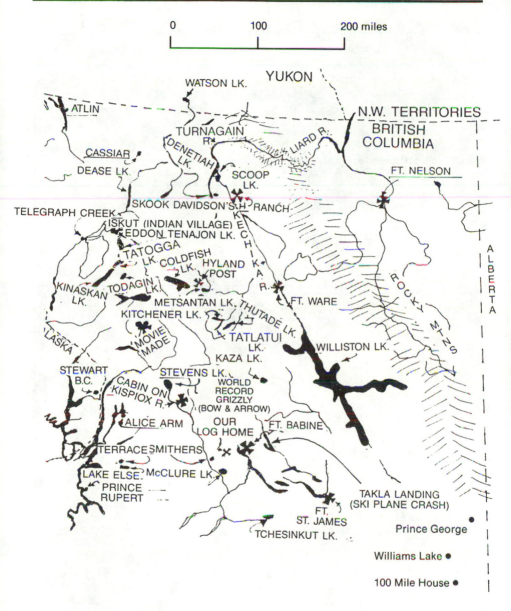

Grandfather William Charles Rydblom standing behind his father, Edward and his mother Ingeborg. Grandpa was born in Sweden in 1888 and came to the United States when he was about 4 yrs. old. Mother was his first child, I was his first grandchild and my son, William Scott Whitesitt, who we named after Grandpa, was his first great grandchild. The happiest days of my boyhood were spent with Grandpa at his cabin on beautiful Lake Coeur d'Alene. He was my fishing pal and best friend.

Grandfather William C. Rydblom and Larry in front of his home at E. 1404 Mallon, Spokane, WA about 1942.

Aunt JoAnn and her brother Uncle Bill Rydblom Jr., my boyhood hero, in Coast Guard uniform, 1942. Warmhearted JoAnn and I have been very close since my earliest memories.

Larry standing on the left and Grandma Ester Rydblom with her grandchildren. She was a special warmhearted lady, we were close. She was a Swede.

Larry with the duck boat at Grandpa's Lake place. Harrison, Idaho in the background.

The Whitesitt Family. Father, Val, holding his son Bob. Mother, Jeanne, holding her new baby Nancy and Larry in the foreground. About 1947.

My sisters Nancy and Jill Whitesitt. They would slip out the second story of our home and dance on the roof top on those warm summer evenings at our home on E. 2428 Mission, Spokane, WA.

Aunt Sue Rydblom-Clark, Grandpa and Larry in front of Grandpa's cabin on Lake Coeur d'Alene.

Eleanor Rott and I near Grandpa's cabin. I sure had a crush on her, she was a neat country girl.

Lake Coeur d'Alene, Larry, Aunt Sue in the middle and Eleanor Rott on the right. Harrison, Idaho in the background.

Olympic National Park 1953. Jim Goerz front, Ben Mitchell, Larry, Lee McLaughlin, Mr. Bowdy (Chops) and his dog.

Enchanted Valley, Olympic National Park 1953. We hiked 13 miles to this lodge surrounded by beautiful waterfalls.

Larry sitting on his favorite green 1941 Chevy, about 1955.

My good high school friend Lee, standing with his sister Nancy -- behind their parents LeRoy and Lucille McLaughlin. I became close to this warmhearted family over the years.

Navy days, Wikiki Beach 1957. My good high school buddy Gary Johnson on the left. We joined the Navy together. My friend and classmate Gordon Smith is on the right. Pearl Harbor was our home port.

A shipmate and Larry on their ship the U.S.S. Hassayampa AO145, in the vast Pacific Ocean about 1957.

Our wedding Feb. 18, 1959. Left, Kathy's older sister Helen Park, Kathryn Ann Park, Larry Whitesitt and his brother, best man, quiet, easy-going Bob Whitesitt.

Larry and Kathy holding their newborn son, Scott, and cousin Danny McDaniel.

Our home for the summer. Desert Lookout overlooked Glacier National Park, Montana. My sister Jill is by the tent. Summer of 1959.

1960 - Larry, Kathy holding Scott and their cousin Danny in the cock pit of their new airplane, a tail dragger, called a Piper J-3 CUB.

Larry and Scott at Trail Creek, where they camped out in a tent for a few weeks before going to their summer home, Faucett Lookout, which overlooked Lake Pend Oreille in northern Idaho. Spring 1961.

Faucett Lookout, northern Idaho 1961.

Scott and our faithful dog Smokey at Faucett Lookout 1961. Scott was lost and I said Smokey find Scott and he led us directly to Scott and may have saved his life.

Larry at Desert Lookout.

Kathy, Scott, Larry and Smokey on the Oregon Coast, on their way to California, fall of 1961.

CABIN ON THE KISPIOX

Laury and Brent Goerz and Scott Whitesitt on our trip north to fulfill the dreams Jim and I had in high school; to go north build a cabin and live off the land. Our 1953 Chevy, spring of 1964, Canada.

Cabin on the Kispiox, that we built in the summer of 1964 and lived in for about 2 years. No electricity, no running water and no rent to pay.

CHAPTER II
FLYING ADVENTURES
IN BRITISH COLUMBIA

By February of 1967 I had 39 hours dual and 162 hours solo. When I flew my Chief, I pretended I was a commercial pilot and pictured in my mind all the excitement of that occupation. Many years later I read a book called *Psychocybernetics* by Dr. Maxwell Maltz, who believes your mind will take over like a computer and accomplish those things you visualize yourself doing.

During this month Ralph Hermanson, owner of Caribou Air Charter of Kelowna, British Columbia, came to Smithers. He planned to bring in a satellite flying school, since there was a group of people wishing to obtain their licenses. He talked me and another man, Gary Wilwan, into coming down to Kelowna to obtain our commercial and instructors' ratings and fly forestry patrol. As soon as we got our licenses, he wanted us to instruct.

February 28, 1967, I began flying at Kelowna in a Luscomb with an 85-horsepower Continental CF-HHA. I was building the necessary time to earn my commercial and instructor's ratings. Doug McCall, a former Canadian Air Force pilot who flew on their aerobatic team, was one of my instructors; Bob Bluet was the other. I began long flights, building up time; I flew to Smithers and then to Spokane. By April 23 I had 85 hours dual and 245 hours solo.

In April Len Mellon, a designated flight inspector for the Canadian Department of Transport, checked me out for my commercial and instructor's ratings. Now I had a green commercial and instructor's license. The job with Caribou Air Charter didn't materialize, but, as it turned out, that was fortunate for me and my future.

In the middle of May, 1967, I was in the local Smithers grocery store when I saw Jack Hodge. Jack was an excellent bush pilot and a first-class engineer with a friendly, kind manner. He was the base manager for Omineca Air Service at Maclure Lake, which is a few miles south of Smithers. "Larry," he said, "we need a Super Cub driver. Why don't you come out to the base tomorrow and go for a check ride with me, and we'll see how it goes." My heart picked up a few beats as I said I'd be there!

I arrived at the appointed time, just as Jack was leaving on a charter trip in the Beaver float plane. Bill Harrison, the owner of the company, was standing on the dock. He was the man who told me three years before they wanted pilots to have two or three thousand hours before he would hire them. "Come on, I'll do a few circuits with you," he said.

FLYING ADVENTURES IN BRITISH COLUMBIA

We went up in the Super Cub on floats. Fortunately for me, I had just completed an intensive course of dual and solo flying for my commercial and instructor's rating. I had practiced landings, take-offs, and flight maneuvers till I thought they would come out my ears. After putting me through my paces, Bill said, "You seem to have a good feel for the airplane, considering the amount of time you have. Tell you what: you come out and go on trips with Jack and the other pilots and learn the country; maybe we'll have something for you."

On June 5, 1967, I made my first official flight for Omineca Air Service. I flew Carl Fay, a paying passenger, to Alice Arm (an inlet off the ocean) and then flew back to Maclure Lake in the float-equipped Super Cub CF JUE!

Bill and I made a trip in the Cessna 185 CF-OXE to Todagin Lake in northern B.C. and did a couple of hours of circuits and landings on Maclure Lake. Bill asked if I thought I could handle the Cessna okay. There was a trip to Babine Lake that involved picking up some men, flying to Terrace and then down the coast to Nanaimo on Vancouver Island, staying overnight and coming back the following day.

"Of course," I said. "Sure!" I tried not to show any apprehension. I was awash with feelings of excitement and the satisfaction that he trusted me to fly this high performance plane. I drew my course with a pencil on the maps, figuring out the proper heading to take, and prepared myself for an extended trip.

The weather was clear all the way down and back; I didn't get lost, and the trip ended successfully. From then on, I flew the Cessna 185 most of the time during the rest of the year. It paid more than the Cub, was much faster, and was just a nice airplane to fly.

I remember clearly the first flight I made out in the bush shortly after my check-out in the Cub. It was with Jack Hodge in the Beaver to Morrison Lake, which is just east of Fort Babine on Babine Lake. The lake was just as remote and wild as I had pictured a bush pilot's destination would be. "Larry," I said to myself, "this is what it's like to be a bush pilot!" At last I'd arrived.

I began flying into places like Fort Babine, an Indian village on the north end of Babine Lake, accessible by air or water only. Fort Babine had one of the few remaining Hudson's Bay trading posts. An old gentleman, Mac, ran the store. As soon as he retired, the Hudson's Bay Company was going to shut down the store, as they had done to most other isolated trading posts. I flew the mail several times a month to Fort Babine and then went on to Takla Post on Takla Lake, forty miles east. Jack Newcomb and his Asian wife ran Takla Post. It used to be a Hudson's Bay post, but Jack Newcomb was a free trader and an independent. In the winter months when the lake was frozen, he couldn't freight supplies up the lake, so I flew groceries and supplies in by ski plane.

We purchased ten acres of mostly timbered land about ten miles north of Maclure

Lake from a man named Fletcher. In the fall I got a free permit from the Forest Service and felled the trees for my log home. At last I would have that log home that I had told Kathy I wanted back in 1959 before we were married.

Ted Strand, a husky Norwegian from the old country, helped me pick out the correct trees. I downed about fifty trees, cut them up into the desired lengths, and rolled them on poles. I then used a spud—a chisel-like blade about four inches wide attached to a wooden pole—to peel each log so they would dry out over the winter.

In the spring the logs were skidded to my ten-acre building site. I used a draw knife and peeled each log again so it would be shining and smooth. We dug out a full basement. Putting up forms for the basement and then pouring concrete was a new experience. I had lots of help; in fact, I was more a laborer and helper than a boss. Drew Wookey, jack of all trades, put in the foundation. Next we put floor joists across, butting up to the logs that had been put down first. After the floor was nailed on, Ted went to work putting up round after round, doing most of the work himself; I was busy flying, and Kathy was working for Lawrence Perry, a local attorney, as a legal secretary.

Ted built the log house as they did it in Norway. Each log was concaved so it would fit snugly over the log below. The corners were designed so the whole log cabin would settle evenly. There was no chinking, and fifteen years later the logs were still as tight as when they were first put up. A thin strip of fiberglass insulation was put between each log. I brushed linseed oil on each log as it went up. When the log home was completed, I used one part of Olympic Cedar Stain, which had a linseed oil base, to three parts of linseed oil. It made a nice, natural-looking protective coating, and after fifteen years it still looked very nice. At last we had our log home. It was beautiful.

Tommy Walker, an outfitter and big game guide, was so impressed with Ted's workmanship that he made arrangements for Ted to build a cabin for him in northern B.C.. Ted built Tommy's log cabin and liked that area so well that he moved up there permanently.

Ted was a bachelor about forty-two years old. He was a free spirit and loved to trap and hunt and roam the wilderness. One day I flew the C-185 up to Eddontenajon Lake, where Ted lived. Gordon Eastman, a former Walt Disney photographer, now had his own film company. He was at Eddontenajon Lake to do a film about wolves. He had a pack of young, partly grown wolves for the movie, and Ted and I flew down the lake to view them.

That was the last time I saw Ted. He was living where he wanted, and he loved the far north country. One day he left his cabin up north and went cross country skiing, hunting for goats with his Samoyed dog. They were caught in an avalanche, and their bodies were not discovered until the following spring. Ted was an honorable and skilled craftsman from the old country, and the log home he built for me still stands as a monument to his skill and artistry.

FLYING ADVENTURES IN BRITISH COLUMBIA

In July of 1967, I had a trip to Bone Lake in the C-185 for Phelps Dodge Mining Company. We ferried material and men into this roadless area south of Francois Lake. It's in a mountainous area, and at times the winds are tricky to contend with. Art Schiller, my passenger, was going to do some work on their single sideband radio, which he had installed. Art also installed single sideband radios in all our planes and our bases, and they were much clearer and stronger than the double sideband radios. He worked for Spillsbury & Tindle out of Vancouver, B.C.

Art was an interesting man. He flew a Messerschmidt during World War II over North Africa. One battlefree, sunny day as he was flying over the desert, everything was going well when his world exploded. His plane was shot down by a British RAF Fighter Pilot. He opened his parachute (The other crew member was killed.) and ended up as a prisoner for the duration of the war.

After the war he was doing some work on a home in Vancouver, B.C., when he and the owner started telling war stories. Art went into detail about being shot down. The Englishman asked him the date and time of the incident and then went to a cupboard and brought out a log book. The Englishman said. "Art, that's the exact time and place where I shot down a Messerschmidt." After all those years, Art met the RAF officer who shot him down, and they became friends.

Art now hated flying, and he was concerned about the weather. "Do you think it's okay?" he asked, as his knuckles turned white from hanging onto the door rest.

"Yes," I said, "it's not too bad." Well, we arrived okay, stayed awhile, and then headed back. Art again didn't know if we should go.

"The weather doesn't look good, does it, Larry?"

"It's okay, Art," I replied. It really wasn't that bad; the ceiling was low, but visibility under the clouds was good all the way home.

During that summer Bill Harrison had an engine failure in the Beaver OBU but landed safely on a lake. A few minutes before, he had been flying reconnaissance low over some heavily timbered and rocky country. If his engine had gone then, they would have had a serious, maybe fatal, accident. The engine had about four hundred hours since major and, I was told, came out of a Beech 18, which uses the same R-985 450-horsepower radial engine. I flew Bill home in our other Beaver JOS.

On a nice summer day in 1968 on Maclure Lake, Sheldon Luck, a famous early-day bush pilot then in his sixties, flew in as the pilot of a converted PBY called a Cansol. Sheldon was one of the finest and most experienced pilots in this type of work; he was a living legend, well-known and respected in the aviation world. He was the father of Grant Luck, who was the base manager after Jack Hodge left. Bill Harrison and his partner Alec Davidson bought the PBY flying boats from a company called Flying Firemen to use as water bombers to drop water and chemicals on fires.

In the fall of 1968 Bill Harrison asked if I would be interested in going to

Tasmania, an island off Australia, as a copilot on one of the Cansols. I gave a quick affirmative, and he continued, "We may have a contract for this winter down there." It didn't materialize.

The following summer one of these Cansols crashed while working a fire, and both crew members were killed. Alec and his copilot were flying a Super Cansol, which had larger engines and hauled about twelve hundred gallons of water; the other Cansols hauled eight hundred gallons. A wing tore off while they were dropping water on a fire on Vancouver Island; they were both killed. Sheldon Luck was flying the other plane. A season or two later I heard another one of the Cansols and crew were lost on a fire--a very risky business. When the smoke got thick, it wasn't uncommon to have a plane hit a snag in the smoke. Visibility was poor, as they had to get so low to make an effective drop. The longevity of a pilot in this line of work is short.

In late August 1968, I met two men at the float base. Jim Conway had a weekly fishing television program called the *Outdoor Sportsman* out of Portland, Oregon. Larry Bardett was the photographer who filmed the action. They were going to fly to Tommy Walker's camp at Cold Fish Lake and then to other lakes to do some fly fishing.

After loading their gear in the Cessna 185, we left the lake and were soon north of the last roads. Fort Babine was a few miles east as we continued to climb, and we soon crossed the Babine River. The Skeena River was below, and Thutade, Tatlatui, and Kitchener Lakes were off the starboard wing about twenty miles to the north. Cold Fish Lake, about eighty miles away, was our destination.

When I made my first trip to a new area, I drew the course on a sectional chart and kept it on my lap during the trip to keep from getting turned around. After a while the country became familiar and the rivers, lakes and mountains became well-known landmarks. This country was familiar, as I traveled this route often.

We flew over a pass that's forty-five hundred feet or so, picked up the headwaters of the Spatsizi River, and followed it for about thirty-five miles to Mink Creek. There we took a left, and Cold Fish Lake came into view about six miles west. Cold Fish was about six miles long, and Tommy Walker's camp was at the northwest end. Circling the camp, I saw a white-headed man walking toward a small dock. The largest log cabin sat in the middle, with smaller cabins on either side.

Flying away from the cabins, I looked for anything on or below the surface of the lake to make sure my intended landing area was clear. Seeing no obstacles, I made a wide descending turn to the left: one notch of flaps, and then another notch, twenty degrees of flaps on final, slowing down to about eighty miles per hour indicated. Leveling off above the surface, a little more back pressure on the elevator control column, brought the nose up to the landing attitude. There was a slight thud, and spray flew up on either side of the floats as we taxied on the step (planed on the surface) with power for a few hundred yards. As I throttled

FLYING ADVENTURES IN BRITISH COLUMBIA

back; we settled in the water and taxied slowly to the dock into the wind, and I leaned the mixture until the engine stopped, then turned off the electrical switches.

Tommy grabbed the strut as I got out and tied down the plane. The flight was 2:05. Tommy's wife called from the lodge with the welcome, "Coffee's on." Tommy's snow white hair, lively eyes, and friendly manner made us feel welcome.

Tommy Walker had moved up here in 1948 from his former guiding area near Tweedsmuir Park in central B.C. He said it was just getting too crowded, and the game wasn't as plentiful as it used to be. There are some record size caribou in this area, as well as sheep and goats whose coats are red from rolling on the side hills along *Spatsizi* (which is an Indian name for Red Goat) River, with its characteristic iron ore stains.

Tommy Walker's book *Spatsizi* tells his story. In 1948, Tommy first arrived at Cold Fish Lake after a nine-hundred-mile trek by horseback. George Dalziel dropped in with his floatplane and introduced himself; he came back later that day with some rainbow trout for Tommy and his wife. Later Dal, as he was known, flew for Tommy in a Waco on floats, flying freight to Cold Fish from Telegraph Creek. Dal lived in Telegraph Creek in the winter months because of the mild winter and then moved to his log home on the southern shores of Dease Lake, which I later came to know well.

Steel Hyland was a well-known pioneer of this area and a good friend of Tommy's. He and his wife Lou lived west of Cold Fish Lake. They had a beautiful log home on the west side of Kinaskan Lake. They also had cabins they rented out to sportsmen. On several occasions, while flying for B.C. Hydro Resource people, I overnighted there, and Lou fixed some good home cooking. They were warm, friendly people, and Steel always had a happy laugh. They let you know you were welcome any time.

The Hylands had owned Hyland Post and had traded with the Indians there. Steel had spent many a happy day as a youngster helping John Creyke, who hunted and guided in the area. *Kinaskan* Lake means "a lake you have to raft"; the adjoining lake north, *Totogga*, means "Second Lake," and the adjoining lake north of that, *Eddontenajon*, means "little boy drowned." These are all Indian names.

Tommy had a ranch east of Cold Fish Lake, near Hyland Post. Jim Morgan looked after the ranch and did some trapping in the winter. Jim was an original, an honest-to-goodness mountain man.

Tommy also had a store near Totogga about forty-five air miles west of Cold Fish. He obtained for me wholesale a lightweight, blue down-filled sleeping bag that I used on my flights as part of my survival gear. Later, when I wasn't flying, I used it on my bed as a comforter.

Sitting around the kitchen table, Tommy told Jim, Larry and me about some good places where we could expect some lively fish and could get some good footage. There was talk of Kitchener Lake and catching fat rainbow trout where the creek from Stalk Lake enters Kitchener. We agreed to give it a go the next day. We also marked Tatlatui Lake, planning to fish the outlet, which is part of the headwaters of the Firesteel River. After a tasty meal, we retired to a cabin. In the morning after breakfast we cranked up the 185 and soon left Cold Fish behind. Picking up the Spatsizi, we followed it to Hyland Post. Continuing east, we were soon over the Stikine River, which we followed almost to its headwaters at Lasluie Lake. Then we continued south. Kitchener Lake was twenty-four miles ahead. The valley floor at this point was about thirty-five hundred feet above sea level, and we were at fifty-five hundred feet. Kitchener's elevation is about forty-two hundred feet.

Passing Stalk Lake, we began our descent and could see where Stalk Creek flowed into Kitchener Lake; it looked like a good place to beach the aircraft and fish. It was open and appeared to be flat and sandy. We landed, heeled the floats onto the fine gravel, and tied a rope from the plane to some bushes.

Camera . . . action! Larry, the photographer, had the camera ready; now if the fish would only bite.

I had watched Jim in the past on television. I remembered the heavy breathing coming across on the audio, his bearlike body wading those icy lakes and streams. He wore tennis shoes instead of waders because he felt waders were just too dangerous. He used to say, "If you step in a hole, they fill with water and it would be easy to drown." Jim didn't seem to mind the icy waters filling his shoes as he stood fly casting into the lake, letting the waters from Stalk Creek carry his fly out into the lake. He takes his fun seriously, and it was a pleasure for me to watch an expert.

Soon the fish started to bite. Jim hauled out some fat two-to four-pound rainbows, quickly releasing each one. Larry was busy with the camera. The weather held, and we spent several hours here. I caught some good ones, and Larry even included me in some of the shots. Imagine—I was getting paid to fish and fly, or fly fish, or fly and fish! In any case it was a fun trip, and we all got along great! The high country was refreshing and the scenery fantastic; I'm sure the people who saw this program were a bit envious.

It was hard to believe that a little over a year ago I had been paying to rent a plane. Now I was getting paid to do something I loved—flying an airplane into remote wilderness areas and getting to fish besides. It was unbelievable; I was having the time of my life.

Jim had a remarkable lifestyle. He was also a pilot, and Cessna Aircraft gave him a new plane to use free, just for their advertising. Tommy Walker let us stay free at his camp for his advertising, and my employers let him fly free for our advertising. Besides this, he was making money having his fishing made into a movie.

"Jim," I said, "that sounds like a good set up."

"Yes," he said, "I haven't figured out a better lifestyle. I get paid for doing what I enjoy—fishing."

For a change of scenery and a different kind of fishing, we cranked up the fuel-injected 260 horses in the C-185 and took a short ten-mile flight down to Tatlatui Lake. Jim did some stream fishing at the north end, following the outlet for several hundred feet. The fishing wasn't as good, so we left after a couple of hours. We flew back to Cold Fish Lake and had better luck at a couple of places along the lake and at the outlet along Mink Creek.

Canadian Broadcasting Company (CBC) was also staying at Tommy Walker's camp, doing a documentary on the Spatsizi River area. They hired me to do some of their flying. Over and over they had me fly low along the lake and zoom over camp, until they had the required footage.

Filming a deserted Indian village at Metsantan Lake was next. The Indians who once occupied Metsantan came from the band of Bear Lake Indians called Sasuchan or Sasuton, a subdivision of the Sekani tribe. *Sekani* means "Dwellers of the Rock"; they lived on the headwaters of the Pasco and Liard Rivers and on some of the neighboring western slopes of the Rocky Mountains.

The story of the village was sad. During the early forties, the game seemed to disappear; the people began to starve. Eventually they all left and settled around Eddontenajon Lake and a village called Iskut. Tommy said the Indians lived in the village when he first arrived in 1948, but even then they were having a struggle surviving and were short of food.

We flew along the same route that we had followed to Kitchener Lake. The noise of the engine was partially blocked by my earphones but was still loud. Ahead a blue sliver appeared: the blue teardrop-sized lake on my map, Metsantan.

Looking like a village gone to sleep, the cozy cabins took form as we approached the lake. After landing, we glided to shore. It was quiet as we stepped off the floats. We were soon walking through the silent village. Not a word was spoken for a time as we kept our thoughts private. As I gently pushed open a sagging door, a metal object caught my eye. A gold pan hung on the wall of the log cabin. The room was sparse; the people had lived a simple life. The other cabins were alike, each with its own gold pan. Entering a larger log building, I noticed some dusty books on a table. Opening one, I saw it was an old primer. A Hudson's Bay calendar, almost three decades old, hung on the wall. Gone were those young, expressive brown eyes that once found a new world in these books.

The village was quiet now. No barking dogs, no hunters returning with game, no children's voices echoing across the lake. The hushed log cabins were fading monuments to a time past. As we flew toward the afternoon sun, the village faded and became a memory.

We departed Cold Fish and retraced our route back to Maclure Lake. Our memories were of new friends, new country, and many fishing stories to relate to friends and loved ones—not of fish that got away, but of fish we caught, recorded on film, and then turned loose to swim those cold northern lakes and streams.

FLIGHT OF THE RED BEAVER

My boyhood hero who was in the U.S. Coast Guard during the war years, Bill Rydblom Jr., saw this movie on TV at his home in Tillamook, Oregon, and was surprised to see me fishing with Jim.

October 27, 1968—leaving Maclure Lake behind, the Cessna 185 CF-OXE climbed over the Babine River. It was a cloudy day as I headed for Stevens Lake, located at the head of the Kispiox River. Bill Love and a hunter, Rex Hancock, a dentist from the southern U.S., were waiting for me to pick them up. As I pulled up to shore, I saw a dark brown fur on the bank. Loading this huge grizzly bear hide on board was a heavy task. The head was massive. Bill said it was a world class bear—in fact, it was the world record grizzly shot with a bow and arrow. The skull was only 1-7/16 inches smaller than the world record shot with a rifle. Wally Love, Bill Love and Jack Lee guided a Dr. Hambrick from Madison, Wisconsin, on another bear bow hunt in 1965; the bear they got during that trip was the world record grizzly until this bear was shot in 1968. After a somewhat bumpy ride back, the happy hunter departed for home with a story about a record grizzly that didn't get away.

Wally and Bill Love and their brother-in-law, Jack Lee, called themselves Love Brothers & Lee, Big Game Outfitters. They first went into the Thutade and Tatlatui lakes area in 1948, making a hard three-month trip cross country on horseback from Hazelton. They guided fishing parties at Sustut Lake for steelhead from 1959 to 1963. The fishing was fantastic, but heavy fishing by others led to its shutdown in 1964. Wally, Bill, and Jack were excellent guides and worked a lot with bow hunters. Fred Bear came up often. Fess Parker, the Daniel Boone of television fame, went out with the Loves, made a movie, and shot a grizzly.

Russ Baker, a well-known bush pilot, flew their first hunter into the Love Brothers and Lee camp on Thutade Lake from his base at Fort Saint James in a Junkers airplane made in Germany. He picked this hunter up at Tatlatui, which is close to Thutade, a month later in a brand new Beaver—the first Beaver off the line. He was really proud of it. Tommy Walker hired Russ to do much of his flying in his number one Beaver. Russ later started Pacific Western Airline from this bush operation.

Mining activity in the Lake Babine area was red hot in 1967, and 1968 was even hotter. People were staking claims everywhere, it seemed. A geologist flew in from Vancouver late one day to restake a claim by Babine Lake that was to expire at midnight. Because it was late, he decided to go in the morning. As we taxied up to shore, we saw a string of men emerge from the bush with lights on their heads. Too late—they had restaked his claim after midnight, and at 8:00 a.m. it was theirs. Mining stock was going wild. I noticed it wasn't the content of the claim so much as the promoter in Vancouver who caused the stock to rise crazily, often on worthless properties.

Once I was alone below the glacier that rises above Smithers, watching a cold glacier stream cascade down the alpine meadow. I felt that I was part of the surroundings here long before I was born. The rocks, the rushing waters and the meadow were part of my being before my physical birth.

One day flying north of Hazelton, a few miles from the Skeena River, my grandfather, who had passed away a couple of years before, was with me in the cockpit. I expressed my feelings to Grandpa about my love of flying and this being my first flying job, and he understood. Grandpa played an important part in my aviation career. He co-signed a nine hundred dollar note so I could purchase my first airplane, a J-3 Piper Cub, at Felts Field in Spokane. When I passed my exams and obtained my private pilot's license I took him for his first airplane ride. My mother was his first child, I was his first grandson and Scott was his first great-grandson, and he treated us wonderfully. Growing up, spending time at Gramp's cabin on Lake Coeur d'Alene across from Harrison, Idaho, I spent some of the happiest days of my youth. We were good buddies and fishing partners. He was an expert fisherman and a first-class human being with a heart of gold.

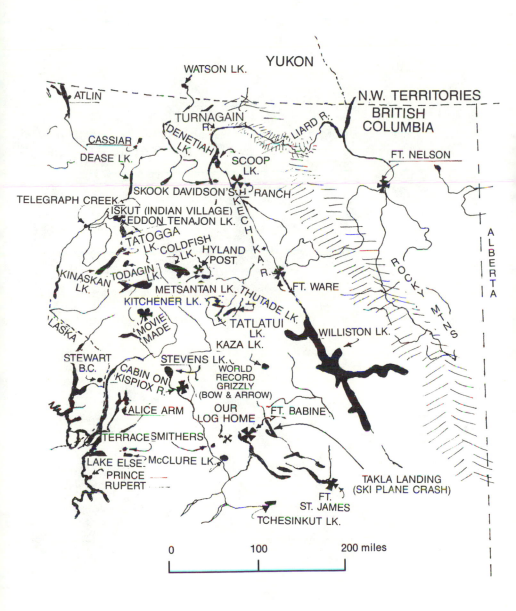

FLYING ADVENTURES IN BRITISH COLUMBIA

Wenatchee, Washington winter of 1967. Dennis Rae and I with the Luscomb CF HHA that I used to build up flying hours for my commercial pilots license & instructors rating. We flew from Wenatchee to Smithers, British Columbia.

Dennis and I on final to the Williams Lake, B.C. airport in the Luscomb CF HHA, winter of 1967. Dennis did about 50% of the flying and had a good feel for flying. He later obtained his private pilot license. Dennis, his wife Connie, and I were classmates at NW Christian High School in Spokane, WA

Our Fleet at Omineca Air Service at McClure Lake B.C. 1967, my first flying job. Foreground, Super Cub, Beaver, Otter, Beaver and Cessna 185, all float planes.

Jim Goerz my good high school buddy at lower right with some goat hunters he guided, high in the mountains of northern British Columbia in the Smithers area.

37

The world record Grizzly bear taken with a bow in the fall of 1967 at Stevens Lake, by a dentist from the southern U.S., named Rex Hancock. The guide was my neighbor in the Kispiox, Bill Love. The skull was only 1 7/16" smaller than the world record taken with a rifle. I picked the hunter and trophy up at Stevens Lake, in northern British Columbia.

Scott and his beautiful mother Kathy, in the early 1970's. The first time I ever saw Katherine, she was galloping her horse bareback, across a meadow toward me, and by the time she dismounted, I fell in love with this dark haired beauty.

FLYING ADVENTURES IN BRITISH COLUMBIA

Ted Strand a Norwegian from the old country is standing on top of logs as he carefully concaves each log to fit perfectly, like they do in the old country. There was no chinking and it was perfectly tight after 15 years.

The dream Kathy and I shared before our marriage of one day having a son and building a log cabin in the north was now completed. On the left is Uncle Jess McDaniel, father Val, Larry, Kathy, Scott and our faithful German Shepherd, Gretchen II.

CHAPTER III
LEARNING TO FLY FLOATS

After my first year with Omineca Air Service, they added two float-equipped de Havilland Otters to their fleet, which now consisted of six aircraft. Grant Luck and Bill Lopeschuck usually piloted these noisy single-engine birds and were kept busy flying men and supplies into mining and hunting camps.

The Otters, like all the others in the fleet, were STOL (short take-off and landing) type airplanes and were ideally suited to floats, skis, or wheels. They were taildraggers (equipped with tail wheels), as were the others. Most modern airplanes have a nose wheel (tricycle gear) and are much easier to land and take off. Flying a taildragger takes a greater amount of skill and finesse, especially on landings and take-offs. Directional straight line control must be maintained or you can soon lose it, sometimes ground looping (one or more circles) after touching down. Normal landings with a taildragger are done on all three wheels at the same time—a three-point landing—and they require a certain skill. Sometimes wheel landings on the main gear, especially in gusty windy conditions, is safer. Actually you fly the plane on the runway, use forward elevator control to pin it, keep it on the runway, and then let the tail wheel down gently.

Most modern trainers in flying schools are tricycle equipped, and the students don't really learn what I think is fundamental: basic taildragger instruction. Most pilots who trained when I did or before started on taildraggers such as J-3 Cubs, Champs, Taylor Crafts, and Luscombs and learned the basic stick and rudder, seat-of-your pants kind of flying. One reason the German pilots in World War II were so good was that they all started out on gliders, where stick and rudder use is essential, and soon understood the basics.

Center of gravity (CG) is located behind the main landing gear on a taildragger, and this causes it to ground loop if you're not careful. I did that once as a student in a J3-Cub. The CG on tricycle gear is forward of the main gear near the nose; this makes it easier to taxi, take off, and land.

Modern-day trainers such as a Cessna 172 or 152 can be slopped on the runway carelessly, yet usually don't bounce. They track straight down the runway with minimal effort on the pilot's part. In the air these modern nose wheel types fly easily, with little rudder control needed in turns. The pilot never really understands or appreciates the basic fundamentals of stick and rudder flying that a taildragger offers. The young men who bought my taildragger, after flying only Cessnas, soon got into trouble; they let the Aroneca Chief get away while landing and bent the landing gear and fuselage.

Our smallest airplane was the two-place, tandem-seated Piper Super Cub. Outwardly it looked like my first airplane, the J-3 Cub. The Super Cub is a fabric-covered, highwing lightweight ship with flaps and a peppy 150-horsepower Lycoming engine that gives it fantastic performance. The stick control column in it is my favorite; it's light and responsive on the controls and a delight to fly. It stalls at 38 mph and cruises on floats at about 85 mph. With excellent visibility, it makes a good patrol plane; I spent many hours in one on forestry patrol. It got in and out of smaller lakes better than any of our aircraft. Because this was the plane in which I made my very first charter trip as a green commercial pilot, this Cub will always hold a special place in my memory.

The Cessna 185 CF-OXE that I began flying regularly two weeks after I made the first charter trip in the Cub was a sleek silver and red bird and was the fastest in the fleet. I was proud of her and was accused of washing the paint off, as I was usually washing and cleaning the inside and the windscreen when I wasn't flying. This silver bird cruised at 135 mph or so on floats, was fairly quiet, and, because it was tight and had a good heater, was by far the warmest in the cold winter months when our fleet was on skis.

The Cessna, like the Beaver, has a constant speed prop. The pilot sets the prop to fine pitch (least angle) for take-off and gets the maximum rpms for the shortest distance necessary to get airborne. Once in the air, the pilot reduces power and selects a lower rpm (coarser pitch); the prop now takes a bigger bite of air and cruises at a greater airspeed.

The Cessna is legally a six-place airplane, but for practical bush flying on floats, we never flew more than three passengers besides the pilot, because with gas and gear it wouldn't get off the water, and it was easily overloaded. It had a 260-horsepower, fuel-injected engine and left the water at about 60 mph; later 300-horsepower models performed better.

The Beaver, my favorite, is an all-metal high wing airplane, designed to carry a pilot and seven passengers. The engine drives a Hamilton standard constant speed propeller, crankshaft and propeller rotation being clockwise. The super charger is an engine-driven single stage centrifugal type.

The 9-cylinder Pratt and Whitney R-985 develops 450 hp at take-off at sea level with 2,300 rpm and 37.5 inches of manifold pressure. It burns about 20 Canadian gallons per hour.

The wing span is 48 feet, the length is 32 feet 9 inches, and the gross weight of the sea plane is 5,090 pounds.

On floats the Beaver indicates 120 mph and trues out at 7500 ASL around 130 mph at the power settings of 28-inch manifold pressure and 1800 rpm. Stalling speed with landing flaps is 45 mph. Take-off distance at sea level, with still air and a 50-foot obstacle, is 1250 feet for land planes and 1610 for seaplanes. Service ceiling for the land plane is 18,000 feet and 15,750 feet for the seaplane, although I have personally taken the Beaver up to 19,500 on floats with some flap and no oxygen, monitoring the effect by writing which became illegible after 15,000 feet or so. The Beaver has a thick ,high lift wing which enables it to get airborne quickly, but makes it relatively slow.

Cruising range with the seaplane is 405 miles, which makes allowance for a 10-minute warm-up and take-off, a climb to 5,000 feet and a 45-minute reserve.The stall is gentle, and, if yaw is permitted, the aircraft has a tendency to roll. Elevator trim is adjusted by a trim hand wheels on the cockpit roof, and the rudder trim is on a wheel just aft of that.The wing flaps are of the slotted type and extend from the wing roots to the inboard ends of the ailerons, which droop in conjunction with the flap movement. The wing flap lever is hydraulic and is located to the right side of the pilot's seat. Late one evening the base manager loaded the Beaver for me with an external load of long drill rods. Early the next morning, in the cool thick air, I began my take-off run! I rocked the floats with the elevator controls, several times back and forth to help it get on the step (the planing position), and with left aileron I lifted first the right float to help break the suction of the water and then the left float, before becoming airborne. Sometimes with a heavy load on hot muggy days when the air is thin, this is the only way you can get off the water. I successfully flew off Maclure Lake and delivered my cargo. I determined that I had approximately a two-thousand-pound payload on the trip and figured that the mining company got its money's worth.

The single-engined Otters we had were about twice the size of the Beavers and hauled almost double the payload. Eventually I flew an Otter, but these noisy airplanes that required so much time loading were cumbersome and never a favorite of mine.

One exercise I practiced on occasion was to turn the Beaver engine off and make a deadstick landing on a lake. It's amazing how quickly it decends. Sometimes I would fly close to winding shorelines below the tree tops to work on my stick and rudder coordination.

Landing or taking off in cross-winds on floats requires the same procedure as on wheels. Use aileron in the direction of the wind to keep from drifting sideways (perhaps taking out the floats); use opposite rudder to keep your nose straight.

Late in fall in freezing conditions the water rudders would freeze upon take-off, and you had to kick the rudder paddles to break them loose. Also during this time of year carburetor icing became a problem, and carb heat was needed on occasions to keep the engine running smoothly—or to keep it from quitting!

Most of my flying was on float-equipped airplanes. Because of the added friction due to the larger surface of floats and the water friction, it takes about a 25 percent longer take-off run to get airborne.

(Reference used FAA Flight Manual 1965) In the air the seaplane handles practically the same as the landplane. It is not quite as snappy in flight maneuvers, does not require quite as much use of the ailerons to hold it in a sideslip, and is likely to be somewhat less directionally stable. Otherwise no difference will be noted, and any manuever that can be performed with a landplane can also be performed with a floatplane. Handling the floatplane on water and during take-off is, of course, very different from taxiing and taking off in a landplane.

When taxiing, water rudders are more effective at slow speeds because they are then working in comparatively undisturbed water. At high speed, the stern of the float churns up the water, and the rudders are less efficient; furthermore, the speed through the water tends to make them swing or retract.

There are three positions of the seaplane while taxiing: the idling position, at seven or eight mph the nose up position, and the planing position. In the first two, the elevator control should be held full back.

There are dangers involved in making turns at high speed or in a strong wind. Any seaplane, if not held against it, will weather vane-turn into the wind, or, as we call it, weather cocks, and it constantly is endeavoring to assume this position at slow speed and when taxiing across or downwind. Consequently, as soon as the controls are neutralized, the plane will swing abruptly into the wind. Centrifugal force tends to make the plane turn over toward the outside of the turn, and the wind striking the side of the plane assists this tendency. If an abrupt turn is made while taxiing downwind, the combination of the two forces may be sufficient to turn the plane over.

The seaplane is put into the nose up position by holding the elevator hard back and opening the throttle until the rpm's reach about half the maximum for that airplane. This position is desirable when taxiing in rough water since it raises the propeller clear of the spray, and it is also sometimes necessary to use this attitude when attempting to turn away from a strong wind.

The third position is the planing position with a minimum speed of around 20 to 30 mph to keep it on the surface. The plane is placed in this attitude by holding the controls hard back and opening the throttle all the way after the water rudders are raised. The raising of the nose is brought about by the force of the water on the forward bottom of the float, and, as the speed increases, the force of the water on the rear portion of the float bottom becomes greater until the rear of the plane is raised and it begins to plane, at which time the back pressure is eased. While planing the airplane is supported on the water, rather than in the water. The speed increases rapidly, and, if not retarded, the airplane will take off.

Turning while in this planing position can be accomplished, but very gentle turns should be used, because the centrifugal force in a steep turn is high and may easily be sufficient to cause the seaplane to capsize if the outside float digs into the water. Turning left, I use left aileron to keep the weight on the inside float (turning right,

right aileron, etc).

On small lakes I sometimes use a step turn, so-called because the airplane is planing on the step portion of the floats. The step is located about half-way back, where the float makes a right angle up and then continues back in a tapered manner to the end of the float. Once the step turn is completed you are at, or close to, flying speed and can get airborne clearing the end of a short lake, whereas a straight line take-off from the normal idling, taxying position might be impossible!

Sometimes because of strong winds it is necessary to shut the engine off and sail backwards into a beach or dock. If the winds are really strong the engine can be left idling so that you don't back up too fast. Lowering flaps and opening the cabin doors will increase the air resistance and add to the effect of the wind. The water rudder should be raised. By using ailerons and rudders—and practicing—you can back into some very restricted areas that would be impossible to reach without sailing.

Landing a seaplane is normally done into the wind, and after awhile you learn to read the wind on the water and can tell the direction accurately. For instance, on the lee side of the lake you will notice it's calm close to shore, and on the other side you can see waves wash right up to shore.

A seaplane may be landed in an approximate level position to a nose high, full stall. The best position, when the water is fairly smooth, is such that the step and the stern of the floats touch the water at the same time. However, a smooth landing may be accomplished in almost any position, as long as the stick is moving back at the instant of contact. A full stall landing is entirely safe, but is not as smooth.

After contact with the water a seaplane will go through the same series of positions as in the take-off, but in reverse order. It will plane for a short distance, then take the nose up position and finally the idling position. If you need to travel a good distance after touch down, then taxying on the step is in order.

All airplanes have three axis. The first is the longitudinal axis extending through the airplane from nose to tail. The airplane rolls around the longitudinal axis. The bank, rolling the airplane for a turn, is controlled with the ailerons, which are a hinged surface, usually near the end of the wing on the back portion. Turns are made in an airplane by banking in the direction of the turn. This is done by using the ailerons to roll the airplane toward the direction in which the turn is desired. Pressure is applied to the aileron control in the direction of the desired bank, which causes the aileron on the wing in the direction in which control is applied to raise, while the aileron on the opposite wing is lowered or depressed. Lift is decreased on the wing on which the aileron is raised and increased on the wing on which the aileron is lowered. This results in the airplane banking in the direction of the applied aileron control.

The lowered aileron on the high wing produces greater drag than the raised aileron on the low wing and causes the airplane to yaw toward the high wing, away from the turn; that's where the rudder comes in. The rudder controls this adverse yaw and helps make a smooth, coordinated turn possible. By applying rudder in the direction of the turn, a clean entry can be made. Returning the airplane to straight and level flight smoothly is accomplished by again controlling any adverse yaw with the use of the rudder. This time the opposite rudder away from the direction of the turn is used as you roll the airplane to straight and level flight, completing the turn.

The second axis is called the lateral axis and extends horizontally through the airplane (wing tip to wing tip) and is at right angles to the longitudinal axis and vertical axis. The hinged surface on the back portion of the horizontal stabilizer is called the elevators, and they control the pitch, which is the movement around the lateral axis, to establish a desired angle of attack for climbing, descending, etc.

The third is the vertical axis. This extends through the airplane from top to bottom, at right angles, too, and intersecting both the longitudinal and lateral axis. Yaw is the movement around the vertical axis and is controlled with the rudder, (the hinged surface at the back of the vertical stabilizer) and is used to help the pilot make a smooth, coordinated turn by controlling adverse yaw created by the ailerons and to make minor corrections in a heading of a couple of degrees or so. Left and right rudder pedals on the floor control the rudder in the air, as well as the tail wheel or water rudder when taxying.

The lift of an airplane is developed by forcing downward a mass of air with a force equal to the weight of an airplane. To do this the wing must pull air down from above and force air beneath its lower surface. In order to produce this lift, the wing must be thrust forward through the air above a certain minimum speed. The sum of the forces lifting from the top of the wing, pushing up from beneath it and retarding it as it is forced through the air, is called the resultant force on the wing. Since the wing does not always proceed directly forward through the air without raising or settling, the flow of air across it is not always from the same angle. The direction of the air as it flows over a wing is called relative wind.

In level flight there are two principal horizontal forces which act on an airplane: thrust and drag. The thrust is provided in the conventional airplane by the engine, acting through the propeller, and the drag by the resistance of the air to the passage of the airplane with all its componant parts.

When flying level at uniform speed, the forward acting thrust exactly equals the backward-acting, total drag. There is no acceleration, since any forward force which might be produced by the thrust is neutralized by a backward force produced by the drag.

If the throttle is opened so that thrust becomes greater than drag, this will cause a forward acceleration or increase in speed until the drag increases to again exactly equal the thrust.

One of the most common fatal causes of airplane accidents (usually close to the ground) is called a stall and occurs with the abrupt loss of lift, when the angle of attack increases to the point at which the flow of air tends to tear away from a wing or other airfoil.

Banking an airplane in a turn requires more lift, and the stall speed increases, which makes turns right after take-off with low airspeed especially dangerous and causes many fatal accidents. A 75^0 bank doubles the stalling speed. In a turn, back pressure on the elevator control column must be used (increased angle of attack) to maintain level flight, due to the loss of lift in a turn, which decreases the airspeed.

The load factor for any airplane maintaining a constant altitude in a 60^0 bank is 2 G's, which means twice the weight of gravity, or twice the weight of the airplane. The load factor increases at a terrific rate after a bank has reached 45^0 or 50^0. The wing must produce lift equal to this load factor if altitude is to be maintained. At slightly more than 80^0 the load factor exceeds the limit of 6 G's, the limit factor of an acrobatic airplane. After the load factor of any airplane is exceeded, structural failure can occur, and in some cases wings are literally torn off an airplane.

Another way this load factor can be exceeded is by diving and then zooming up rapidly, which once on a water bomber popped rivets out of the wings. It has literally torn wings off when pulling up in a climb after dropping water on a fire.

There are four basic fundamentals of flying techniques: straight and level flight, the climb, the glide, and the turn. All flying consists of the use of one or more combinations of these fundamentals. An excellent coordination excercise I practice is to keep the nose pointed on a distant mountain and roll the airplane from side to side, with aileron keeping the nose straight with the rudders. While flying I try to pick out places to land, should the engine quit. On floats ,because of the large surface area, you're much safer landing on most surfaces and much less likely to flip on your back than if you were in a wheel plane.

Flying off rivers is probably the most difficult type of seaplane flying, because of so many variables such as currents, winding narrow channels, rocks, sometimes silty, murky waters that are impossible to see through, and the wind.

Landing upstream, into the current, gives a pilot excellent control; you can slow down, even go backwards as you manuever to a landing site. Going downstream you have to go much faster to have the same water rudder effectiveness, and the danger increases substantially. If you're heading upstream and into the wind, it's sometimes very difficult or impossible to turn downstream, as the wind and current tends to keep you heading into the current.

One pilot for another company flew into Nahanni Butte, located in the Northwest Territory, one day and landed his Beaver floatplane on the silty, murky river there. Upon take-off he hit a sand bar, and the Beaver ended up in the verticle position, having to be pulled down with a rope.

One hunting camp I flew into on numerous occasions was on the Turnagain River. We landed upstream, but always had to take-off downstream because of obstructions in the river above camp. The Turnagain, as the name implies, looks like a snake. On this narrow, shallow, rocky rim there was a real danger of hitting the other shore or rocks with the floats or of the wing hitting a tree on the bank. When turning downstream, the outfitter would wade in the water and help turn me downstream after I cranked up the engine. If we were loaded, it meant going around the first bend or two on the step (planing position), often on one float until the airplane became airborne and then sometime going around another bend in the air until we cleared the trees.

One pilot who flew an Otter for another company related a terrifying experience he had one day. "Because I flew the Otter floatplane most of the time, which has a very flat landing attitude, I wasn't used to our company's Cessna 185, which has a higher nose up landing attitude. I was with the president of a mining company when we landed on Summit Lake. As I landed the Cessna and the floats dug into the water, we ended up vertically looking straight down into the lake, not knowing which way we would go. But we were lucky, and the plane came down rightside up!"

I have found while flying with a heavy load in the Beaver floatplane—especially if it's tail heavy—that a bit of flap will raise the tail and help the airplane to pick up a few miles per hour. Mostly bush flying is common sense, and, of course, experience helps eliminate some risks. But this you get only with time. I was fortunate to have good, safe training by Jack Hodge and some of the other pilots when starting out as a green pilot.

CHAPTER IV
WINTER FLYING ON SKIS

A few more trips up north into some hunting camps and the busy, short guiding business shut down for the season. The lakes had begun to freeze, and, until the ice thickened, we couldn't fly. We kept busy working on the airplanes, taking care of mechanical and structural work that needed to be done. Eventually the ice was thick enough for us to operate on skis.

We packed down a runway on the snow-covered ice with snowshoes and snowmobiles. The sides of the runway were lined with spruce branches, which enabled us to see the strip from the air and also helped our depth perception, as snow, especially on gray days, is similar to glassy water landings on floats: very poor depth perception and a good possibility of a mishap. Other strips in the bush, such as Fort Babine and Takla Post, were also lined with tree branches. Because there were sometimes rough ice, snow ridges on the lakes, and uneven snow strips, I usually touched down on the strong main gear first and let the weaker tail ski touch last. On take-off, forward pressure on the elevator controls lifted the tail ski ,and then slight back pressure on the elevators let the ski plane fly off the snow.

Les Cox, the game warden of Smithers, and I flew in the Super Cub on skis to do a moose count in January. I had met Les earlier at Marty Allen's ranch when we lived in the Kispiox Valley; he occasionally drove up to check things out and stopped to visit, but we got to know each other better in the close quarters. We flew low, sometimes rolling our lively ship on its side to get a better look at those dark masses of fur against the white snow background.

Milt Warren and I flew out on a cold February day in the ski-equipped Super Cub JUE to do a wolf kill count east of Smithers around the Babine Lake area. We were looking for moose kills and getting a rough count of moose. Then on February 29, Milt Warren, Bill Russell of the B.C. game department, and I climbed into the ski-equipped Cessna 185 to continue the moose count: looking at moose kills, determining their age, and looking to see if they were killed by wolves. The Cessna was a lot warmer and more comfortable to fly than the Cub.

Later in the winter I flew with Ray Seridic, assistant to Les Cox, to drop off poisoned meat to kill some wolves. The outfitters had complained, saying the wolves were killing the game and ruining their hunting area. Ray thought maybe the outfitters were responsible, but, to keep peace, the Game Department set out a token of a few poisoned baits. We landed at a few lakes on the ice and dropped off some bait.

WINTER FLYING ON SKIS

As we approached Mooseskin Johnny Lake, twenty-five miles south of Smithers, all looked well—that is, until we touched down, sinking almost to the wings in light snow. It looked like a long walk out on snowshoes. I told Ray to push on the strut, and I applied full power. We were able to get back on our tracks and out of there in a hurry, a bit shaken. Often when flying in northern B.C. on skis, I spotted wolves on lakes or open fields. They were and are a favorite of mine—such a part of the wilderness scene, they truly belong and serve a useful function in nature's scheme of things. Sometimes I would see large packs of twenty or more—grays, blacks, and a few all-white ones.

On one trip with fisheries personnel we flew to Morrison Lake on skis in the Super Cub. Flying back over Babine Lake we saw several wolves run out toward the middle of the lake. I came in about fifteen feet above the ice, behind a huge silver wolf. As we got within fifty feet or so his head turned to look at us, and I knew he was trying to figure out what to do. When we were about twenty feet away, he turned sharp left, and we flew by. His beautiful, strong body going at top speed across the ice is still a picture in my mind that I recall from time to time. A priceless moment, it's the closest I have ever been to a live wolf in the wild!

Our airplanes were equipped with straight skis, so unless a runway had snow or ice on it we couldn't land. On skis there were no brakes, so you just slid until the plane decided to stop. The tail ski acted as a tail wheel; when rudder was applied it turned, unless it was frozen or stuck in the ice or snow.

Ski flying could be hazardous. Early in the season it was hard to tell how solid the ice was. Later in the year the ice got rotten with large holes that we tried to land between, hoping we didn't fall through the ice. We always carried gas blow pots to preheat the engine if we got stuck overnight. We carried an engine cover to direct the heat from the blow pot to the engine. Snowshoes and survival gear were staples. It was sometimes necessary to snowshoe a runway in order to get the plane going fast enough for take-off.

Once, early in the winter season, I was checking the ice across from Fort Babine on Babine Lake to see if it was thick enough to handle the ski-equipped Super Cub so we could start flying mail in. I was out from shore about fifty feet when all of a sudden, without any warning, I fell through the ice. I was able to climb up on the ice and ran to the shore, up a bank and back to a cabin to dry off. Another time, Bill Harrison lost the engine in the Cessna 185 CF-OXE, a ski-equipped plane that I usually flew, and barely made it over some trees, landing on the ice, just a day or so after I had flown it. Luck and good fortune seemed to be going my way.

One cold winter day I flew our ski-equipped Beaver JOS to Hyland Post, thirty miles east of Cold Fish Lake. This was in Tommy Walker's hunting area and was called The Ranch. Jim Morgan, a genuine mountain man, was spending the winter there looking after things. I landed on a field next to a log cabin. Because of an inversion (cold air on the ground and warm air higher), it was minus sixty degrees.

FLIGHT OF THE RED BEAVER

I left the engine running as I unloaded the food and supplies he ordered and, of course, the mail. He was doing some winter trapping and had several furs. I bought two wolf hides, one all white and the other silver, which I have to this day.

After taking off and gaining a few thousand feet, the temperature went up thirty or forty degrees; it seemed warm after the minus sixty degrees on the ground. This was the coldest air I had ever flown in. We had a policy of not flying if it was much colder than minus ten or twenty degrees; the cold temperature was hard on the airplanes and made for hazardous flying.

When flying a ski-equipped plane during the winter months, extra precautions were required to ensure the plane would be ready for flight. Ice and snow on the wings reduce the lift (because they affect the shape of the airfoil) and have on many occasions caused fatal accidents, so we pulled rope over the wings to loosen and remove the snow and ice before flight, as well as using a push broom to sweep off the loose snow. To keep the skis from freezing to the snow and ice when the plane was on the ground, we had poles laid out and ran the skis partially up on them. After the last flight of the day with the Beaver, we switched on the dilution system, which transfers some gas into the oil system, making the oil thinner and enabling the cold engine to turn over more rapidly in the morning and start much more quickly. Flying skis is usually more work than pleasure. Skis stick and freeze on the ice, if you don't run them up on a pole when you stop. Sometimes water gets between the snow and ice, and the slushy cover prevents the airplane from obtaining flying speed, so you just sit and wait for better conditions, which can be a bit of a pain if you're on a remote wilderness lake two hundred miles from home.

There is always danger, especially during the beginning and the end of winter, when the ice is marginal and you hope you don't break through and lose a plane. On one occasion, early in the season, we put the Cessna 185 on skis and slid it out on the ice. A couple of hours later we saw it at a crazy angle in the lake; one ski had broken through the ice, and the plane was in the water. Fortunately, it wasn't deep, but about that time the Old Man, as we called the owner, Bill Harrison, flew over and landed with the Super Cub, which was lighter. He was a bit upset, to say the least. We got the Cessna out of the lake undamaged and back in the hangar; we left it there until the ice got thicker.

March 28, 1969, Mike Smith and Gene Winoski, from a company called Ipec, met me at Maclure Lake. Ipec worked for B.C. Hydro checking snow depth to determine water flow for the coming year. We flew in the Beaver CF-JOS to Kaza and Tsaydaychi Lakes and to Germansen Landing, where we overnighted at Westfalls' place. He was originally from Sandpoint, Idaho. He and his wife manned a weather station for the government and were warm, gracious hosts whenever I stayed overnight. Wes had a Champ on floats and later purchased a Cessna 180 on floats that he flew off the river at Germansen Landing.

The following day we flew to Tutizzi, Johanson, Fredrickson, and Pulpit lakes and then on to Fort Ware, where we overnighted at Art Van Sommer's home. Art was well known in the north. He freighted supplies up for his store during the summer months when the Finley River was open. He sold the goods to the natives at the Indian village at Fort Ware. During our stay I had a chance to get to know him a bit. He talked slowly and easily, and I could tell he was well versed on the area and, of course, on the Finley River, which provided his livelihood. Art was a congenial host, and my stay was enjoyable. On March 30 we departed; we landed at Sikanni Chief, Lady Laurra, Germansen, and finally Maclure Lake, our home base.

April 8, I prepared for a flight in the ski-equipped Cessna 185 CF-OXE. My destination was Takla Post. Jack Newcomb, the owner, wanted me to fly in some groceries and supplies. During the winter, flying was the only means of getting supplies in; during the summer it could be freighted up the lake.

I invited Jim Goerz along, as it was only a forty-minute flight, a quick turnaround, and then the return flight—about two hours total. Jim mentioned he had to work that afternoon, in about three hours. "No problem, Jim," I told him. "We'll be back in plenty of time!"

The soft snow covering the ice on Maclure Lake was packed hard. Several of us pilots had snowshoed back and forth, making a decent airstrip. After sweeping the snow off the wings and fuselage and untying the wings, we hopped in. The preheated engine started after several shots of primer and a touch of the starter. Taxiing to the north end of the strip, which was marked with spruce branches, I did the runup. Full power, and soon the tail rose as we accelerated quickly in the winter air.

The Cessna seemed to jump off the snow, and we climbed rapidly in the dense, cold air. The air was so clear that distant mountains seemed much closer than they actually were. The cowl flap was almost closed to keep the engine warm. Usually the cowl flaps are full open in a climb to help keep the engine from overheating, but not in cold winter conditions.

Enjoying the sunny day, we flew through Chapman Pass and soon crossed the south end of Chapman Lake, now covered with ice and snow. We passed north of Old Fort Babine on Babine Lake and soon saw the smoke rising from cabins and the store at Takla Post. Making a lazy left banking turn, I looked over the sleepy village. All seemed peaceful.

The snow-packed strip on Takla Lake was several hundred feet from shore and was also marked with spruce branches. Flying north down wind, I slowed to ninety miles per hour indicated with one notch of flaps, turning base, another notch of flaps, and on final I used three notches—thirty degrees of flaps—and approached at about eighty miles per hour indicated. Touchdown was smooth and all seemed normal.

After about a hundred feet or so the airplane started turning left on the ice, and I tried to correct it with first partial and then full right rudder—with no effect. The right wing soon struck the ice as the right landing gear buckled under the plane. Because the prop was still turning, it struck the ice and bent at the ends. It happened so fast that only now did I turn off the switches.

Gas poured over our clothes. "Let's get out of here, Jim!" The door was jammed from the impact, gas was pouring from the wing tank on us and on the engine, and panic set in as I thought of fire, the thing pilots dread the most. After several tries, I finally kicked the door open, and we ran across the ice, expecting an explosion. All was quiet as we caught our breath. The right wing was bent up on the ice about eight feet from the wing tip. The prop was bent backward towards the cockpit, and the horizontal stabilizer on the same side was bent on the end. I had no idea what had happened.

No one from the village was there; maybe it was fortunate, as they could have been injured by our wild ride off the marked strip. A fine fix: we were about sixty-five air miles from home, and Jim had a job to go to in a couple of hours. Our "two-hour trip" took a couple of days. We were finally picked up by another plane, and the C-185 CF-OXE was flown out by helicopter. It was sold and eventually ended up in the bottom of the ocean, I was told.

Investigation revealed that a supporting component inside the fuselage had a hairline crack; it just let go at that particular time. Bill Harrison said it wasn't my fault and didn't hold it against me, since I had no control over a structural failure.

I was somewhat shaken up, having never before been involved in an accident. I took a much-welcomed vacation of six weeks to Spokane. It was the end of winter; spring breakup was to come shortly, so it was a good time to leave.

WINTER FLYING ON SKIS

Larry standing beside the Beaver CF JOS in March of 1968, on the Finly River at Ft. Ware B.C. while flying a Charter for IPEC. We stayed overnight with Art Van Sommers, a legendary river boat man that ran a trading post here at this Indian Village.

Larry standing beside the wrecked Cessna 185 ski plane CF-OXE. Jim Goerz went along for the ride, and it was a wild one. I was flying freight to the fur trader Jack Newcomb who ran a trading post for the Indians here at Takla Post, northern British Columbia, when the right landing gear collapsed.

CHAPTER V
FORT BABINE

The Indians at Fort Babine are a subtribe of the Carrier tribe. The name was derived from a native custom whereby a widow was obliged to carry the ashes of her deceased husband with her in a basket for three years. The Carrier tribe is located around Eutsuk, Francois, and Babine Lakes and as far south as the neighborhood of Quesnel.

One of my fun jobs involved flying the mail to Fort Babine, where they still had an honest-to-goodness Hudson's Bay trading post, similar to ones I read about as a kid growing up in Spokane. This was one of the last trading posts in existence. Mac, the storekeeper, was only three years away from retirement, and the store was to be shut down when he retired.

The store's supplies were rather sparse: wooden shelves filled mostly with canned goods and, of course, flour, salt, sugar, and other staples. Prices were high, and I believe most Indians were in debt to the company. Credit was still the number one commodity with these Babine Indians.

There were no roads at the fort. A Catholic church stood impressively on the hill, overlooking the village and Babine Lake. There were Indian cabins on either side and up the hill from the company store. The store itself was close to the lake.

My Cessna was loaded with every size box and package known to man, I think. They completely surrounded me and were stuffed in all the corners and cracks available. Fortunately, it was a light load; the only problem was space.

The natives were fascinated with the airplane, and many were waiting eagerly to see if those items they had ordered from the catalog had arrived. With lots of help at the dock, the 185 was soon securely fastened, and I was surrounded by children of all sizes, as well as men and women. With all this help, the plane was soon unloaded.

"Pleeze, take some fish to my sister at Takla Post," said one native woman. Takla Post, forty miles east, was the next stop on the mail run. Having a little room, I loaded up some salmon that was very ripe and something to which I couldn't have gotten close enough to eat.

I got lots of help pushing off. I told the natives to watch the tail when I started up so they wouldn't get knocked down; that had happened before, fortunately with nothing but their pride hurt. Takla Landing looked a little rough, as there was a fair wind blowing. The lake was long, and the spray was blowing off the tops of some good-sized whitecaps. I thought I'd try for a little smooth stretch that I remembered close to shore and work down to the dock from there. The water was hard as I hit the troughs with a thud, but it soon slowed the airplane and, just idling now, we actually went backwards.

This was the tricky part, coming up to the dock and not damaging a float. Jack Hodge once said, "Larry, hurry all you want in the air, but take your time docking." Once, just after getting checked out in the Beaver, I went on a flight to Fort Babine. The wind and waves were whipping up a bit. I was used to the C-185 and the shorter radius of turn. A wind was also working against me. Because of that, I didn't quite get turned parallel to the dock before I hit; the front of the float got a bit of a wrinkle, and I got a good talking-to. It was a while before I flew the Beaver again.

Easing into the dock, I was able to secure the plane with no problems this time. The stinky fish came off first, but I knew from past fish runs that the smell would not leave so quickly. For several days I would be reminded of the fishy mail run.

Jack Newcomb, owner of the store called Takla Post, and his Asian wife were some of the nicest people I knew. Takla Post was owned by the Hudson's Bay Company at one time. Jack was an independent trader. His wife was a happy, well-adjusted woman who evidently didn't mind the isolation.

After a cup of coffee and a little local news exchange, the outgoing mail was loaded. I started the engine as Jack held me out a few feet from the dock to keep the floats from banging against the logs. The fuel-injected engine caught after a couple of cranks. I eased out a bit, staying close to the bank where the water was calmer. Full power, a few solid thumps as I hit some big waves, and we bounced into the air.

One warm, sunny morning as I was unloading the mail at Fort Babine, an Indian man of about forty years approached me. "I want you to fly me to Fort St. James. I have one hundred dollars for the trip," he said.

We jumped in the C-185 and flew to Fort St. James, where he bought a case of beer. The case of beer and flight cost came to ninety-seven dollars. Later, one of the pilots told me that before I arrived, this Indian put on quite a performance with the Indian social worker who happened to be in Fort Babine at the time. With tears streaming down his face, he said his family had no food and he needed the one hundred dollars to keep them from starving. A check was issued, and ninety-seven dollars went for a case of booze. Fort Babine was a dry village.

One winter morning on a mail run to Fort Babine, I noticed some very hung over and quite subdued natives. Evidently there had been a weekend drunk. Coming down the hill was a naked Indian woman in a dog sled—just the sled, no dog—with a native man holding onto the handles. Into a log cabin went sled, naked woman and man. He tipped the sled over and the woman rolled off in a very undignified heap. Quite a performance so early in the morning, I thought to myself, as I went about my business at the Hudson's Bay Store.

Another time, again in front of the Hudson's Bay Store, the doors of the houses opened, and boys of various ages began gathering in an opening between the houses and store to play ball. There was no shoving, shouting or putting one another down as I've seen white children do. Instead, each took his turn catching, throwing and hitting the ball, a marked contrast to behavior I remembered from my childhood.

The Indian people I observed at Fort Babine and elsewhere enjoyed simple pleasures and needed very little to be happy. They enjoyed now, today, and seemed unconcerned about the tomorrows. This was evident in their wood supply, as they seldom had any stockpiled. Money was to be spent. Credit was cherished at the store; most of the Indians charged merchandise. The Hudson's Bay Company had them dependent on its goods, much the same as their ancestors were.

I admired these Babine Indians, especially the older ones who worked and remained independent. One native in his eighties had a facial bone structure that an artist would love to paint. His chiseled face showed depth of character, self-reliance and wisdom. He was a real gentleman, proud and self-sufficient, with the regal bearing of a chief, which he may have been. He lived on his own place with his daughter. He logged in the winter, skidded the logs with a horse to the ice on the lake and made a boom which held the logs until the ice melted. In the spring a tug hauled away his winter's work.

The Babine Indians were primarily fish eaters. They netted salmon near the mouth of the Babine River. Forty miles to the east the Takla Lake Indians lived near Takla Post. They were primarily meat eaters, shooting lots of moose. Occasionally they got salmon from their cousins at Fort Babine when I flew some over on a mail run.

Father McCormick, my friend the flying priest, flew into Fort Babine and surrounding isolated areas administering the Catholic doctrine to area natives. We had some good times. I convinced him to begin a running program when he was in town; we ran from the base at Maclure Lake down the road a few miles.

One day, as Father McCormick and I headed into town to have a drink, he said, "Larry, don't call me Father. I want to relax and have a good time." Dressed in regular clothes, he and I went to a local establishment and proceeded to down a few. Some of the teachers at the Catholic school were there. All but the prudish one joined in; we had a great time. Father was an intelligent, interesting man; once he told me he might consider marriage someday.

A few years before, the Protestant Church sent competition in the form of a Protestant missionary with a plane. The missionary began converting Father's natives. Up until that time, Father McCormick had traveled by boat, but it was much slower than the competing plane. To stay ahead of the game, the church sent Father out to get a pilot's license. Father came back with a Super Cub, and became a flying priest. He stopped some of the natives from leaving the church, as he could now visit each parish more often. Of course, the image of the flying priest made a good impression on the natives. One winter as Father was preparing to take a nun for a ride, she walked into the turning propeller, which was almost invisible, and was killed.

John Morganthayler, the engineer, was fixing a fresh brew of coffee when I got back from one of my fishy mail runs. John was a hardworking, gruff aviation mechanic with a heart of gold. He knew his job well and worked long hours after we shut down, so the planes would be ready to fly the next day. His wife lived in southern B.C. and worked in a store. He went home occasionally, but I think they got along well when they were seven hundred miles apart, or so it seemed.

Since I was a fairly new pilot, John tried to be helpful and let me know when I did something wrong. He warned me about problems that could develop; I appreciated all the information and help I could get. I was thirty years old and had been flying commercially for a little over a year. Because I had owned planes of my own, and maybe because of my age, my inclination was to be on the cautious side and not to take unnecessary chances.

Bill Harrison told me once, "Larry, when it gets busy, I expect things to get done, but I'll never ask you to take a flight that you feel is beyond your capability and would never hold it against you if you turn down a trip for that reason." And he never did.

Mom and Dad came up every summer now, and Dad took Scott fishing. They brought their camper, and every morning our dog Gretchen was waiting outside for the pancakes they always made. Gretchen let them know when she felt it was time to get her breakfast.

My sister Nancy came up one year with her first son Jon, who was a baby at the time; so did my brother Bob. Later Jon would come up with Mom and Dad, and they would take Scott fishing and have a great time. They said it was the highlight of each year.

Mom, Dad, Kathy, Scott and I flew into Kitchener Lake, the same lake I flew into with Jim Conway and Larry Bardette when they made fishing movies for *Outdoor Sportsman*. We caught many rainbow trout; some were wormy, however, so we didn't keep any. We then visited the Love brothers for lunch at Tutade Lake. Wally Love related a story to us. "Four of us went from the cabin to the lake to catch some fish. We surprised a mean-looking Grizzly bear, and he headed right for us. I yelled, waved my arms and he charged right by me, brushing my leg. I'm sure if I had turned and run, he would have attacked me." We also visited Mr. & Mrs. Woods at Johanson Lake. I flew them and their dog in earlier in the C-185. They were almost out of food, so we gave them some of ours. Mrs. Woods taught school in the Kispiox Valley. Mr. Woods was a true Englishman and had an English Land Rover 4-wheel drive that usually seemed to be in the shop. They were neat people, warm, kind and generous. It was a beautiful trip, and, except for the wormy fish, we all had a good time. I had begun to appreciate my parents, now that I had a child of my own and could realize how much they had done for me over the years. We spotted many salmon from the air in the rivers and streams as they were beginning to spawn.

One summer Dad, Mom, my Aunt JoAnn and Uncle Jess McDaniel, Aunt Sue and Uncle John Clark came up for a visit. I flew Dad, Jess and John into Babine in the C-185; they caught a lot of trout. My dad was the cook; he declared that if there were any complaints, the complainer would become the cook. John said one morning, "Val, these pancakes were lumpy and the dough was raw, but it was just the way I like it." They garnered many happy memories on that trip, even though Dad pushed Jess into the cold lake for lack of anything better to do. Aunt Sue used to send me cookies and cake when I was overseas, and Kathy, Scott and I stayed with them in California for a month when John was in the Air Force. They made us feel right at home, so I was glad to do something for them.

My Aunt JoAnn was only 10 years older than I, and we were always close. Her husband Jess took me on my first hunting trip with a gun; I shot my first duck with his 410 shotgun. We became good pals over the years.

The Super Cub CF-JUE looked a bit like a toy airplane when it sat beside the Beaver and the C-185, but the size difference was deceiving. With its 150-horsepower Lycoming engine, it got off much more quickly than the rest of the fleet. It was a good plane for getting in and out of short lakes and doing reconnaissance work because it could be flown very slowly, and the visibility was terrific. It was, however, a bit cramped and could haul only one passenger. Four or five hours on its spartan seats left me not wanting to sit down again for a long time.

I had some parts to fly into a mining exploration company working out of Kaza Lake. The Cub was gassed and rode easily on the water, looking eager to go and have some fun. John gave me a push out. The powerful Lycoming engine caught quickly, and I taxied to the north end. Runup was normal, and I felt good about the plane.

The hundred-mile flight to Kaza Lake, which was north of Takla Lake near the Omineca River, took a little over an hour. Climbing rapidly, as we were lightly loaded, I trimmed for level flight at six thousand feet. I always figured extra altitude was like money in the bank. If the engine quit, I had more time to pick out a spot to land. In addition, it was usually quicker to go higher; I could fly over the mountains instead of around them, saving time and fuel.

Crossing the Omineca, everything appeared to be fine, and I was relaxed as I started my descent, looking foward to fresh coffee at camp and, if I was lucky, a piece of pie. The lake looked almost square as I flew over the camp to let them know I was there and to check for obstructions before touchdown on the lake. Everything looked good, and my landing was smooth. Lucky day—in front of a camp, you tried to make it look good. Most people judge a flight by a smooth landing; while it's nice, it's certainly only one part of flying.

I unloaded and went to the kitchen tent; a cup of coffee and a piece of pie were waiting for me. I was fat and happy. "Well, John, I'd better be getting back. Thanks for the pie. You do good work," I said before heading back to the plane.

Take-off was normal, and I soon left the lake behind and climbed toward the southwest. Everything was normal—in about an hour, I'd be home. Suddenly my windscreen turned black, and smoke began filling the cockpit. I immediately slammed the side window open so I could breathe fresh air and see. Oil was spraying the windscreen so heavily that the oil supply would soon be gone, and the engine would quit. I turned back toward the lake. I desperately wanted the airplane to be over the lake now—if it would just keep running for a few minutes, I could make it.

The lake was closer now. Just a few minutes, engine, and we'll both make it. Well, Larry, it's your lucky day. The lake was finally below, and I was okay. I knew I could glide to a safe landing.

The camp residents met me with puzzled looks. The windscreen was completely black, and I had my head out the window, but I was happier than I'd been for a long time.

Under the cowling I easily located the problem:broken oil line. I called Bill Harrison on the camp radio, explained the problem, and told him what part I needed, then relaxed and enjoyed my good fortune. I was alive, and the airplane was safe. It was at times like this that I said, "Larry, I don't care if I ever fly again." That attitude usually lasted only a day or so and was forgotten until another close call shook up the bad flying memory bank.

Flying was a bug that got into my blood and liked it there—most of the time. I grew another gray hair or two during those moments when I couldn't see and when that ever-present threat—fire—seemed imminent. But for whatever reason, it wasn't my time. I had no control over what happened.

Left, Uncle John Clark, Uncle Jess McDaniel and my father in front of our log home, in the Driftwood Valley N.E. some 8 miles from the Seaplane base. I flew them in Omineca's C-185 Float plane to Babine Lake for a few days of fishing at a friends cabin.

Our neighbor and guide from the Kispiox, Bill Love on the left. Center is Fred Bear, maker of Bear Bows, and the actor Fess Parker of Daniel Boone and Davy Crockett fame. Fess got his grizzly bear on this hunt, in northern British Columbia.

Scott and his faithful dog Gretchen II. They spent the night in this Igloo he built, about 1968.

Kitchener Lake northern British Columbia 1967. My father is on the left, mother, Kathy and Scott on the floats of the C-185 CF-OXE that we flew in on. We had a wonderful day of catching large Rainbow and seeing this pristine high mountain lake country.

CHAPTER VI
ADVENTURES IN THE YUKON

Work was slow, and we had too many pilots for the work available in the summer of 1969, so we got in very few hours flying. In the middle of July I drove to Bill Harrison's home and gave him my two weeks' notice. I planned to go to Seattle for an instrument rating, so I could fly for Interior Airways in Alaska on a Hercules aircraft. An Interior Airways pilot had told me my chances of going to work for them would be good if I had an instrument rating.

A few days later Grant Luck, the working base manager, offered me an attractive salary to go to work for B.C. Yukon Air Service at Watson Lake for the remainder of the season. With little hesitation, I accepted. I had requested a transfer earlier to do this, but they had wanted me to stay at Maclure Lake.

Scott and I departed Smithers for Spokane, arriving on July 25. Scott was to stay at Grandma and Grandpa Whitesitt's. August 2, I left Spokane in my VW, on course to Watson Lake, Yukon Territory. During the long, dusty and muddy drive up the Alaska Highway my windshield broke, but I arrived at last at Watson Lake. I drove several miles past it, not believing the few sparse buildings were my destination. It was the fifth of August. I turned north at Watson Lake and drove another six miles to B.C. Yukon Float Base. I was finally here and ready to begin my first flight in the Yukon.

Yukon is an Indian name meaning "the greatest." It's one of the coldest areas of the world. The winters are long and dark, and harsh blizzards are frequent. It gets down to 60 degrees below zero. In the southwest corner is a fantastic area called Klauane National Park, so remote that 90 percent of its features are unnamed. The park is over eight thousand square miles, half the size of Switzerland. The highest mountain, Mount Logan, has an elevation of 19,520 feet, and ten other peaks are over fifteen thousand feet. There are more than two thousand glaciers; it's the largest ice field in the world outside the polar regions. More than seven hundred kinds of flora grow here. Dall sheep (white) live in the Yukon—as do wolves, grizzlies, moose and caribou.

The Yukon Territory has 186,000 square miles and extends north from the B.C. border to the Arctic Ocean, over 600 miles. From Alaska on the west to the Northwest Territories to the east, its southern border measures 583 miles. Compared to the Yukon's population of 23,500, or one person for every 8 square miles, Alaska would seem densely populated with 534,000 people, or about one person per square mile.

ADVENTURES IN THE YUKON

The adjoining Northwest Territories to the east, where I flew often, has a population of 52,238 people, one for every 25 square miles. The Yukon and Northwest Territories, both Canadian territories, have 1,508,900 square miles, about three times the size of Alaska.

After my long trek to Watson Lake, I really appreciated the vastness and the remoteness of this land. Being basically a loner, with a love for the wilderness, I felt a closeness, a kinship, at home here in the Yukon.

B.C. Yukon was started by pioneer aviator George Dalziel in the 1940's. At the time I joined B.C. Yukon he ran a guiding service, flew a Super Cub and was still very active.

I flew with a fellow by the name of Jim Thibaudeau longer than any other pilot, from 1969 to 1975. The first time I met Jim was at B.C. Yukon's seaplane base in 1969. Jim's friendly grin, warm Yukon welcome and handshake greeted me as I walked through the door. It was the beginning of my Yukon adventure, and I was to get well acquainted over the years with this bush pilot.

Jim was about twenty-five years old, 5 feet 10 inches with a trim, well-built body. He was a handsome man, and I noticed that women gave him more than an occasional glance and made complimentary remarks among themselves about his good looks. He wore cowboy boots, blue jeans, a blue shirt, and an Air Force flight jacket. Jim had a good touch and feel for an airplane, and you knew right away he was in control. He was the kind of bush pilot that Hollywood would portray, and, in fact, he did some flying for several films. He lived with one film maker for a year or so and flew his Super Cub, making a movie about a bush pilot who crashed in the wilderness. He also flew Watson Lake Flying Service's Red Beaver CF-IBP in a film depicting a true story about a man and woman from Alaska who crashed near Aeroplane Lake, eighty miles south of Watson Lake and just west of the Rocky Mountains. This couple survived longer without food than anyone ever has in the wilderness.

Jim and I each flew Beavers for B.C. Yukon. His was one of the best performing Beavers in the country, and he was proud of his plane. The following year Jim went to work for Watson Lake Flying Service, and I flew his favorite plane that year.

Jim was sweet on a girl named Lynn, a cute bank teller. She was totally taken by this handsome Yukon pilot. One memorable night there was a party at the seaplane office. The northern lights were brightly rippling across the sky like giant colored curtains, and Jim said that some nights when it was cold you could hear the northern lights. Jim and Lynn got into a friendly wrestling match, and Jim ended up on top.

This was my first season in the Yukon, and I felt that at last I was seeing the real North and was beginning to feel at home in this vast, spectacular country of my boyhood dreams.

Ernie Harrison was my boss when I arrived. He was a man in his forties, of medium height and very friendly. He gave me my first flight the day I arrived. Ernie's open, friendly manner and experience as a bush pilot were well known in these parts. He was half owner of B.C. Yukon Air Service with his cousin Bill Harrison, my former boss and owner of Omineca Air Service.

Shortly after arriving in Watson Lake, Ernie Harrison said, "Larry, you have a trip to Moodie Lake, a hundred miles south in the Rocky Mountain Trench, for Frank Cooke." I was to take B.C. Yukon's Beaver CF-JBP and fly some freight to Moodie Lake.

It was August 10, 1969, and this was my first trip to this area, so I had my sectional maps on my lap. The weather was lousy after take-off, and I had to climb over the cloud cover, but I could see holes in the layers. I was flying, feeling good and following a river when I noticed the river was running the wrong direction, according to the map. I discovered I was not sure of my location. In other words, I was lost!

A short time later, I saw a lake through a hole in the clouds and thought I spotted a couple of pack dogs by a cabin. This made me feel better; I could land and ask directions. Upon landing, I taxied the Beaver to shore, tied up, and proceeded to climb up the bank, intending to walk over to the cabin. As I topped the bank, I met a large mass of fur coming toward me only fifteen feet away. I froze. The grizzly didn't like my looks any better than I liked his. I walked slowly backward to the plane, and he went the other direction, much to my relief. Looking at my map I figured I was probably at Scoop Lake; Moodie Lake was about 15 miles southwest.

I flew on to Moodie Lake and met Frank Cooke for the first time. Frank, a lean six-footer, who looked like a cowboy—which he was—had wrangled horses since his childhood. He was a nice-looking, intelligent individual, friendly, well-organized, and seemed completely in charge of every situation. I explained my encounter with the bear and asked, "Frank, are there any pack dogs by the cabin?"

He replied, "No, but I'll bet they were bears, and they probably wrecked my cabin." Frank rounded up a hunter, and we flew back to Scoop Lake to deal with the grizzlies.

Frank describes this event: "I remember it like it was yesterday, and it was the first time we met. You flew in and asked me if there were big dogs or some other animals down at Scoop Lake, and I said there shouldn't be, and no people either. Having lived in the north for so long, I thought there had to be a bear fooling around. I also knew in my mind that they would smash a window and get in my cookhouse and wreck everything, which is exactly what they did. I asked the hunter if he wanted to have some fun, and he said, 'Doing what?' When I explained it to him, he became excited and said, 'How can we get down there?' I told him I would hire you to fly us down to Scoop Lake to take a look, and then we would fly back to Moodie Lake. So I chartered the Beaver, and away we went.

"When we tied up at Scoop Lake, I remember looking out the window of the

Beaver, and sure enough, there was one grizzly in the yard. I wasn't going to let the hunter shoot him, but I looked over at the cookhouse door and saw that it was open and all the windows were knocked out and knew there would be a mess in the cabin. The bear started to run, and I said, 'Shoot him!' He did and killed him. The gun had no sooner gone off, when out the door came another grizzly, and then out the window another. I hated to shoot them, but I knew I had to, as they would never leave and are very destructive. One started down the lake, but the other one started toward us at the lake shore by the plane.

"I said to the hunter, 'You take the one going down the lake, and I'll take the one heading for us,' as he was close, and I wasn't sure how good he could shoot. I don't like being in too close to a grizzly with a strange hunter in case he wounds him; grizzlies can be very dangerous at close quarters. I knew my gun and knew I could kill with one shot, and I did. He shot, and—sure enough!—he wounded his bear. I walked over to the dead one and then finished off the one he had wounded. I can't remember his name, but he sure was excited. He had never seen or participated in that kind of event. It was just another day to me; I have seen lots of these real dangerous situations in my life."

I sat down on one of the bunks to write out a flight ticket. My pants suddenly became very damp, and a strong odor penetrated the air. The bears had urinated on the mattress, and, confined in the warm cockpit of the Beaver, I had to endure this odor all the way back to Watson Lake.

Frank reminisced, "I remember one evening at Moodie Lake, there were twenty of us having a big barbecue in front of the cabins on the lake. I had a big black work dog called Zero at the camp to warn me if anything was around. We had a big fire going, and it was just starting to get dark. Everybody was singing and having a few drinks, but I always kept my eyes peeled for anything wrong, since that was my job, and I always kept my gun handy. It was my responsibility to see that nobody got hurt or got into bad situations. I looked over at the dog, and he stood up and looked up the trail going around the lake. He growled, and the hair stood up all over his back. He was a great dog! I picked up my rifle, told the women and kids to go into the cookhouse quick! I knew there was something coming down the trail. I told the hunters to get their rifles, and they thought I was kidding. Frankie and Terry knew I wasn't, so they got their guns. Sure enough, out of the edge of the clearing came five grizzlies, just like they owned the place.

"The big bear charged, and I shot it right in the mouth. When it went down, it hollered, and the rest charged. I yelled, 'Kill them,' and we did. One bear pretty near got Mac Cooke, who was only fifteen years old at the time. I didn't see Mac behind me when one bear came in sideways toward me. Mac hollered, 'Look out, Dad!' It was pretty dark, and I swung around and shot him not two feet from me. When I looked around, Mac was out in the lake in water up to his waist. Everything was all over in a matter of two to three minutes, and the women and kids all came down to look. We all had a laugh at young Mac, but it was a good lesson to a lot of people, including Mac, especially for him to remember in his guiding in later years.

"All main camps should have a good, proven dog around. He is worth his grub, to look after the camp. I saw a bull moose kill an Indian guide when I was a young boy on the middle river out of Fort Saint James, B.C. I have a great respect for a bull moose in a fight, more than I have for a grizzly bear, as a moose fears nothing during breeding season and will kill you quick in the right kind of situation. Even chopping wood to make a campfire will at times bring him right on the run, and he is very fast and dangerous, especially if he has been fighting and is hurt. He will charge through camp at night. In good moose country during rutting season I always put my camp in heavy timber so the moose can't tear it apart. If he does come in, you can get behind a tree. Out in the open, you have no place to go, and if you have to get your gun, you are helpless. Skook Davidson taught me as a young boy to always know where my gun was, and to put it where I can get to it quickly. It is not a case of being scared; it is a case of self-preservation and caution.

"As an outfitter or guide, it is your job to look after people and to see that they are never put into bad situations, as most people and hunters you take out are from cities and just don't understand what can happen. All young guides should have to take a course and be taught how to handle people and what people expect of them, as every person who comes to your camp has a different personality. It is your job to talk to them all separately before you leave on a hunt so you know who needs more attention. I blame our own B.C. government for not making this mandatory. If it were done, then our game department would eliminate over 80 percent of their problems that are created by dumb guides, especially drinking among the help and things like that. The outfitter should have to make out a report to the Game Department on every assistant guide at the end of every season regarding that guide's progress, and then they could assess each guide. That way our guiding industry would improve dramatically, and they would know before issuing an outfitter's license if a man was capable or not. This would also give the guide an incentive to perform better, and the guiding industry would automatically improve itself. The way it is now, an outfitter can pick up any drunk off the street, buy him an assistant guide license, and turn him loose with people. Customers end up spending a lot of money in Canada, and it is just a big disappointment when they go home bewildered and sad after a poor hunt. Many of them have saved a long time for a hunting trip."

Frank Cooke was born in Victoria, B.C. in 1927. He was sixteen years old when he started working for Skook Davidson at his ranch on Terminas Mountain about 120 miles south of Watson Lake, along the Kechika River in the Rocky Mountain Trench.

Frank started his own guiding business in 1965 with his headquarters at Moodie Lake, one hundred miles south of Watson Lake. He purchased part of Skook

Davidson's guiding territory from him. He built his first main camp at Moodie Lake, and for a time his son Terry Cooke flew their own Super Cub off a rough airstrip there. In British Columbia the Game Department gives each outfitter a designated area that is his alone to use for guiding non-resident hunters, who are for the most part from the U.S., Mexico and Europe. Resident hunters of B.C. can hunt by themselves anywhere in the province without a guide.

Later Frank moved his headquarters to Scoop Lake, where he had a two-thousand-foot airstrip built that could accommodate DC-3's and smaller aircraft; of course, seaplanes could also land on the lake. Cabins, a cookhouse, and a building with showers and indoor plumbing were built near the old cabin where we had encountered the three bears. Frank's family included his sons Frank, Jr., Terry, and Mackey; his daughters Diane, Tammy, Gloria and Donna; and his wife Hattie.

Frank described his relationship with Skook Davidson, a man who was a legend in his own time.

"I met Skook when I was seven years old in Fort St. James, B.C., where my father Frank Cooke, Sr. was a provincial policeman. I used to spend all my holidays from school as a young boy helping Skook pack horses for survey parties and freighting on the Manson Trail. It was 150 miles to the mines, and we used four-and six-horse teams in the winter and big freight wagons in the summer. Skook also had sixty head of pack horses. In 1944, I left Fort St. James with Skook for the Kechika Valley with fifty pack horses, and we ended up at his home place by the end of September. We left on the tenth of May, traveling through the bush and mountains, rafting the rivers and swimming all the horses. We wintered at the home place in the Kechika Valley, and the next spring we drove our horses out to Lower Post and up to Teslin Lake, and started the B.C. Yukon Boundary Survey with forty head of pack horses, moving camps and cutting out the boundaries. That fall we drove the horses back down the highway over to Lower Post, swam the Liard and Dease Rivers, then drove our horses back to the Kechika Ranch and wintered there again. We drove our horses out the next year and worked all summer and went back and wintered there again.

"In 1948, I married Hattie at Lower Post, and I worked for Skook over all the years 'till I bought out everything west of the Kechika in 1965 and started my own big game guiding service and built up Scoop Lake from straight bush.

"I spent many a tough trip on the trail with Skook Davidson, and he obtained his first hunting party in 1947. He was the toughest, hardiest man in the bush that I ever met in my lifetime. He was very fair, but very strict, and could fight like a wildcat; he backed down from no one. He was born in Longside, Scotland, in 1882 and came to Canada when he was fifteen years old. His name was John Ogilvie Davidson. Skook was a nickname given to him by the Indians. It comes from the Indian word *Skookum*, meaning "strong," which he lived up to.

"Skook came to live in the Kechika Valley in the northern end of the Rocky

Mountain Trench and established his Diamond J. Ranch at the foot of Terminus Mountain in 1939. He remained there until 1972 when ill health forced him to go to the Whitehorse Hospital and then to a private hospital in Vancouver, B.C., where he died. (I remember Skook calling in on the radio, usually every day, while flying for Watson Lake Flying Srvice).

"Skook worked on all the big cattle ranches in the Caribou Country and packed mules for old Cataline all through the Caribou gold rushes. He was a packer and freighter throughout the north 'till I met him. He went all through the First World War and was well decorated for bravery. He was a special policeman for the north while I was with him. He loved his horses and treated them like his own children. He never married or had any children.

"I knew Grant McConachie personally as a young boy. Grant's bush operation, which consisted of a Waco airplane at that time, later became Canadian Pacific Airlines. I gassed his airplanes up many a time just for a ride.

"My father, along with Russ Baker, started what became Pacific Western Airlines. Russ was operating a Junkers out of Fort St. James and later bought the first Beaver off the production line. I flew the north as a boy with them, in old Fokkers, Fairchilds, Wacos, Tri Motor Fords, and Norsemans. I babysat their children when they went out to dances at night and used to sit and listen to them, night after night, when they were all young men trying to get started in the flying business. My father was the only policeman north of Fort St. James, and everyone gathered at our house. My mother was a cousin of Winston Churchill, and Skook also knew him personally and drank rum with Winston during the First World War. He also went for a flight with Billy Bishop over France during the first war."

Frank was a Golden Glove boxer, and not only could he handle himself well, but he taught his sons to fight. They're all good with their fists.

During the first part of my stay at B.C. Yukon, I detected some sort of conflict between Ernie and Bill Harrison. Ernie soon left Watson Lake and departed for his home at Fort St. James. Sid Baird, a partner with Bill Harrison on a helicopter venture, took charge of the base when Ernie left; Sid became my boss. Sid was one of the smoothest and most knowledgeable helicopter pilots I ever met. He had an excellent reputation in the north with clients and companies he worked for. He, Bill Harrison, and some others bought Frontier Helicopters in Watson Lake and ran a very successful, safe operation in the area for many years. Sid was movie star material—extremely handsome, tall, dark-haired and broad-shouldered, with a quiet nature. He was a born leader and conducted the helicopter business well. I respected and trusted this man. His wife and children lived at Watson Lake, about a block off Main Street, which is actually part of the Alaska Highway.

Jim Thibaudeau and I were living in our respective Beavers, having no place to stay. Actually it was enjoyable in some ways. The interior of the Beaver is quite large, and we could stretch out full length in our sleeping bags with foam underneath. The waves lapping against the floats at night gently rocked us to sleep. However, baths in the lake were a bit on the cold side. When Sid found out Jim and I had no place to live, he quickly obtained a room for us at a the Signpost Motel in town. We shared a room and each had clean sheets and a place to shower every day. After a long day at flying, it was nice to come home to.

My first trips in a Cessna 180 were made shortly after arriving at B.C. Yukon. The Cessna 180 wasn't nearly the performer the Cessna 185 was; the engine was smaller, and the load capacity was less. Most of the time, much to my delight, I flew one of the Beavers CF-JBP; it was a bush pilot's dream. Jim Thibaudeau flew the other Beaver CF-IGF, which was an exceptional performer. At that time Jim was only twenty-five years old and had already been flying for a few years up here.

Before we obtained a de Havilland Otter DHC-3, we used to carry some heavy loads. We counted the number of rivets under the water on the back of the floats. That would tell us how much more we could safely load aboard. We carried plywood, drill rods, boats, canoes--all these could be strapped to the floats and flown safely, if they were properly tied down.

Once we got an Otter, we cut down on the Beaver's payloads. The Otter was like a big Beaver with a much greater load capacity, larger cargo doors and a much bigger hold. Bulky items fit inside, and we could eliminate a lot of external loads.

Bill Harrison hired Dennis Ball ,who arrived at Watson Lake in 1969 with an Otter that Bill had purchased for B.C. Yukon. Dennis had been flying back east near Lake Larounge and knew all about flying in the flat country.

We partied frequently here at Watson Lake, and I had a regular snort at the end of most flying days. The Yukon had the highest alcohol consumption rate in Canada, and Watson Lake had the highest rate in the Yukon.

August 13, 1969, I flew the Beaver into Dalziel's hunting camp at Bluesheep Lake in northern B.C., about a hundred miles south. Dal had lived many lives, and I judged him to be in his mid-sixties. He owned the oldest original building in Watson Lake, a log home. He was here in the 1930's and was the first to fly in and explore the Mackenzie Mountains extensively. He didn't say much, but I sensed he had many stories, experiences and knowledge beneath his calm exterior. His wife June was friendly and a gracious host.

Inside his log home was a fantastic trophy room. He had the second and fifth largest stone sheep in the world, fully mounted, animals from Africa, a tiger, various sheep, including one Marco Polo sheep from Afghanistan, bears, moose, and other animals that he had shot.

In the early days Dal shot game and flew it into the mining camps so they could have fresh meat. He started B.C. Yukon and had one of the first Beavers in the country. He now flew a Super Cub with long range tanks so he could keep tabs on his large hunting area and get the camps set up. Our flying service flew the hunters in and out about every ten days or so, the length of an average hunt. Dal ran a first-class operation and was well organized. In a couple of years, he was to buy a completely rebuilt Beaver from Kenmore Air Harbor and fly it himself into his hunting camp.

Flying was like living in another world. Looking down and seeing shapes and forms in miniature reminded me of my size and put my problems in proper perspective. Winging over this country untouched by roads, houses or smoke-stacks, breathing the clean fresh air and drinking the sparkling pure water without thought of pollution brought a feeling of unmatched contentment.

Today's trip was into Little Dal Lake, named after George Dalziel, located in the rugged Mackenzie Mountains in the Northwest Territories. Four hunters, anxious to go, and their gear were on the dock, I thought to myself that it was really a pleasure to take these men into the remote areas. They had planned a year or more for this trip. Some of them had saved for years, and for some it was one hunt in a lifetime; they looked forward to thoroughly enjoying themselves.

I began the loading, putting sleeping bags and other light items in the rear and heavy things toward the front. Weight and balance were very important and could prove fatal if managed improperly. Because there was so much gear, groceries and supplies from the outfitters, I took the back seats out and soon had the gear aboard and a place on the freight for the three passengers to sit. The passenger who was to sit up front climbed in first, then the others climbed in the back. I shut the back door, shoved off from the dock and climbed into the cockpit. A shot of prime, switches on, starter engaged. The 450-horsepower Pratt & Whitney engine snorted and caught, and soon the reassuring roar drowned out all other sounds. Putting the earphones on, both to protect my hearing and at times to protect me from unwanted questions from passengers, I took off and began a shallow climbing turn to the west, circling the lake to gain altitude before heading north.

Little Dal Lake was one of my favorites. About forty-five hundred feet above sea level, it's near the headwaters of the Redstone River and about fifty miles northeast of the South Nahanni River, some two hundred miles from Watson Lake. This is tundra country. Grooves made here by tracked vehicles years ago are still visible, and the ruts get larger as the years go by. It is very fragile country; care must be exercised to keep it from being damaged by men. This is also Dall sheep country. They're the white sheep, the same that were found in Alaska. Caribou, grizzly and moose are also hunted here, but today's hunters were primarily after sheep.

Flying on a northernly heading, I climbed to eight thousand feet in order to fly a straight line and maintain safety. One pass we were to fly over was over six thousand feet, so it was nice to have altitude. Today we could fly straight over the top; other times when the weather was bad we followed valleys, sometimes several before we could find one that was open.

Crossing the Hyland River forty miles north we soon saw some high peaks ahead. Mount St. James MacBrien at 9,062 feet was visible. Below this peak is Glacier

Lake, where I often dropped off mountain climbers who scaled this and other peaks nearby in the Mackenzie Mountains. There are some fairly extensive ice fields and glaciers around Mount St. James. The sight was awesome and sobering if you had to fly the area in bad weather.

We crossed the Yukon-Northwest Territories border about thirty-five miles south of the Nahanni River. We were in some of the most rugged mountains and certainly about the hardest to navigate in, as each valley and mountain looked like the next one, especially in bad weather.

Dennis Ball was lost once for four hours in the same area while flying B.C. Yukon's Otter. His comment was, "I don't like these Mackenzie Mountains, and I hope I never go down in them." Dennis had flown in eastern Canada in the flat country, and mountain flying was a new experience for him.

Even though I had good altitude, I watched my map closely as I crossed the South Nahanni. From here to Dal Lake it was tricky navigating; it was easy to take a wrong valley and get lost. Some of the creeks were improperly marked on the map and actually ran a different direction, something you had to keep in mind in bad weather.

We flew over the high pass north of the Nahanni River and were over the headwaters of the Redstone River. A deep blue speck ahead turned out to be Little Dal Lake, and we began our descent. As we circled the lake we saw the outfitter, Chuck Hayward, and a guide waiting at the lake for us. The lake was not large, but was almost treeless, and the approaches were fairly flat on either end. The Beaver settled down like a large white duck, and we taxied toward the makeshift pole dock. After unloading the freight and passengers, we all talked for a few minutes. Chuck looked through the mail and gave me the outgoing mail. A couple of successful hunters climbed aboard for a return trip out.

Besides my liking for the country around Little Dal Lake, it was a good paying trip. In addition to a good base salary, I was also paid by the mile. The trip back was uneventful; we returned by the same route. As we taxied up to the dock, the engineer waited to give us a hand tying up the airplane. After the passengers got out, I handed them their gear and then the Dall sheep horns and cape. Their flight left shortly, so we gave them a lift to the airport. They departed with smiles on their faces and stories to tell their less fortunate friends.

At the end of a long day, a Watson Lake Hotel meal and coffee hit the spot. I met Jim at the Signpost for a drink. Our table was soon filled up, the drinks started flowing, and not a few stories were told about our flights in those far northern skies. We finally walked to our room and crashed; we had some early flights and a long day ahead of us.

September 30, 1969: I was to fly into Little Dal Lake and pick up the last hunting party, then fly them back to Watson Lake. Little Dal could freeze any day now, so Chuck Hayward could delay no longer and have any certainty of getting the men and his horses out. When I landed, I learned that the guides had already left with the horses. It was a two-week trip to get to the mining town of Cantung. From there the horses could be trucked to Alberta, where Chuck lived.

Since there was so much gear, B.C. Yukon was supposed to fly in both a de Havilland Otter and a Beaver, but it was so busy they couldn't. Jim Thibaudeau had flown in earlier in his Beaver and taken what he could, leaving the rest for me. There were seven caribou racks, four hunters, a large stack of hunters' gear, and supplies from the camp that Chuck wanted flown out. Sometimes you went an extra mile for the outfitters; after all, it was the last flight of the season and he needed all these things taken out to avoid winter damage.

The first thing I did was put the seven caribou racks inside the Beaver. That filled up the inside, and I couldn't get the hunters, their gear, or Chuck's gear in. I then unloaded the horns and tied them to the floats--it was a horny Beaver, with racks hung everywhere and in every direction. We could just barely get the gear and men in; it was an overload even without the horns. I rocked the floats several times with the elevator controls, to get on the step, and then used the left aileron to lift first the right float and then the left float to brake the water friction and become airborne.

It took about the whole lake, which was at a high altitude and not very big, to get airborne. We staggered into the air, and then the fun began. The caribou racks disturbed the air flow around the Beaver and caused so much drag that when I got level the gauge indicated only eighty miles per hour instead of one hundred and twenty. The plane was shaking badly, but we were flying.

It was already late in the afternoon; night came quickly in the fall. We were using much more fuel than normal and were flying much slower than normal with a great deal of drag, sucking the gas up at an alarming rate. This was usually a flight of about 1:50, but I could see it was going to take much longer: I hadn't figured on that when I left Watson Lake. The four hunters were all pilots. Pilots were usually the worst passengers in an airplane.

We made it over the Nahanni, struggling to keep flying. The plane was buffeting badly and barely flying. It was going to take about an extra hour to get home; I was getting concerned, as we emptied two tanks and part of the remaining front one.

As we crossed into the Yukon, darkness became a second concern; the light was rapidly fading. We all glanced nervously at the gas gauges, which were draining very rapidly, and it was questionable whether we would make it.

I had maintained an altitude of about seventy-five hundred feet so I could glide a good distance, and there were some lakes along the route we could land on if we had to. Finally the darker shape of Watson Lake came into view. Still maintaining lots of altitude, I began our descent. The gauge was showing empty on the front tank.

There was no moon out, and it was pitch dark as we descended over the shore of the lake. I used power and maintained a landing attitude, not able to judge distance below the tree line. We made a smooth landing and everyone, especially me, breathed a little easier.

As I looked back after landing, I thought how stupid I was trying to take everything out in one trip, but I had no idea that those caribou racks would cause such a problem. The hunter/pilots made a comment later to the outfitter about this hazardous trip, and his reply was, "Well, you made it, didn't you?"

We did make it, and I learned a good lesson. I didn't repeat that performance again. From then on if I had to fly horns, I would put only a couple outside. That way the flight characteristics were closer to normal and acceptable. I tied them on outside only if I couldn't possibly get them inside the plane.

After tying down, I didn't really care if I flew again, a feeling often experienced after a bad trip. However, after a good sleep, flying looks better the next day and you know there is no other type of work that can compare. Hopefully you learn from your mistakes or poor judgement and become a better pilot.

The last flights of the season were spooky for me. The weather was usually bad, and I wondered if I had used up my luck. I spent long days of flying and loading and unloading without any time off, maybe averaging four or five hours of sleep each day all summer.

When I woke up the morning after that last flight into Little Dal Lake, I was glad to be alive and glad that I was going south to my log house in Smithers, B.C. It was about a three-day trip, and I was anxious to get started. I enjoyed this new country, met new friends, and was glad I was still in one piece. All and all, it was a memorable season, something I'd wanted to do for a long time.

When I arrived home after that long drive on the Alaska Highway, which was now mostly mud, it was good to relax with my family, catch up on what they'd been doing, and sleep in my own bed. My plans were to go south to Boeing Field in Seattle to obtain a U.S. Commercial and Instrument Rating and then my Airline Transport Pilot Rating.

It was October 31, 1969, and I was getting ready to depart Boeing Field for my first flight in a Cherokee PA-28. My instructor, Jim Gill of Galvins Flight Service, knew his job well and was an excellent pilot and good instructor.

To me it was like driving on the freeway. Airplanes were all over the sky, and I kept a wary eye out landing and taking off, but then I was under the hood learning proper instrument flight techniques. It was a whole new world as I learned to believe the gauges. The first nine hours or so were preparation for the U.S. commercial check ride, which I passed successfully November 5. Then I started the basic instrument course in earnest.

Tracking, VOR intercepts, ADF tracking, ADF approaches, ATC clearances, ILS, and holding patterns swam in my head. Finally on December 31, 1969, the last day of the year, I obtained my U.S. Instrument Rating. I passed the written test earlier with good marks, thanks to an excellent teacher who made it clear and enjoyable.

Driving back to my log house in Smithers, my spirit was light. I had reached another goal and had a U.S. Commercial and Instrument Rating. It was good to be with my family again; Scott was such a fine son. We had a good time taking it easy, and we got caught up on events. I stayed home and did some cross-country skiing, but soon my restless spirit longed for the Yukon. I looked forward to returning and flying once again in the vast wilderness.

One winter day Scott and I loaded our packs, put on our cross-country skis and left our log cabin, heading east. Our destination was Silver King Basin in the mountains east of our log home. It began to snow, and the going was getting tough. We crossed an open creek, and now the snow stuck to the wet skis. After six hours we still hadn't come to a cabin that we were told was at Silver King Basin. We talked about just sleeping in the snow, we were so tired.

Around every bend we expected to see a log cabin, but it was nowhere to be found. Finally, after nine hours of skiing uphill, we came around one more bend, and there was the cabin on the right side of the trail. It looked like a little bit of heaven.

We were cold, extremely tired and starved. The cabin had gaps between the logs, and the snow lay in little rows on the floor. The thin sheet metal stove was full of holes. We got it going until it was hopping up and down. I took out a can of the moose meat from our Kispiox cabin. I heated that and some peas. Scott to this day remembers canned moose meat and peas with a sour expression.

After a hot meal we zipped our sleeping bags together and cuddled all night, thankful to be here with full stomachs. We were a little too cold to sleep much and spent a lot of time wide awake. Ten-year-old Scott kept up with me all the way and was a good trail companion, not complaining, just trooping along right behind his dad. I love that boy and felt fortunate to have such a fine son.

The morning was clear, and the newly fallen snow created a winter wonderland. Going down was so easy that we reached our log home in a couple hours. We had lost about fifteen pounds between us through dehydration, I guess. We quickly polished off almost a box of oranges and whatever else we could get our hands on.

I left for Fairbanks, Alaska, about the first of March to see about a flying job. I hoped to get on with Interior Airways, flying as a crew member on a Hercules. It was sixty degrees below zero when I got off a commercial jet at Fairbanks. I went to the office of Interior Airways to apply for a job, but they had been laying off workers and wouldn't be hiring for quite some time. The layoffs were caused by environmental concern among citizens' groups and certain government agencies regarding the North Slope oil exploration that was big a part of this company's business.

I hitchhiked a ride from Fairbanks to Watson Lake with a trucker. Along the way, we stopped at a rather seedy-looking Chinese restaurant at Whitehorse for breakfast. While eating, I noticed some dark objects in my oatmeal and quietly asked the waitress to come over to my table. She was in a dither about her relief that had not shown up for work. In an angry mood, she asked, "Well, what's wrong with you?"

"Oh, there's mouse turds in my mush." The restaurant got deathly quiet as all the patrons' ears perked up, and they contemplated their breakfasts with sober expressions. We finally got back on the Alaska Highway.

At B.C. Yukon Air Service, I talked to Grant Luck and was hired to fly with Ron Wells on Transprovincial's Otter, which was temporarily leased to B.C. Yukon. Ron, an old-time bush pilot, and I flew diesel fuel for a mining camp. We would roll the forty-five-gallon drums out of the large cargo door opening and let them drop on the snow, where they remained until they were used. It was cold, and the snow was deep. We each flew a leg--Ron flew the load in, and I flew the plane out empty and helped load and unload. We filled up at Toad River on the Alaska Highway and flew in to the Churchill Mining site on wheel skis.

Ron was the best Otter pilot I ever met and handled the Otter like a Super Cub. He wore thick glasses and was hard of hearing. One of his favorite things to do with a passenger he didn't know, who was sitting in the co-pilot's seat, was to pretend to lose his glasses and grope around with his hands looking for them, unable to see.

A near whiteout caught us at the end of the job on our way home. I had the maps out navigating. Ron was flying just above the blowing snow. At times we could see only a few hundred feet ahead. We arrived in Smithers after winding for hours through some narrow valleys.

The snow was slow leaving, but spring finally arrived. The ice was gone from the Bulkley River by May. The moose that we saw behind our log cabin during winter were gone now to the higher country. My restless spirit, dormant during the winter, now stirred, and I longed to be flying in the Yukon Territory once again.

On May 18, 1970, I packed flight jacket, log books and some clothes in my 1967 Volkswagen bug. Smithers fell behind as I drove east toward Prince George, then north for Dawson Creek and the beginning of the Alaska Highway and another season in the Yukon.

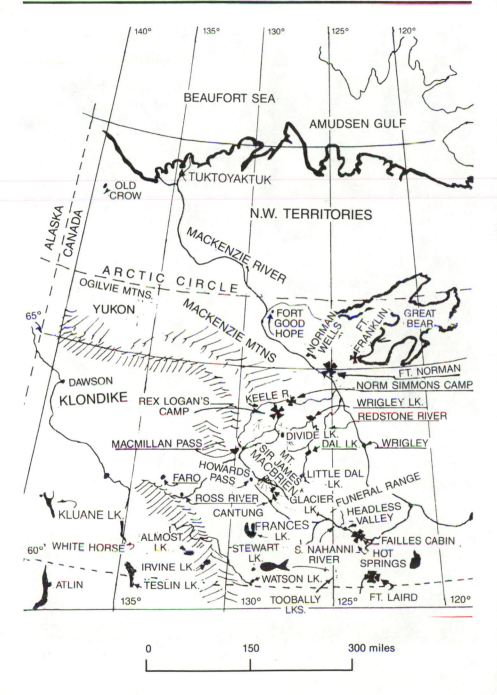

Scott and Larry at Grandma Whitesitt home on E. 14822 32nd, Veradale, WA, August 1969. Scott stayed at Grandma's for a visit while Larry headed north to Watson Lake, Yukon for the first season flying in the Yukon.

Family August 1969. From left, front row, Uncle Jess McDaniel, cousin Danny McDaniel, Scott Whitesitt, Jon Furlotte, Kenny Clark. Back Row: Bob Whitesitt, Nancy and Doug Furlotte, Dennis McDaniel, JoAnn McDaniel, Mom and Dad back row Sue Clark and Larry far right.

Larry heading north up the Alaska Highway, on course to Watson Lake, Yukon, for a season of flying the Bush.

Larry standing on the floats of the Beaver CF JBP that he flew during his first year working for B.C. -Yukon Air Service in the summer of 1969, at the Company Seaplane dock on Watson Lake.

The wide spot on the Alaska highway called Watson Lake, Yukon. The town is in the lower center. The Island on Watson Lake can be seen in the distance. B.C. Yukon Air Service is beyond the Island and Watson Lake Flying Service is right of the Island.

South Nahannie River about 1971. Larry standing about 150 yards above Virginia Falls N.W. Territories. The boat was carried board by board on Albert Faille's back from the bottom of the falls. Note the rapids, Virginia Falls is twice as high as Niagra Falls.

Larry standing on the floats of the Cessna 185 that he flew to Bone Lake, B.C. After unloading the Seaplane and while taking pictures the plane drifted out. Note the wet pant legs from wading after the plane.

ADVENTURES IN THE YUKON

Flying the Beaver over the mighty Mackenzie Mountains. They were the toughest to navigate in because the valleys and mountains looked so much alike. Many a pilot lost their lives in these mountains. I came close to buying the farm more than once near here.

Larry and the Beaver CF JBP at Little Dal Lake in the heart of the Mackenzie Mountains NW Territories. I'm starting to tie up 7 caribou racks to the outside of the floats. It was the last flight of my first season in the Yukon and I came close to losing it, on a very dangerous flight home.

CHAPTER VII
WATER BOMBING WITH THE BEAVER

Watson Lake lies on the west side of the Rocky Mountains in what is called the Trench. Flying up to Alaska, most pilots fly visual over the Alaska Highway, cutting through the Rockies northeast of Prince George to Dawson Creek and following it to Alaska. If you fly north and a little west of Prince George, you can fly in a direct line to Watson Lake and stay in the Rocky Mountain Trench all the way. This route is much shorter; however, it is over some very isolated wilderness area, so there is a certain risk factor if mechanical or weather-related problems arise.

My love of the Rocky Mountains was acquired when Kathy and I spent our honeymoon summer on Desert Lookout, looking into Glacier Park in northwestern Montana. Now I was often flying into this same rugged mountain range and had a new appreciation of the beauty and of the potential danger, as the winds and weather were often severe. Caution and care were dictated, as well as avoidance when nature unleashed her fury over the peaks and down in the valleys.

The Rockies here look very similar in shape and size, although not quite as high as in Montana, until the range crosses the Yukon border. There the mountain formation changes shape; the mountains are more rounded and noticeably shorter.

Flying the Rocky Mountains is no different from other mountain flying, except that, because of their size and shape, the weather can be more severe—especially the wind. When flying across a ridge, I use an angle of about forty-five degrees or more. If there is a downdraft, and some can be quite severe and violent, I can break off and turn back without a problem. Flying straight across and encountering a bad downdraft could result in a crash against the mountains before the airplane could be turned back. Once the ridge is safely crossed, you can fly directly away on your intended course.

Air flowing over mountain ranges is similar to water. It follows the contours, rising on one side, flowing down the other. A good, safe pilot uses the wind to his advantage and, hopefully, enjoys a long lifetime of safe flying. Thinking ahead and trying to anticipate problems before they accumulate, especially in mountain flying, will help a pilot to increase his chances of survival. I believe you should always plan for a way out; never be ashamed of turning back or, for that matter, of just sitting on the ground until you feel you are well within the limits of your flying ability.

Jack Hodge, who was the manager of Omineca Air Service and invited me to go for a check ride in the Cub which led to my first job, was here in Watson Lake. I was glad to see Jack, as he was an interesting, experienced pilot (as well as an engineer) and had always treated me well.

Jack was flying an Aero Star, a fast, light twin-engine airplane that was used as a bird dog for the World War II A-26 bombers, converted to water bombers that were working a fire near here. Jack made a run over the fire first and then radioed the 26s of any problems before they began their runs. The A-26 required only one pilot, and it looked like an exciting flying job.

The lead pilot told me I should consider getting into this type of work, as I was the kind of pilot, with my bush flying experience and hours flown, that they were looking for. He seemed to me to be a bit of a hot dogger, as he always tried to pin it on the very end of the runway when he landed, sometimes landing short and sending up a huge dust cloud as he hit the dirt and grass.

This lead pilot was working a fire after leaving Watson Lake. He would fly above a ridge and follow down a canyon, dropping his load as he descended. He decided to fly up the draw with a full load and got behind the power curve, stalled out and killed himself within two weeks of our conversation.

The other pilot, a "recently ex-Canadian Air Force" type, was flying up the Frazer River about two weeks after he left Watson Lake, got in some bad weather, and tried to climb through it. He almost made it, but hit the top of a peak. The chief pilot for this same company was also killed in a DC-6, along with two crew members, while dropping water on a fire. He evidently stalled in a turn, again within two weeks of my conversation with the A-26 pilot who encouraged me to get into this type of flying.

The rustic-looking B.C. Yukon seaplane office was built out of panobode-type logs. We had a long dock and a storage shed. At the airport by the main terminal was a large World War II hangar that B.C. Yukon owned, where major work was done on the airplanes. Frontier Helicopters, which was owned by Sid Baird, Bill Harrison and others, also used this hangar for helicopter maintenance.

A radio operator and dispatcher monitored the single sideband radio, kept in touch with the pilots as they flew to their various destinations, and gave advice on weather. If there was a problem with your airplane or you got into bad weather, it was great to know someone was at the base to take your call and help out.

Mark Goostry, a warm, likeable eighteen-year-old new pilot with a sunny disposition and quick smile, was flying the Super Cub for B.C. Yukon. One warm summer day he crashed into a mountainside by Wolverine Lake in northern B.C. We were having a few drinks at the base when I was told about the accident, which rolled the Super Cub into a mass of fabric and metal while Mark walked away without injury. My comment was, "Good, now we're rid of that poor performing Super Cub." It was a dog, and the margin of safety was little, as the cruising speed wasn't much higher than the stall speed. I also commented, "Now, maybe we'll get a good performing Super Cub." Mark later in his flying career was flying a Twin Otter on floats betwen Vancouver and Victoria, British Columbia when he was killed. The flaps were down as he made the approach to land. All of a sudden, the connecting rod to one of the flaps broke due to corrosion (mechanical failure), causing the airplane to roll and crash into the ocean. Mark and nine of the eleven Japanese passengers were killed—the co-pilot survived. Mark loved to fly and was doing what he enjoyed when the end came.

Dennis Ball was flying the de Havilland Otter most of the time. Occasionally I made a trip with the Otter, but I preferred the Beaver, although it was interesting to fly different types from time to time. Max Sanderson, an old-time Beaver pilot and then helicopter pilot for Cannex Mining Company, gave a definition for a good Otter pilot—someone who wore a size four hat, was four feet tall, and about as wide. He felt the way I did toward that back-breaking, noisy machine.

Grant Luck and Sid Baird were in charge of operations, and Grant helped out with the flying. We all got along well. Flights often began at 0400, and sometimes we flew as late as 2200. We were paid a good base salary and five to ten cents a mile, depending on the type of airplane flown. The season was short, so we tried to get in as many miles as possible.

One hot summer day Grant told the engineer to put the water tanks on the Beaver. A forest fire had broken out by the lake and was threatening to burn up the town of Watson Lake a few miles south. A ninety-gallon dump tank was mounted on each float. There was a tube running from the tank down to the water that filled the tanks in a matter of seconds while the plane was on the step. (The step, which is located in the middle of the float and looks—appropriately enough—like a step, is where the airplane rides when it planes at high speeds.)

After the installation, a senior pilot decided to fly the first few drops, and we taxied for take-off. Fortunately the engine quit before we took off, as the fuel selector valve was inadvertently on an empty tank. He selected the full tank, started the engine, and we were soon on the step and filling up the tanks, then on our way to the fire.

Diving down on the fire and pulling the release cable, we zoomed up as the heavy weight of the water instantly left the tanks. It was rather exciting, acting like a bomber. After a couple of drops, the senior pilot got off at the dock, and I finished the day dropping water on the fire. It was a nice change, and it made me imagine I was in a war and dropping bombs. A helicopter with a long cable and bucket was also being used. The fire was put out, and the town was saved from becoming a burnt spot on the map.

This was a bad year for fires. We flew forestry personnel and equipment to areas without roads, as they tried to control the many fires burning through this vast area. The Cub was used to fly a forestry patrol route, looking for telltale smoke. On floats, the Cub hardly seemed to move, and four or five hours in its hard seat was about all anyone wanted.

On June 19, I began loading our single-engine Otter. Kathy and Scott soon arrived to join me on a trip into Bluesheep Lake, about a hundred miles south, for a mining company. It was a pretty flight, with the last few miles through a windy, narrow canyon. The lake wasn't visible until the last minute or so before landing.

Bluesheep Lake is small, which keeps you on your toes and makes for an interesting approach and landing. The Otter is a noisy beast and has a much flatter landing attitude than the Beaver, which takes some getting used to. It had a 600-horsepower radial engine and did a good job for bush-type operations, carrying about double the payload of a Beaver.

Throttle back, landing flaps, and we touched down on the east side of this puddle. By the time we were off the step, we were at the other end of the lake. Some men from the mining exploration camp met me at the shore, and we soon unloaded an assortment of mail, groceries, and mining supplies. Coming out light, having only some core samples and mail, the Otter was on the step and in the air before half the lake was used up. One day one of these men swallowed battery acid ,thinking it was water, and his throat started to swell closed. I flew in and brought him to Watson Lake, where he was treated successfully.

Scott and Kathy flew in Omineca Air Service's Otter once with Bill Harrison out of Maclure Lake. I tried to get Scott and Kathy on flights whenever there was room, if the person chartering the plane didn't mind. Kathy was busy expediting for George Dalziel. She picked up supplies and passengers that flew in on CPA and delivered them to the base. Occasionally we had a drink with Dal and June in the evening at their log home. Scott was now ten years old and, as always, enjoyed himself wherever he was. Scott and I were very close, and he made a good co-pilot. He also pumped the floats and helped clean my airplane.

Norm Simmons, a game biologist for the Canadian government, called our base from Norman Wells, Northwest Territories, and requested the Beaver for a few days. July 9, 1970, I prepared to depart for Norm's camp on the Keel River. Kathy and Scott were going with me on this flight. It was new country for all of us and the furthest north we had been yet, not far from the Arctic Circle. The Keel River camp was located about 80 miles southwest of Norman Wells and 290 miles northeast of Watson Lake. It would take about two and one-half flying hours to reach there.

We followed the Hyland River almost to the Northwest Territories, crossed the South Nahanni River, and followed the Brokenskull River to the headwaters of the Natla River. Following the Natla we soon flew over Rex Logan's hunting camp, just below where the Natla enters the Keel River. From here it was about a hundred miles downstream to Norm Simmons' camp, which was a few miles above Nainli Creek.

I could see a small dock on the north bank of the Keel. The cabin was located on a bench that ran parallel to the river. The river appeared very swift; white water tumbled the surface, and some mean-looking rapids and jagged rocks were visible about four hundred feet below the dock. It was going to be a "stay on your toes every second" landing and docking. But I enjoyed the challenge and looked the river over carefully as I circled and planned my approach. The river told a story that I read very carefully, looking for the deeper, safer channels before making my landing. It was a wild river, and I treated it with the respect it deserved.

The river was in a mountainous valley, and the only reason Norm Simmons didn't fly with a charter company out of Norman Wells was that they didn't like mountain flying and landing on treacherous rivers. Pilots like that were what I called "flat land pilots," flying the level country east of the rugged Mackenzie Mountains.

My decision was made, and we made an approach, slowing down to about seventy-five miles per hour indicated on final. I touched down and came off the step just before the dock. I needed lots of power to hold my own against the current as I started to work my way carefully toward the dock. Nudging up to the dock, I left the power on until I was securely tied, not daring to shut down until then.

Norm, a friendly, straightforward kind of guy, was doing a study on Dall sheep here in the Mackenzie Mountains. They used a cagelike trap to catch the sheep and then measured and checked them over. After putting tags and, I believe, radio transmitters on the sheep, they turned them loose.

Norm updated me on his study. Perry Lynton had been flying a Helio Courier for him, using it to spray the sheep with red dye so they could keep track of their habits. He had kept his plane on a makeshift strip on the bench by the cabin, but a flood washed the plane away, completely destroying it. Norm and his assistants climbed up in the attic of the cabin, as the main floor was underwater, and waited out the flood. Perry's plane was uninsured, and he suffered considerable loss, as the Helio was a very expensive plane.

We stayed a couple of days. I flew Norm to Norman Wells, where he picked up supplies and took care of some business, and then we flew back to camp. Norman Wells had an oil refinery; during World War II a pipeline was laid to the south, and for a while oil was pumped. Old pumping stations can still be seen along the old Canal Road. I also flew the Beaver to Fort Good Hope, an Indian Village on the Mackenzie River near the Arctic Circle.

Norm had a very large, magnificent malamute dog that must have weighed 150 pounds or more. The malamute, a close descendant of the wolf, doesn't bark much, but howls like a wolf. Norm's was a good-natured, quiet dog that had a presence and knew he was the boss of his domain. Scott talked to an old Indian man who worked for Norm and first came to the Keel in a skin canoe when he was a child. He and his wife lived in a cabin nearby, and their sled dogs would sometimes start howling. The old Indian woman would go outside and tap on a stump with a stick, and they instantly quieted down.

After several side trips for Norm, Kathy, Scott and I departed for Watson Lake and arrived there after a smooth, uneventful flight.

I had an interesting flight one day with Dave, the forest ranger at Lower Post, B.C. About fifteen miles south of Watson Lake just inside the B.C. border, Lower Post is an Indian village. Dave chartered B.C. Yukon's Cessna 185. I flew to Lower Post, landed on the Liard River, picked up Dave and two other forestry employees, and departed for Denetiah Lake. We did some fishing on a stream at the west end of the lake, which flows into Denetiah from a small lake about a half mile to the southwest. This was the best fishing I had ever experienced, and I have the picture of our catch, which was also used in Frank Cooke's brochure on fishing.

We caught about seventy-four rainbow trout in a couple of hours and kept thirty-two that weighed between two and nine pounds. The ice had recently gone out, and the fish were active and struck hard. We fished until we had our fill, then we flew back to Lower Post, and I dropped them off on the banks of the Liard River. I returned to B.C. Yukon's floatbase with my fabulous fish story, documented with a picture from the trusty Argus C-3 35mm camera that I purchased years ago from a destitute sailor on my ship in the South Pacific. In fact, all but a few of the pictures I took while flying in the North were taken with this solid camera.

In August I flew the Beaver into Fort Simpson, which is located at the junction of the Liard and Mackenzie Rivers. There was a fire nearby, and I flew fuel into it for the aircraft and helicopter that were fighting the fire. I flew over eight hours that day and was fairly tired after many hours of loading forty-five-gallon drums of aviation gas in and out of the Beaver. The day went quickly and after a good meal at a local hotel, I got a room there and was soon asleep. Morning came quickly, and I started another day of hauling fuel to the fire. After another rather long day, I returned to Watson Lake.

The long summer days passed quickly as I worked seven days a week with many long hours. Eight hours of flying time usually required a good sixteen-hour day because of loading, unloading, and waiting time. September 23, 1970, I flew the Cessna into Wolverine and Dease and back to Watson Lake on the last flight of the season for B.C. Yukon at Watson Lake. My total time now was 2620 hours.

In October I returned once again to Galvin's Flight Service at Boeing Field in Seattle and began training for my Airline Transport Pilot (ATP) rating, the highest rating in aviation. After putting in four days in a Cherokee 140, I began flying an Aztec PA-23, which was a twin-engine executive-type airplane that I used to train for the ATP rating. It was more difficult to fly—much faster—and it kept me on my toes. On every flight it seemed my instructor pulled an engine while I was under the hood or in actual instrument conditions. In addition to flying with instruments, I also had to contend with a lost engine, and it kept me busy just trying to stay up with the airplane and stay on course.

The written test for the Airline Transport Pilot rating was very difficult, and I had to learn nine formulas by heart just to work out the math and engineering problems. Math was never a strong point of mine, and this test was most difficult. After much study and restudy, I finally passed the written. On December 7, 1970, my log book says, "ATP passed—Frank Benedict." Frank was the designated inspector for the

FAA and took me on the flight check ride. This is similar to an instrument check ride, only you have to be much more precise in the flight maneuvers and in your ability to hold the correct altitude and course. Red letter day! I was now the proud owner of an Airline Transport Pilot rating.

I returned to Smithers for about one month. Because of some long-term problems in our marriage that couldn't be resolved, a separation and finally a divorce on April 30, 1971, ended a period in both our lives that saw a lot of good, as well as difficult times. When we said our vows, I believed in a lifetime marriage and commitment and didn't think this would ever happen.

Our son Scott, a fine young boy of eleven years, was a joy to both of us. The hardest part for me was to realize I wouldn't be with him on a day-to-day basis, and I knew I would miss him terribly.

We had our son and our log home. We flew into some of the most remote and beautiful areas of British Columbia, the Yukon, and Northwest Territories. Many good memories were mine to relive, and we had our special son.

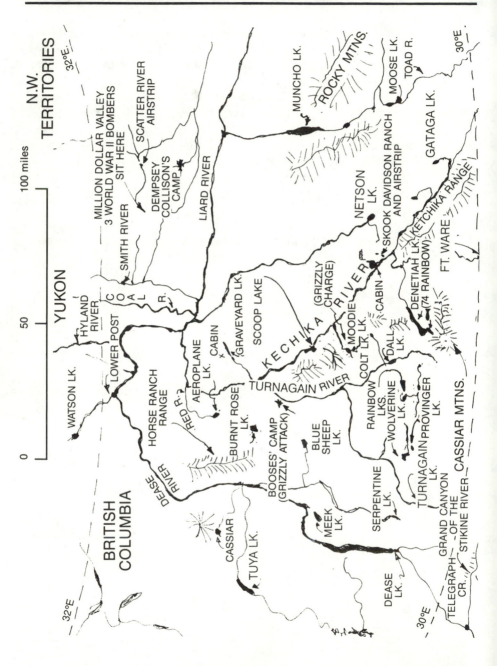

Scott, age 10, following me on a cross country ski trip to Silver King Basin east of our log home in the Driftwood Valley. He kept up with me all the way, some 9 hours of skiing up hill. He was always a good companion on the trail and in the air.

Scott front row, left, Kathy, Prime Minister Trudeau, Lynn Thibaudeau, wife of Jim, who I flew with in the Yukon, airplane engineer's wife, Mrs. Dennis Ball, her husband Dennis flew B.C. Yukon, Otter, her son and my Uncle Floyd Smith. Summer of 1970 in Watson Lake, Yukon.

WATER BOMBING WITH THE BEAVER

George (Dal) Dalziel, an early day bush pilot and outfitter on the left, Kathy, Larry and Dal's wife June Dalziel. Marco Polo sheep in background, in Dal's log home, Watson Lake, summer of 1970.

From left - forest worker, Dave the forest ranger at Lower Post and Larry at Denetiah Lake, B.C., spring of 1969. We caught 74 Rainbow and kept 32 between 2 and 9 lbs. George Dalziel (Dal) was rumored to have planted rainbow trout here and in many other lakes in the area.

CHAPTER VIII
JIM & STAN—
WATSON LAKE FLYING SERVICE

On May 31, 1971, I made my first flight for my new employer, Watson Lake Flying Service. I was checked out in their red Beaver CF-IBP. The town of Watson Lake was named after fur trader Frank Watson, who set up a post in the area during the 1890's. Watson Lake was founded with the construction of the airport in 1940. Airplanes that were flown to Russia on the lend-lease program to help in the war effort stopped here for fuel. Many ended up in the bush, due to bad weather and inexperienced pilots, from fighters to bombers. In fact, one valley east of Smith River was called "Million Dollar Valley" because of the planes that crashed there. Three bombers were trying to locate the airport at Smith River in a snowstorm. They followed their leader, and all three landed in Muskeg in the wrong valley--the next valley to the east. I saw the bombers on many occasions when I flew into Dempsey Collison hunting camps in the Scatter River country east of there. They are lined up, one behind the other, in a neat row, the engines long since removed.

When the Alcan Highway was completed in 1942, businesses were established in Watson Lake to cater to the tourists who would eventually use the highway. Today the tourists often stay overnight before continuing on to Whitehorse to the northwest or Fort Nelson to the east, both 250 or more miles distant.

The town is also a center and jumping-off place for prospectors, hunters, and fisherman who often charter flights with Watson Lake Flying Service to fly into remote lakes or airstrips scattered throughout the Yukon, Northwest Territories, or northern B.C.

The Yukoners are a casual, laid-back kind of people. If a job doesn't get done today or tormorrow, it can always be done next week or next month. For people used to fast service, this is not the place to come. But if you want to be accepted for yourself, this is the place to be. The Yukoners accept individuals for what they are as persons, not impressed by money or some high position on the outside. Many wealthy men of high position that we flew out to fishing and hunting camps soon learned that they were treated like anyone else.

I once flew the chairman of the board of Standard Oil of New Jersey and several of his underlings to a camp in northern B.C. with the red Beaver. We stayed at this camp for about a week or so. They brought in quite a bit of high-priced booze, and the cook got into the sauce during the night. When we sat down for breakfast the following morning, these oil men were in for an unwelcome surprise that I found quite amusing. The cook was in another world and feeling no pain. In fact, I don't think he could feel; it was surprising he could stand. The pancakes that didn't get flipped on the floor were mostly raw, and these men just weren't used to anything like this.

They had to pay for three hours of flying each day even if they didn't fly, so I mentioned one day that maybe they would like to see some of the country and use up the time they were paying for. This struck them as funny—three hours wasn't much to them, and they weren't concerned about the cost. We flew through the mountains looking for mineral deposits and stopped to do some fishing. They were treated the same as anyone else by the people in the north and by our company.

Jim Close is a real Yukoner and proud of his roots. Jim was about thirty-five, with a twinkle in his eye and an unending repartee of one-liners. He was a congenial, walking encyclopedia of flying history and of the Yukon characters, many of whom he knew personally. He was warm-hearted and often too easy in extending credit to people who were down on their luck. Trappers, outfitters and others who needed to fly into the bush but were without funds found a sympathetic ear and an airplane to drop them off at their various camps and homes.

Jim was the front man, the visible one, that most people first saw or talked to when booking a flight or arriving at the float dock. He was the organizer and an excellent aircraft engineer.

In the many years I flew for Jim and Stan I never had an engine or structural failure. Once the hydraulic system went out in the Beaver and I had no flaps when I landed, as they operate hydraulically, but that was the only system I can recall that quit working while I was actually flying.

When Jim and Stan first started the flying service in 1962, Jim was doing some of the flying and was written up in a local paper for a rescue operation he performed. His expertise as the engineer for the company eventually consumed most of his time, and he gave up being an active pilot; however, he still flew enough to check the airplanes he worked on.

Besides engineering, expediting, meeting customers, and gassing airplanes, Jim also operated the lifeline to the many camps, mining companies, and other isolated individuals by monitoring the radio. He checked weather on a regular basis with these people so he could advise the pilots on the flyability in the different areas, as well as taking their orders and passing on messages. He was usually the first to arrive and the last person to leave the seaplane base.

Stan Bridcut, Jim's partner, was in his forties, lean and wiry with a quick grin and quiet demeanor. His flying experience covered a long span, and he had a wealth of knowledge about bush flying that took some prodding to uncover; he didn't talk much about himself. Because of his light frame Stan could haul a larger payload, which is especially important in the smaller planes where every pound makes a difference. I could tell when Stan was flying. His landing approaches were smooth, well planned, the touchdowns gentle. He knew the country well and was very cautious about the weather. Although he had a few engine failures, he always managed to walk away. Stan liked to prospect and spend time in the bush. In his early flying days he flew a PA-14 for a mining company, and prospecting was in his blood.

Stan and Jim have the oldest flying service in the Yukon that is still in operation with the original owners. They started out with a PA-14 and a Cessna 180. The flight office was a small building about fifty feet from the lake. It consisted of a waiting room, a storeroom, a kitchen, a front office with a combined back radio and record room.

Wally Waulkonan, a big Finn, was our engineer. Wally did most of the maintenance on our airplanes, including engine changes, normal inspections every fifty hours, and daily troubleshooting. Wally was well-qualified, having worked many years in Meadow Portage, Manitoba, in an engine overhaul shop. He worked for B.C. Yukon Air Service from 1967 to 1970 and has been employed since then by Jim and Stan. Jim Close and Wally worked closely together on airplane maintenance.

Late in the fall, flying floats became a cold job in the drafty Beavers with their poor heaters and the temperature near freezing. Wally made the best hot rum, called "Old Sam," and had it waiting for us pilots after we finished the last flight of the day.

Jim Thibaudeau, whom I first met when we both flew for B.C. Yukon Air Service, flew for Watson Lake Flying Service while I was there. One day after flying, the three of us went into Wally's Finnish sauna, cooked bright red and then ran down to Watson Lake with nothing on but smiles on our faces and jumped in. The water was like ice, but after the shock I felt as if I were reborn--a fantastic high.

Wally and his wife Marge and children live near the seaplane base and have a comfortable home on the water, close to Jim Thibaudeau's lake place north of the base. Wally's good-natured and nice to be around, and I was glad to have him working on the Beaver I flew.

Jim flew the Beech 18 on floats most of the time and was a very competent pilot. He had recently married Lynn, and the young couple was well liked by clients and by the local people at Watson Lake.

Bob Mitchell, a young pilot with a few seasons under his belt, flew the Cessna 185 and was also cutting his teeth on the Beaver, which of course he liked. Later Bob went to work for Canadian Pacific Airline, so this was a stepping-stone for him.

John Poiser flew the Super Cub and the Cessna 185. I got to know John well and eventually introduced him to his wife-to-be, a schoolteacher from the Seattle area. John and I lived together for a time at Stan's cabin on the Lake. John was a good pilot and very conscientious, and I liked being around him.

Many interesting people from all walks of life began the adventures of a lifetime at the float base: hunters, prospectors, geologists, canoeists, mountain climbers, park officials, fishermen, photographers who want a picture of Virginia Falls and maybe some glaciers and ice fields near the South Nahanni River. Occasionally we flew the Royal Canadian Mounted Police out when someone disappeared. What I enjoyed most was sharing with these people, some of whom had saved for a once-in-a-lifetime trip, the beauty and peace that this wilderness setting offers to those who come. It was one of the most rewarding parts of my job: showing them this magnificent country and sharing my love of flying.

One nice thing about the Beaver is the feeling it gives people of a stable, trustworthy plane. Once passengers ride in a Beaver, they're usually hooked and almost always prefer it to a Cessna or other bush plane. The steady roar of the 450 horsepower radial engine, the sturdy construction, and the fantastic STOL (short take off and landing) performance make this an engineering marvel and a winner with most. This was even more evident with pilots who flew the bush. I know it is my favorite airplane of all time, and I trusted old CF-IBP, my red Beaver, with my life.

On May 3 I flew the Super Cub PA-18, CF-HCM, to Lucky Lake to check the ice condition on a reconnaissance flight on floats. Then in the next few days I spent almost two hours on a forest patrol, again with the Super Cub.

Watson Lake Flying Service, Jim and Stan, and the many pilots I flew with over the years there enriched my life and hold forever a special place in my memory that I would draw on from time to time. The fabulous Yukon and the warm-hearted, good-natured Yukon people here at Watson Lake and throughout the North are printed deeply in my being, and I'll always have a special love for this country and warm feelings for these people.

Single after thirteen years of marriage, I found myself in a different world at thirty-two, living in a place where there were about fifteen men to every woman. However, being a pilot had certain benefits. I often flew badly injured people from Watson Lake to Whitehorse, which had a modern hospital, and a nurse would accompany the injured patient. Through these encounters I was able to meet some of the nurses and dated a few. I was also able to meet some of the schoolteachers, and of course I met some ladies through trips booked with Watson Lake Flying Service. Occasionally I met a single lady in the bush.

One day I flew to Frances Lake, which is about one hundred miles north of Watson Lake, with a young couple returning to their home on the east arm of the lake. They lived in a log cabin year-round and had been out only for a few weeks to work and earn enough to get their staples for another year. They had a commercial fishing license and could net fish for their needs and for the dog team's food. They told me about a young woman who lived south of them on the lake. She lived alone and had built her log cabin with her own hands. The more they talked, the more interested I became, and I decided I wanted to meet the woman who had the guts to live alone in this roadless wilderness setting.

I flew the Beaver south and soon spotted the log cabin nestled in some timber close to the lake. An attractive, well-endowed young lady met me. After showing me her rustic cabin with its dirt floor, she asked if she could fly back to Watson Lake with me. The plane was empty and I said sure, come along. We became friends and had a platonic relationship for years. She eventually married and had a child. She followed her dreams and carved out a home in the wilderness with her own hands.

Toward the end of June I flew some people into Seaplane Lake, which is by the Flat River in the Northwest Territories. I flew into this lake on many occasions over the years. We were flying my favorite airplane, the red Beaver CF-IBP. My passengers were going to raft down the Flat River to the South Nahanni River. I also flew the white Beaver CF-WMH into Burnt Rose Lake, eighty miles south, near the Turnagain River where the outfitter Johnny Drift had a hunting camp.

Later that day I flew into Don Taylor's place on Stewart Lake, forty miles north in the Yukon Territory. He had constructed a nice lodge and some cabins. Don, a local politician, represented Watson Lake and the surrounding area. He spent much of his time in Whitehorse during sessions, pushing the needs of the people in his district. He was developing a sport fishing business and planned to retire here one day. The fishing is good, with red trout colored like salmon from the freshwater shrimp they eat. Don was always friendly and I enjoyed flying for him. He had strong feelings about the government of the Yukon, of course, and worked hard for his district.

July sixth I flew into Windy Point, where a big game outfitters' hunting camp was located beside the Turnagain River. The Turnagain is, as the name implies, a river with many turns. It is shallow and a bit tricky at Windy Point. Landing upstream and working against the current to shore isn't too bad; however, because it is so shallow and has large boulders it is imperative to land in the deepest channel. Take-off is a bit tricky on this windy, narrow river. If the wind is blowing downstream the airplane wants to stay weathercocked into the wind and current, and you can lose a lot of distance trying to turn downwind for take-off, if, as is the case on portions of this river because of obstructions upstream, you have to take off downstream.

Earl Boose's camp on the Turnagain near Sandpile Creek, which I often flew into, required a downstream take-off in an easterly direction. The wind is usually from the west there, so I normally had a tailwind, and it could get tricky turning and then getting airborne with a sharp bend fairly close downstream. It was then a matter of full power with a tailwind and a fast current, with the pilot white-knuckling the controls as you went around the first bend on the step or maybe flying and trying to get altitude so you could climb above the trees along the bank before another sharp bend gave you another gray hair or two, or worse.

A green eighteen-year-old pilot put our Super Cub in near Windy Point. It hit so hard that the wings actually broke off the fuselage and dropped the wingtips into the water, and the floats broke loose from the struts and bent upward. Neither the pilot nor the passenger were injured, but the pilot ended up gassing planes for the remainder of his time with Watson Lake Flying Service. A picture of this mishap is in an album there—it looks like a bird shot out of the sky.

Over the next several days I flew to Twin, Nome, Allen, Davis and John I Lakes. I also flew the Cessna 185 CF-YIG into Tobally Lakes, which are eighty miles east of our base and in the Yukon Territories. Larry Schnig had a fishing camp there where you could catch huge lake trout, large pike and Arctic greyling.

One beautiful summer day I flew to Virginia Falls, a favorite place of mine, with some people who wanted to take pictures. Virginia Falls, which is twice as high as Niagara Falls, is located about 150 miles northeast of Watson Lake in the Northwest Territories.

This flight took about an hour and twenty minutes. We flew at about seven thousand feet, passing over the Hyland and Coal Rivers and Skinboat Lakes, north of McMillan Lake, and across the flat about sixteen miles south of the falls. As we circled the falls, the passengers got some good pictures. We began our letdown and on final flew over the falls and landed just above the rapids, about two thousand feet above the falls. Taxiing into shore, I jumped out and securely tied the plane down. If it went over the falls, we would have a long walk home.

There was a large boat decaying near the beach. The boat had been hauled up piece by piece from below the falls and reassembled to be used on the water upstream—quite a feat getting it up board by board on a man's back. Albert Faille, the noted Nahanni explorer, was that man.

After a few hours of picture-taking, walking to the falls, and getting some close-ups, we climbed aboard. The reliable radial engine started after a couple of revolutions of the prop. Soon we were on the step, speeding upstream away from the falls. Slight back pressure and the reliable Beaver was in its element. We continued upstream over the river to gain a safe altitude before heading southwest back to Waston Lake. My passengers were impressed and well satisfied with this magnificent set of falls.

The federal government eventually made this area, and the land for many miles downstream past Deadman's Valley, into Nahanni National Park. It was a worthwhile effort to set this magnificent wilderness aside for future generations.

I had a trip to Rabbit Kettle Hot Springs, just south of the South Nahanni River. Summer was passing swiftly—it was already August third. Soon the trees would begin turning gold in the high country. The publisher of an Anchorage newspaper, his wife, and a friend stood on the dock, watching as I tied their canoe to the floats. The canoe sat on top of the float, the bottom facing outward. I used two ropes at each end of the canoe, each tied around the bottom of the float struts, wrapped around the canoe, looped around the top of the strut and then back through the middle to a loop in the rope, and cinched until they were tight as a bowstring. The canoe was then ready to fly safely.

I was always very careful with external loads and never had one get away, but I heard stories of some pilots that did. Once I flew an eighteen-foot boat that weighed about four hundred pounds. I loaded it onto the Beaver from a lake by myself, with much grunting and some mumbling, because it was not only heavy but awkward to handle as well. Antlers were by far the hardest thing to fly with, as they disturbed the air flow so that the Beaver shuddered and didn't like to fly. Such a load slowed the plane down about forty miles per hour to an indicated eighty miles per hour once when I had seven caribou racks tied on the outside.

A canoe or boat slowed me down about ten miles an hour, making it a little wing heavy and causing the airplane to yaw slightly, but it flew relatively well. Sometimes I flew sheets of plywood and lumber in the same manner without any problem. I flew a radial engine, tied to the floats, into a lake in northern B.C. for our Beech 18, when Jim Thibaudeau lost an engine and made an emergency landing there. The company has a picture of it in their album.

When the canoe was securely tied down to my satisfaction, we climbed aboard and pushed out to deeper waters. I engaged the starter and the engine coughed, sputtered and roared to life, ready for another trip. The red Beaver looked a little strange with this object hanging out on the port side, but took it in stride. The take-off run was longer with the external load, but we were soon in the air and climbing on a northerly heading to the fabled South Nahanni River.

The flight was pleasant, as the weather was sunny with excellent visibility. We followed the Coal River to its source and then flew over the Flat River about thirty miles south of our destination. We landed near the hot springs, untied the canoe and pulled it up to shore, then unloaded the supplies.

Our party planned to head downstream to Virginia Falls, portage along a steep trail on the south side to the bottom of the falls, and continue downriver. The distance from the hot springs to Virginia Falls is about fifty-two air miles, but it's much farther by canoe as the river winds and loops.

Deadman's Valley is down the river another fifty air miles. After going through the Grand Canyon of the Nahanni on the other side of the valley, they would reach Kraus's Cabin and Hot Springs, where they would probably have a long, leisurely soak. They would finish the run at Nahanni Butte, about fifty-two air miles east. This is where the South Nahanni enters the Liard River, and there is an Indian village and a school there. They would use a two-way radio at the school to contact us at Watson Lake when they were ready for me to pick them up.

After wishing them well, I taxied out. The empty Beaver seemed to leap into the air after a very short run, and I began a climbing left turn to the southwest toward Watson Lake, flying directly over the mountains. The flight back took about 1:15. It was pleasant--just me and my favorite airplane on another journey over the fabled Yukon and Northwest Territories. Soon we would be back at our base, preparing for a new adventure. What a pleasant way to live my life: doing what I enjoyed most, and getting paid to do it. I was a fortunate man, and I knew it.

Two days after my trip into Rabbit Kettle Hot Springs, a much longer trip into the

Northwest Territory began. The Northwest Territory Forest Service booked IBP to fly from Watson Lake to Fort Simpson, pick up a fire fighter crew and fly them to Yellowknife. There were some forest fires out of control, and fire fighters were needed right away.

The trip to Fort Simpson is 280 miles, and it's another 270 to Yellowknife, about 550 air miles total. Getting paid mileage plus a base salary made this a very profitable trip. I was also getting to see new country, as it was my first trip to Yellowknife, the capital of the Northwest Territories.

The red Beaver climbed quickly to eight thousand feet, and I headed on a northeasterly course to Fort Simpson, which was located at the junction of the Liard and Mackenzie Rivers, on the southwest side. Fort Simpson was a small town. Several newer buildings were visible as I circled over town and checked the Mackenzie River for driftwood before my final approach. Landing to the east, against the current, I found a fair current running. After shutting off the engine I had to jump out of the Beaver on the passenger side and tie down quickly before we were swept downstream.

I met the forest ranger, and we loaded the Beaver with four men and their gear. I taxied out into the river, checked the controls and instruments, raised the water rudders, and applied full power. Because we were near sea level, where the air is denser, IBP quickly got on the step; slight back pressure and we broke free of the mighty Mackenzie River and headed almost due east for Yellowknife.

The weather was overcast, but the ceiling was a couple of thousand feet, so we were fat and happy. I was amazed at the countless lakes and swamps under my wings. The relatively flat country that begins east of the Mackenzie River stretched as far as my eyes could see.

Great Slave Lake is over 250 miles long, the longest lake I had ever seen. Yellowknife is on the north side. To see a small city so far north, surrounded by wilderness, was unusual, and it seemed out of place. After unloading the men and gear, I walked through this northern city. It was much like other Canadian cities farther south. Bank buildings, Hudson's Bay store, post office, Royal Canadian Mounted Police headquarters, and restaurants lined the paved streets. Walking back to the plane after a quick tour, I fueled up and was soon in the air heading west, back to Fort Simpson.

The weather was deteriorating rapidly as I set a compass course. Knowing that I would come over the Mackenzie River, my big concern was that when I did I would make the right decision, turning in the direction of Fort Simpson, unless of course I came out over the town.

The ceiling continued to drop, and I was soon about 150 feet above the trees. Fortunately it was flat country and I could see under the clouds, but the ceiling had dropped so much since flying over earlier in the day that I was getting concerned, especially since this was my first trip to this area and I didn't know the country.

Finally the wide Mackenzie, about one mile across at this point, came into sight and I turned right, downstream, hoping it was the right direction to Fort Simpson.

We flew visual flight rules (VFR), as our airplanes were not equipped for instrument flying. Jim Thibaudeau and I were the only pilots in Watson Lake who were instrument rated. Normally I was able to pick out lakes, mountains and rivers that showed up on my map as I navigated to a new area. It was important to get an accurate fix on my location, but the country was flat and the lakes endless, so all the lakes looked alike as I flew low over them. Flying over the Mackenzie River was an improvement--at least I could land, and if my calculations and a little luck were on my side, Fort Simpson should be showing up soon.

Sure enough, it was my lucky day. Ahead I could just make out some buildings that soon became Fort Simpson. What a relief to find my port in a storm. A quick circle over the landing area and I turned final, landing flaps, quick pre-landing check. Approaching at 80 mph, I soon leveled out and raised the nose to the landing attitude. The floats touched the water, and we settled in like a well-fed duck.

Having been here earlier in the day, I was familiar with the current and easily maneuvered to the dock. After I fueled up, the ranger sent me to Trainer Lake, south of Fort Simpson. I had to bring empty fuel barrels back from a fire near there, along with other gear.

After a rather long day I tied up for the night and walked to the local hotel, where I ate supper and returned to my room. The next several days were much the same, as I continued flying empty barrels from Trainer Lake to Fort Simpson.

Fort Simpson is a rather small town, set in a vast wilderness area. There is a Hudson Bay store, post office, Royal Canadian Mounted Police headquarters, a hotel and restaurant, and several large docks where river boats and tugs tie up. Most of the supplies are brought in during the summer by boat, as the river freezes over each winter. I met some interesting people who called this northern settlement home, and I enjoyed observing their lifestyle.

My work was finished August eighth, and the forest ranger at Fort Simpson released me. Soon I had IBP gassed and was on course for Watson Lake. I flew direct, which took me a few miles south of Nahanni Butte, visible in the sky-blue weather. However, just west of this where the mountains began, we hit some severe turbulence, and I slowed down as the Beaver bucked and fought an unseen foe. Every so often I checked the wings to be sure they were still there and not separating, but the strong Beaver remained in one piece.

We crossed the Whitefish River, then the Beaver River, and Tobally Lakes were visible straight ahead. I was over familiar territory now, and Larry Schnig's fishing camp was visible. The air turbulence had subsided somewhat, much to my relief.

Although I enjoyed trips to new areas, it was always nice to come home to Watson Lake (especially after many days on a freight haul), shower, change clothes, and have a few poose capays—a strong local flaming drink consisting of seven liqueurs—and a good meal. I could rest at my home on the lake where there was no phone, and peace and quiet reigned supreme. I got one day off and caught up on my laundry and other things that needed to be done.

August tenth I had a trip to Chuck Hayward's camp on Little Dal Lake. The hunting season was in full swing. Chuck's area had some good Dall sheep rams, which are the trophy most hunters come up here for. His hunters also shot caribou and grizzly bears, but the sheep were the most sought-after trophy, and the hunts were very expensive. Chuck had a first-class outfit.

Little Dal Lake sits on a plateau over four thousand feet above sea level, with the rugged Mackenzie Mountains rising to the east. It was a favorite of mine when the weather was decent; in bad weather, because of the high mountain passes, it could be very hazardous to my health. I was very careful and especially watchful in bad weather, as most of the valleys look alike and it was easy to get turned around and lost while flying. A few years ago, on a return flight to Watson Lake, a Beaver crashed during bad weather on a high pass a few miles north of the Nahanni River, killing all on board.

The trip up and back took about five hours, including the loading and unloading. The flying time was about two hours each way. The weather was good and the trip uneventful. Dall sheep were visible on the grassy hillsides near Little Dal Lake, and the hunters I dropped off with Chuck were all smiles. They anticipated a good hunt and were probably dreaming about getting a world record Dall sheep.

The hunting season starts earlier here (about July 15) than in the areas south, because it freezes up around the end of September. The outfitters have to leave much earlier or take a chance of losing their horses, as it takes about two weeks to trail them from here to the nearest road.

The next few days involved trips closer to Watson Lake. I flew to Moodie and Twin Lakes, south of Watson Lake about 120 miles or so, for Frank Cooke and Sons outfitters, then made a trip to Eaglehead and another lake for George Dalziel.

On September 9, 1971, I began a memorable trip into Headless Valley that lasted for a couple of weeks, flying men and supplies in from Fort Liard and Nahanni Butte to help fight a forest fire.

I returned to Watson Lake on September 25, and in the next few days flew into Meeting Lake with IBP and to the Turnagain River and back to Watson Lake, then to Skook's Ranch on the Kechika River.

I climbed into IBP on September 30, for the last trip of the season. I tried to make a charter flight, but the weather was bad and I returned to Watson Lake. This season was history, and it was time to pack and head to the outside.

It had been an intersting season up north, and now a new experience in the big city of Seattle was about to begin. In the middle of October I returned to Seattle, and on January 6, 1972, I began attending college at Bellevue Community College in Bellevue, Washington.

My journal entry for the sixth of January declares, "Big Day! I began attending college." The winter at school was an exciting time, and I met some interesting people. I began a growing period as the new ideas at college caused me to change some long-held ideas and think about new issues. I began to question my old set of ideas and considered new approaches to life. Quite a change from flying the bush to being a city dweller!

Reading about women's liberation in magazines and actually seeing it in action on campus were two different things. In the North the family structure was more traditional, with the husband and father the head of the home. Here it seemed the women wanted it all--to be in charge, to dictate their lives, and to heck with men telling them what to do. It was a culture shock, to say the least.

After becoming friends with what I thought were probably hard-nosed independent "women's libbers," I began to see the other side of the coin: they had legitimate reasons for wanting to see some changes made. Of course, their husbands were a bit shaken. I remember one lady in her late forties was going back to school to make a new career now that her children were grown. Her husband couldn't understand what was going on. He was looking forward to a good retirement and spending his days with his wife. She, on the other hand, wasn't satisfied and was determined to have her own life, even if it meant a single life.

I was to spend this winter and the next three winter seasons in the Seattle area. I found a home to rent along Lake Sammamish in Bellevue. Lake Sammamish was just east of Lake Washington, near Seattle. The Canada geese fly down from the north and winter here, and they became quite tame, walking up close to the house where they usually were able to get free handouts. Pity the mallards that tried to get some food if they got within range of one of those Long Necks, as I've seen a Canada goose literally pick one up in its beak and give it a good shaking before spitting it out with an angry HONK!

I was thirty-three years old the first day of classes. Before attending classes that day, I remember sitting at a restaurant, trying to figure out if I should catch a flight to the Hawaiian Islands and spend the winter there before going back to the Yukon or give college a try. In high school I usually just scraped by, because I knew school was a waste of time and that I was going north to live as a mountain man. Jim and I were going to steal those horses at Colville and head across the Canadian border, so school was useless. Finally I talked myself into going to just one day of classes, figuring that then I could split. Having paid my tuition, I thought I should give it one day.

School was fantastic, and it was an exciting experience to realize I could handle it and actually pull good grades. I met some interesting people there who became good friends. One I fell for like a ton of bricks, madly in love once again.

My favorite class was an English course in creative writing. I developed a crush on my teacher; she was a few years younger, and this helped to get my attention.

She wouldn't date until the class ended, and then we had one date, attending my first opera, "The Black Widow." It was interesting, and we had a nice evening. I developed a love for writing and started keeping a daily journal and have done so since then. Writing stories for this class was easy, because I wrote about my flying experiences, of which I had quite a few from several years of flying the bush.

A tall, dark, attractive woman named Barbara caught my eye in one of my classes. She had been a stewardess for Alaska Airlines, on a Constellation (Connie), which was the same airplane I flew in to Hawaii when I went into the Navy. Her middle ear developed problems, due to pressure changes, so she had been grounded and no longer flew. We hit it off well and, because we were the oldest in our class and usually sat together, we were referred to by the teacher and class as "you two." We began dating.

I remember our first date well. I had a Volkswagen bug and picked her up at her beautiful home on Cougar Mountain in Issaquah, which was close to Bellevue. It was a bit strange for this pilot out of the bush to be in a situation like this, but we had a great time.

We dated steadily and became good friends. She drove me to Vancouver, B.C., to catch my flight to Watson Lake in the spring, and we spent a memorable weekend together. Since my Volkswagen had developed engine trouble, I had sold it to a student at college a short time before.

My life seemed to be a series of goodbyes, as I spent part of my year in the far north and part down south, but I enjoyed this lifestyle and wouldn't change it for anything.

Flying north to Watson Lake on a Canadian Pacific Airlines 737, my thoughts were filled with memories of that tall beauty with the long black hair. I would have married her in a minute, and I told her as much. But Barbara was in the middle of a divorce, and another marriage was about the farthest thing from her mind. Memories of this intelligent, classy lady filled my being, and I missed her deeply. We were so close this past year, and we shared that wonderful experience of going to college--stretching our minds, experiencing new ideas and unlimited possibilities. I'll never forget her and those special times together: cruising the Puget Sound on a small boat near Seattle, walks in the countryside holding hands and thinking maybe someday we could share our lives together. She was in a class by herself and a very special friend.

Barbara gave me a parting gift that I'll always treasure, the book *Jonathan Livingston Seagull,* and wrote on the inside first page by a flock of flying seagulls, "This story makes me think of you. L.B.C." She used initials because she said that way you can always keep the book. I read this, my favorite books of all books, from time to time and think of this unique lady who will always be a special part of my life. The story is about those who don't put limits on themselves, those who reach for the stars.

CHAPTER IX
ALLIGATORS TO GRIZZLY BEARS

I began my longest flight as a commercial pilot on June 7, 1971, departing Watson Lake for Fort Meyers, Florida, to pick up a Beaver on floats and fly it back to Watson Lake. A trip from the southeast corner of the United States to the far-off Yukon in the farthest northwest part of Canada excited me with the anticipation of new adventures and new country—and getting well paid for what was almost a pleasure flight.

I flew the commercial airlines to Toronto and from there to Florida. After arriving in Fort Meyers I spent three days, from June 8 to June 11, working with an airplane mechanic to help get the airplane ready for the flight north.

On June 11, I climbed into the white de Havilland Beaver, cranked it up, and began taxiing toward the center of the river. After a satisfactory runup I applied full power before getting airborne and came close to an alligator swimming in the river. I had previously filled two forty-five-gallon drums of aviation fuel, to use as a reserve which I tied securely behind the pilot's seat. There are few seaplane bases in the South, and the extra fuel came in handy on numerous occasions during this long flight. The blue-green ocean of the Gulf of Mexico was under my left wing as I followed the Florida coast. This magnificent sky-blue day, new scenery, and the freedom of at last starting my journey home made my spirits soar!

The friendly skies began turning dark and ominous after about an hour, and I turned away from the coast in order to skirt the darkest thunderstorm. My fuel was getting low, and I wasn't certain where I was, because I couldn't get aviation maps of this area.

Below I saw a narrow canal winding by a few cabins, and I noticed some signs of life. After a normal approach and landing, I tied up to the bank and walked to the nearest cabin. A couple of women looked at me curiously; they hadn't heard me land. I explained my mission and asked for directions to New Orleans, as that was the day's destination. They pointed toward New Orleans and gave me an idea of the distance.

My fuel was low, so I ran a hose with a wobble pump attached from the drums to the belly tanks and began transferring fuel. It took a fair amount of time to fill the tanks, but at last they were topped.

The temperature and humidity were high as I began my take-off run on the canal. At the last possible moment, just before the canal made a ninety-degree turn to the left, I managed to stagger into the air. When I arrived in New Orleans several hours later, I noticed weeds and twigs wound around the water rudders, from skimming along the bushes just above the ground after take-off with the floats. The engine was on the weak side, and I think it had a lot more hours on it than the engine log book showed. In other words, it was about clapped out. Later when the company replaced the engine with a rebuilt one, I undertand it performed well.

I disliked, maybe hated, this Beaver, and so did the company pilots. Luckily for me it was given to a fairly new pilot, Bob Mitchell, who later flew for Canadian Pacific Airline. This was his first Beaver, and after flying the Cessna 185, he thought it was a marvelous machine. I was sure glad to get IBP back.

I stayed overnight in New Orleans and spent most of the evening walking Bourbon Street in the French Quarter. I listened to a terrific jazz band, four black men in their sixties and seventies playing horns--they were terrific. In the morning I worked on the airplane, installing a new battery.

I departed from New Orleans for Memphis, Tennessee, on June 12. I landed on a small lake to refuel, where I came close to a bad mishap, because some wire was strung across the lake and wasn't marked. I just touched down as the wire passed overhead, appearing to be too low to miss, but fortunately I did. After transferring fuel, I departed.

I landed on the Mississippi River a few miles north of Memphis and tied up to an island. I got a ride to the boat landing from a yacht owner, as there were a number of yachts pulled up and anchored along the island where a group of wealthy people were on a weekend outing. I was fortunate to find a man driving up, as it was late and deserted at the landing. He asked me what I was doing. I explained that I had just landed on the river with the Beaver and needed a lift into town. He told me to take his car, because he was going to stay overnight on his boathouse, but to make sure and bring it back by noon the next day. Southern hospitality at its finest, I thought, as I left for Memphis, which was about seven miles away.

That night in Memphis I danced at a night club called The Vipers until the "wee hours" with a nurse. The next day I flew from Memphis to St. Louis and overnighted there, then went to Madison, Wisconsin, where I stayed overnight at a motel owned by an interesting inventor. One of his inventions was a large car with truck tires that you walked into from the rear, standing up straight. It had an oil furnace for heat. While at Madison I had some papers signed by the former owner of the Beaver, releasing the airplane.

An interesting story was told to me by the airplane mechanic in Fort Meyers who had helped me get the airplane ready for my departure. The Beaver had been in a South American country which had a revolution, making the legal removal of the plane impossible. The owner persuaded a U.S. pilot to fly it out of the country, which he succeeded in doing, after obtaining the necessary fuel from various places. Well, he flew it out of the country and into the United States, illegally and at great risk, but didn't obtain the remuneration he had been promised.

FLIGHT OF THE RED BEAVER

From Madison I flew to St. Paul, Minnesota, a three-hour flight. I arrived in good form and spent the night with Mike, the owner of the Beaver, who was leasing it to our company. We went to a local watering hole for a few drinks, where we met a single woman and her pretty daughter. A few stories were told about the far north before we parted company that night.

The next day I departed for Estavan, Saskatchewan. On the way I stopped in North Dakota and filled up the belly tanks from the two forty-five-gallon drums on board. I landed and cleared customs in Estavan, then flew almost to Edmonton. I stopped on a small lake when it got too dark to fly and slept at a nearby motel; all I remember of that stay is waking up and getting a ride to the plane the following morning.

When I arrived at Edmonton, I ended up staying for ten days, because a lot of work needed to be done in order to get the Beaver licensed with a Certificate of Airworthiness. It was a most interesting stay, and my knowledge of human nature increased somewhat. Being single once again opened up a different world for me.

While in Edmonton I ran an ad for a female radio operator to work with me at Dease Lake for the summer. Her job would be to keep tabs on me while I was flying, do some expediting, and make bookings. I was told when I left on this trip that if I could find someone for the job, I was to hire the person.

Evidently the ad I put in the Edmonton Journal and the university papers was written in such a way that it intrigued many women, because the phone rang steadily, and the switchboard operator at my motel was swamped with young ladies wishing to interview for the position. As I recall, the ad read something like this:

> WANTED: Young woman to live at a beautiful, remote
> wilderness lake for the summer and operate the radio for
> a flying company.

Well, for several hours I had appointments every half hour. Some men were digging a trench outside my motel room, and they had the most incredulous looks on their faces as they watched a different woman come and go every half hour!

One cute, young redhead told me about special qualifications she had, "Oh," I said, "and what would that be?" She informed me, with a mischievous twinkle in her eyes, "I give terrific back rubs." She told the truth! The base at Dease Lake was never started, and the Beaver was based instead at Watson Lake, but I'll always have a special memory of my stay at Edmonton and what might have been an interesting summer at Dease Lake.

On June 27, 1971, I cranked up the white Beaver CF-WMH and departed Edmonton for Dawson Creek, a three-hour flight. Battery trouble forced me to stay overnight at Dawson. Then I headed up the Rocky Mountain Trench on a course to Watson Lake. As I had on the whole trip, I carried extra fuel in two drums. I had to make one stop on a lake in the Rocky Mountain Trench to transfer fuel to my front and middle tanks. The trip from Dawson Creek to Watson Lake totaled four flying hours, plus the short stop to transfer fuel.

Such an extended trip across North America was quite an event to begin my flying with this new company. It was seventeen days from departure at Fort Meyers, where an alligator was swimming in the river at take-off, to arrival in the far north Yukon Territory, where the grizzly bear is king! This was also the beginning of a series of new adventures that would forever be special highlights in my aviation career.

Larry flying his favorite airplane The Beaver.

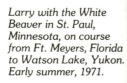

Larry with the White Beaver in St. Paul, Minnesota, on course from Ft. Meyers, Florida to Watson Lake, Yukon. Early summer, 1971.

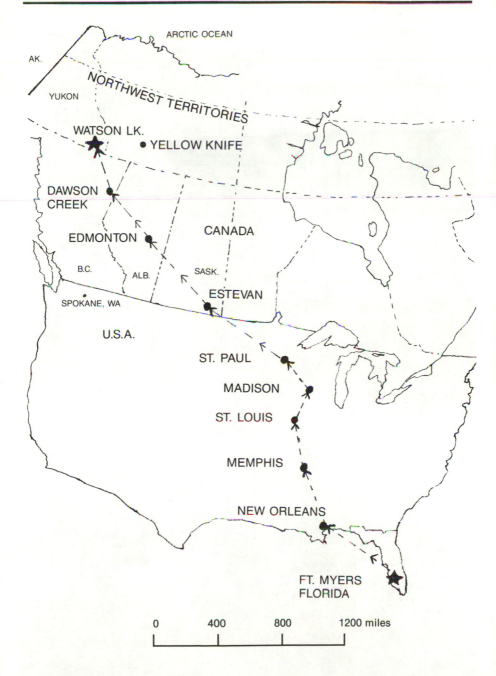

Larry unloading Caribou and Stone Sheep, at the Watson Lake Flying Service Floatdock, early 1970's.

CHAPTER X
DEADMAN'S VALLEY

We received a call from the Forest Service at Fort Liard in the Northwest Territories, requesting the Beaver to fly men and freight into Deadman's Valley to fight a forest fire. Because of limited resources, the remote fires are normally left to burn; however, they wanted to put this fire out as quickly as possible, because it was in the proposed Nahanni National Park area.

This was a new adventure for me, as it was my first flight into Headless Valley or, as it's called on my sectional chart, Deadman's Valley. Deadman's Valley is located just inside the Northwest Territories, in the southeast corner of this vast land. The mighty Mackenzie Mountains divide the Yukon and Northwest Territories and run in a northwesterly direction. Not far from here is the Arctic Circle, an imaginary line on the map which marks the zone where the sun does not set on at least one day of summer and does not rise on at least one day of winter.

The treeline, an area where it's too cold for trees to grow, cuts across the territories from the Mackenzie River delta in the northwest toward the Hudson Bay Coast in the southeast. North of the treeline are vast expanses of arctic tundra, large areas consisting of rock desert that is bare of vegetation except for a short period during the summer when tiny flowers bloom. The rest is mostly covered by grass-like plants, mosses and lichens that provide excellent grazing for herds of caribou and shaggy musk oxen. South of the treeline the tundra is mixed with scattered stands of stunted conifers. White birch, one of the few deciduous trees able to stand the cold, can be found in a few places. Because of the low rainfall and short summer, trees grow very slowly here.

The only really thick forests are south and west of Great Slave Lake in the Mackenzie River basin. Birch, spruce, balsam, jack pine, fir, tamarack, and aspen are fairly common. The winters, though cold and very long, are dry and healthy. With spring comes an immediate transformation from ice and snow to an immense area of thousands of shallow lakes with no outlets. A few, however, are connected with river systems that empty into the sea.

Wildlife includes moose along with Mackenzie Valley, with grizzlies, black bear and Dall sheep in the western mountains. Small game, such as beaver, arctic foxes, muskrats, and other furbearers, is plentiful. Wood buffalo are found west and south of Great Slave Lake; north are the woodland caribou, which are larger than the barren ground caribou, live in small groups rather than in herds, and don't migrate.

The great white Arctic wolves prey on the musk oxen and weaker caribou. On the

111

coast you can find polar bears, whales, and seals. Waterfowl such as geese, ducks, and swans arrive for the summer breeding season, as do birds of prey such as the snowy owl and peregrine falcon. The ptarmigan is one of the few birds that stay north; most of the rest migrate. I often saw them in my flights to Howard Pass, around the mining camp there.

The Yukon and Northwest Territories occupy almost 40 percent of Canadian land, yet this land holds less than one-half of one percent of the total population of Canada.

The South Nahanni River runs through Deadman's Valley. The Nahanni is a very dangerous river of whitewater, jagged rocks and swiftly changing channels, and is reputed to be the most treacherous and fastest flowing river in North America, with an average speed of twelve knots. It has risen as much as seven feet in one hour after one of the vicious rain and wind storms common to this area has unleashed its fury.

The air was smooth, the 450 horsepower Pratt & Whitney radial engine roared reassuringly, and I trimmed the airplane level at about seventy-five hundred feet. There wasn't a road or any sign of man as we headed across the eastern part of the Yukon and then into the Northwest Territories. It's a given time of reflection as I marvel at the Creator's handiwork from this vantage point. We're a tiny speck on this vast expanse of sky and earth.

This first season flying for Watson Lake Flying Service has been chuck full of new adventures, new firsts for me. It started out with a trip to Florida to pick up a float equipped Beaver in Fort Meyers, Florida, and fly it to the Yukon. I met some wonderful, warm and friendly people in the South who helped me in so many ways: people driving me to airports for fuel, a stranger in Memphis, Tennessee, giving me his car to use overnight, and the waitresses saying "Honey" this and "Honey" that.

Then on August 5 I flew to Yellowknife, the capital of the Northwest Territories, and later spent several days flying out of Fort Simpson on a fire. There were interesting trips with canoe parties into the fabled South Nahanni River, into the rugged Mackenzie Mountains to Little Dal Lake with sheep hunters, and trips for Frank Cooke and Sons, outfitters in northern B.C.

Now I was flying to a place I had heard so much about—Headless Valley—and would actually be living here until a fire was brought under control.

Leaving the Yukon in the red Beaver, I crossed into the Northwest Territories near the headwaters of Meilleur River, which flows into Deadman's Valley on a northeasterly direction. The Mackenzie Mountains began on the north side of the South Nahanni River. They are the most difficult mountains that I have ever navigated in, as the different valleys and mountains look almost identical, and it's easy to get turned around and lost. Several pilots and passengers have died in plane crashes near here while flying these mountains in bad weather.

While I was excited to begin the new adventure and operate off the fabled South Nahanni River at Deadman's Valley, I also felt a certain reservation and some apprehension in the Mackenzie Mountains. Flying over the Funeral Range, which is just west of the valley, I noticed the mountains were barren of trees above four thousand or five thousand feet. They had a desolate look, much like mountains I'd seen in Arizona in the dry desert areas. The elevation of the valley is under two thousand feet, according to the map.

Past the junction of the Meilleur and Nahanni rivers a few miles downriver, I saw a cabin on the southside and some people camped nearby, directly across from where Prairie Creek enters the South Nahanni, I think it must be Albert Faille's old cabin. He was a noted explorer and an expert with the canoe. He came to this country in the '20's and stayed some 40 years.

Circling the camp, I checked the river for debris and rocks, picking out a clear channel, and landed below the cabin into the current. As I came off the step, the current slowed me down rapidly and I had to use a fair amount of power to keep from being pushed backward. Maneuvering toward a makeshift dock, I slipped up alongside, and a native on the dock tied me down.

This was an Indian camp, and these Indians were of the Nahane Tribe, which means "people of the West." The Nahane form a major division of the Athapascan linguistic stock. They are located in northern B.C. and the Yukon Territory, between the coast range and Rocky Mountains, with some bands extending to the Mackenzie River.

The foreman, John, was there to greet me. He, the woman cook and the fire fighters were all local Indians. John was the only native who spoke English, so he quickly filled me in on what was happening and what I would be doing.

The fire had already burned a large area, and the government wanted to stop it as quickly as possible, because this area would be part of the Nahanni National Park; any scars would be visible for many years to come. I would be working for the forest ranger at Fort Liard and Fort Simpson and John here at the fire camp headquarters, where I would sleep in a tent.

John said, "Larry, you are to fly on to Fort Simpson and pick up some supplies and return to camp tomorrow." Before leaving, I checked out the camp. The log cabin was used as the cookhouse, and the men lived in tents set up near the cabin.

With some help from the natives I prepared to depart for Fort Simpson. A native held the Beaver to the dock after it was untied, until I could get in and start it up. The engine started easily, the native pushed me out a bit, and I began preparation for take-off.

I enjoy working rivers; it's a real challenge and keeps me on my toes. I get a lot of satisfaction from successfully completing a tough river operation without mishap. So far I'd been fortunate and had no accidents on rivers, although a few hairy times I came close to losing it. Currents, contrary winds, rocks and shallow waters in silty, murky rivers where the visibility is only a few inches are some of the hazards that can put you out of commission quickly, wrecking your plane and maybe taking your life.

Once on the raging Keel River in the Northwest Territories, I was turned loose before I could get the Beaver started. Whitewater rapids and large ugly rocks were waiting to wreck me a short distance downstream. If the old reliable 450 horse-power R-985 had coughed a few times before starting, the Beaver would have been lost—and perhaps me, as well. Fortunately it started quickly, averting a disaster.

My first take-off from Headless Valley was safely accomplished, and I set course for Fort Simpson 110 miles northeast. Flying over the first canyon, I noticed the canyon walls seemed to rise straight up from the river; I thought I might fly low through the canyon at a later date and get a better look. Next I noticed Kraus's cabin on the southside of the river, east of the canyon, with hot springs behind the cabin about one hundred yards or so.

Soon the valley widened out, and Nahanni Butte was visible under my starboard wing; just east of this Indian village the country flattened out as far as I could see, and the mighty Mackenzie Mountains slipped slowly behind.

Fort Simpson is located on a island at the junction of the Liard and Mackenzie rivers. The first fort here, Fort of the Forks, was established by the Northwest Company in 1804. In 1821 the Hudson Bay Company built a post here, and it was named for George Simpson, the Hudson Bay Company governor.

Fort Simpson was visible at last. Since I had been here earlier this season, the river and docks were familiar. A normal final approach (after first circling to look for debris at my proposed landing site) at 80 mph indicated round out, landing attitude, and a smooth landing was accomplished. Sometimes it seemed that when there was an audience watching and I tried hard to impress someone, I bounced! But after flying the Beaver for a while, you get fairly proficient and can usually set it down gently.

After tying up, I walked to the District Ranger's headquarters, about a quarter-mile away. It was getting late in the day, so I decided to overnight and return to Deadman's Valley with men and supplies the next day. I arranged dinner at the restaurant and another overnight stay at the hotel. One nice thing about working for the Forest Service was that I got my board and room in addition to my base pay and mileage, or hourly rate, whichever applied. They were nice to work for, and it was satisfying to know I was able to be a part of a worthwhile effort to protect a future national park from going up in smoke.

After a good night's sleep and breakfast, I loaded men and supplies into the Beaver and made an early departure off the river. Fort Simpson slipped behind, and I retraced my route over now-familiar country.

The flight back took about one hour. Landing against the current, I noticed some natives walking to the pole dock to give me a hand. I always appreciated that on a river; jumping out alone to tie down can be tricky in a strong current.

I soon began flying to Nahanni Butte, picking up freight and then flying back to camp. A DC-3 was flying in loads of supplies to the airstrip at the village of Nahanni Butte. The freight was then brought down to the river, where it was loaded onto the Beaver for the flight to Deadman's Valley.

My work was cut out for me. It's only forty air miles, which meant most of my time was loading and unloading with a 25 minute break of flying in between. Much of the freight consisted of 45-gallon drums of fuel for the helicopters that freighted men and supplies out of our camp at Deadman's Valley to the fire. I usually carried three drums in the Beaver. I always tied them down with ropes. If they slid back while I was in the air, the center of gravity would be too far aft. That happened to one pilot and was fatal.

When I landed back at camp, John, the foreman, informed me, "The other pilot never ties down the drums in his Beaver, but of course he probably knows his airplane better than you do." I didn't say anything, but that "other pilot" had wrecked several airplanes and was on the careless side, probably lucky to be alive. In any case I had nothing to prove and just wanted to safely get this job completed, with no damage to the airplane or pilot.

September 15: I flew to Fort Liard, then to Fort Simpson and back to Fort Liard to overnight. The flights went well, as usual with the red Beaver. Returning to Fort Liard from Fort Simpson, I was in a good mood. I would be staying in Fort Liard overnight for the first time and would have a chance to look around and do some sightseeing at the Indian settlement. In the fall the natives from the outlying villages and camps boarded their children at Fort Simpson, where the children attended school. A young and very beautiful Indian woman took care of them in a large dorm-like building.

It was late in the season. I was in the middle of the bush, away from roads, cities and civilization as most people know it, and I was single. I had nothing to do after tying down my Beaver and eating dinner, so I strolled over to the dorm to talk to the striking, raven-haired beauty. Machelle's English was broken, but we communicated fairly well.

While growing up in Spokane, Washington, I lived a couple of houses away from the chief of the Coeur d'Alene Indians. He had several grandchildren my age living with him. They were all girls, and we were good buddies. I've always had special feelings since then for native Americans. I remember those girls—Evonne, Doty, and another sister—who would show me their skin and say, "See, people don't like us because our skin is not the same as yours." We were in grade school then. I told them, "You're my friends, and to me you are no different than anyone else." My buddies would tease me, but to me the Indian girls were very special friends. We spent much time together playing games and having a good time growing up together.

I spent several more nights here on the banks of the Liard River, and Machelle and I became well acquainted. She was the kind of person a poet or author would call an Indian princess, a delicate beauty.

During the day Machelle brought the children down to the banks of the Liard to watch as I loaded the Beaver and flew away to the north. One day I left for good. Machelle and those nights along the Liard became fond memories of a special time, with a special lady in the far North.

One day at Nahanni Butte I was watching the DC-3 bring in another load of supplies. When the captain shut off the engines, a young, pretty, smiling French girl climbed down from the DC-3. I learned she was a French photographer and free-lance writer wanting to do an article on Deadman's Valley.

Shella flew with me on the trip into our camp and stayed three days, writing and taking pictures. About every three days or so I would fly downstream through the first canyon and take a bath in the hot springs behind Kraus's cabin, so I invited her along. We flew through the canyon, which was about a ten-minute trip, and landed on the Nahanni in front of the cabin. I pulled the Beaver up on the sandy beach and tied down.

Shella and I walked to the cabin and were met by an Englishman and two Frenchmen who were studying the caves along the Nahanni River on a grant from the Canadian government. They told us one cave had about 100 Dall sheep skeletons in it. Apparently the sheep had gone into the cave during a snowstorm and weren't able to get out.

The researchers showed us the various hot springs behind the cabin. Shella said, "I'm too embarrassed to stay and take a dip in front of all the men." She went back toward the cabin with the Englishman and two Frenchmen. I stripped and started to get in one of the pools when Shella's voice broke the silence. She had come back because the men told her to get in the pool right away; the bottom was muddy, and after my bath it would be riled up. Much to my surprise, she disrobed in front of me. I took a picture of this attractive 22-year-old woman with a schoolgirl figure and only a smile on her face.

She let me know up front that she wasn't in love with me and there couldn't be anything but friendship between us. We acted like a couple of school kids playing hooky and had a great time, soaking in the hot springs in the wilderness. She flew out to begin another adventure a couple days later.

A few months later Shella sent from South America a letter and slides she had taken of the Beaver. I still have them. The one I use for a business card is me just taking off the Nahanni in the red Beaver IBP. She was so good-looking that she was probably able to hitch free rides, much as she did with the pilot on the DC-3 and with me. She was full of life and enjoyed it thoroughly.

Another day one of the fire crew, Jim, who was the only white man besides myself, went with me to Nahanni Butte, to help load freight and get out of camp.

We flew Mr. and Mrs. Johnson, the schoolteachers from Nahanni Butte, to Kraus's hot springs, a short distance to the west; we all needed a bath. After landing in front of Kraus's cabin on the Nahanni, we tied the Beaver and walked to the hot springs. Jim and I got in one of the series of pools, and the Johnsons picked out another one about thirty feet away. We were all skinny-dipping, but the separate pools and high banks gave us privacy. We began lobbing a few mud balls through the air. Soon we were in a serious mud ball bombardment. The springs boiled a dark mud color, and we had goop through our hair and covering our bodies. We left the hot springs much blacker than when we arrived, but we laughed about the fun we had all the way back to Nahanni Butte.

Mr. and Mrs. Johnson were a tremendous help; we often used their two-way radio to call Watson Lake. Canoe parties dropped off on the upper reaches of the South Nahanni River reached the Johnsons' and used their two-way radio to call our base for pick-up. I was always glad when we could do something for this couple. Once I flew in to take a canoe party back to Watson Lake, and Mrs. Johnson hitched a ride, so she could get a pair of glasses.

Jim was driving through the Yukon on the Alaska Highway and was stopped because of tremendous forest fires burning throughout the territories. He readily agreed to help fight a forest fire and was flown into this camp before I arrived. Jim was from back East, probably in his twenties, a long-haired hippy type. I soon found out he was an okay guy, and I enjoyed his company.

At night we had a ritual of sitting around the campfire until the wee hours of the morning, watching the northern lights, talking about the States, the North or just listening to the night sounds of the river and bush. Those nights along the banks of the Nahanni River were pleasant, satisfying times.

The campsite and the area close by was wild and beautiful; the fall colors were magnificent along the river. The top half of the mountains, a short distance away, were bare looking, but it was pleasant on the river here by camp.

Besides hauling freight from Nahanni Butte to Deadman's Valley almost daily, I made several trips to Fort Liard and Fort Simpson. Those longer trips were a welcome relief from the short freight hauls.

One overcast day I had several trips from the airstrip at Nahanni Butte to our camp. I had been flying direct, a short cut across some ridges just south of the first canyon, to save time. The ceiling had been dropping, but I didn't really want to fly through the windy, narrow first canyon. I saw some daylight between the clouds and the ridge, so I decided to take that route again.

The clouds enveloped me as I started to fly over the ridge; I could see only the inside of a white cloud. I was above the valley, mountains on either side, no navigation aids. I shouted, "Oh God," thinking I had mere seconds before I crashed into a mountain side. I figured this was it, and that I would soon be buying the farm, for good! Split second terror!!! A helpless feeling. There was a slight drop in elevation ahead, so I maintained the heading and altitude. I slid down the window on my door and stuck my head out, trying to see the ground.

DEADMAN'S VALLEY

The fall-colored tops of trees flashed red and orange periodically. I felt temporary relief when I broke through the clouds a couple of times, only to be plunged back into whiteness. When I finally broke through to clear air, the relief was one of joy, of new life—another chance to live. Fortune once again smiled on me. I'm not sure why; others have not been so fortunate here in the Mackenzie Mountains. I was thankful to God for letting me live. That was the last time I took the shortcut; from then on, I flew through the narrow first canyon, where the visibility was good.

I left Headless Valley for Fort Liard on September 25 with men and gear. The fire was out, and my job was finished here. I unloaded, fueled up and taxied out into the Liard River. The roar of the engine drowned out all sound as I took off upstream to the south. The floats left the water, and Fort Liard disappeared behind the Red Beaver.

I had a souvenir of this sojourn—a beautiful pair of moose moccasins with intricate beadwork, made by a native woman in Nahanni Butte. My size 13 feet fit perfectly into the custom-made moccasins. Additionally, I had many adventures to relive in my mind, two beautiful women I had come to know and a few more grey hairs caused by a close call with death in Deadman's Valley. My memories were mostly pleasant ones, of natives living in the bush, dried moose meat in the sun, of new country, new friends and a safe return of the Red Beaver and this grateful pilot to Watson Lake.

The flight back to Watson was about 190 miles. The weather was good, and I was glad to be on course to a hot shower, old friends and maybe a few poose capays at the Watson Lake Hotel. After what seemed like a long trip, Watson Lake finally came into view. I approached from the east and let down over the trees north of the base. I came off the step at the point of land near the seaplane base and taxied to the dock. After leaning the mixture, the engine quit, switches off, and I stepped off the float to tie IBP to the dock. A memorable trip safely completed; now I looked forward to a few nights in my own bed. I left on September 9, 1971, and was back September 25, safe and sound.

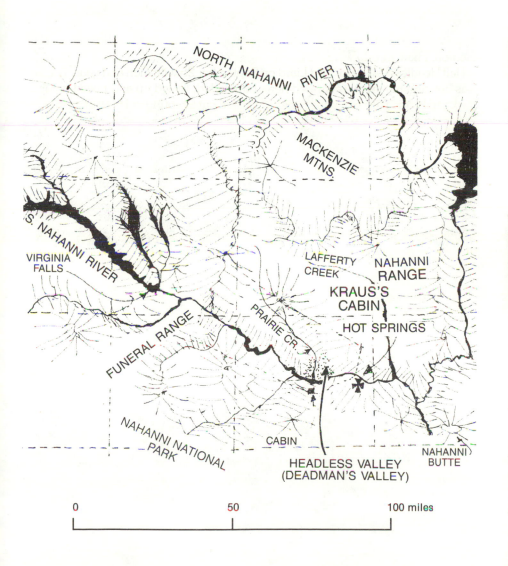

NORTH NAHANNI RIVER

MACKENZIE MTNS.

S. NAHANNI RIVER

VIRGINIA FALLS

LAFFERTY CREEK

NAHANNI RANGE

KRAUS'S CABIN

HOT SPRINGS

FUNERAL RANGE

PRAIRIE CR.

NAHANNI NATIONAL PARK

CABIN

HEADLESS VALLEY (DEADMAN'S VALLEY)

NAHANNI BUTTE

0   50   100 miles

Larry flying freight in the Red Beaver from Nahanni Butte to Deadman's Valley, Sept. 1971.

The Red Beaver and Larry taking off the South Nahanni River in Deadman's Valley 1971, while hauling men and freight from Nahanni Butte to this valley, to fight a nearby forest fire.

Shella taking a picture of Larry taking a picture, while flying thru first canyon on course to Kraus's cabin, in the Red Beaver. The ridge on the right is where Larry disappeared into the clouds, in bad weather. Note the throttle is on the left center, prop lever middle, and the round topped fuel mixture lever, is on the right.

Kraus's cabin 1971. These two Frenchmen and an Englishman were doing a sheep study in the area for the Federal Government. Larry is on the right.

WATSON LAKE Flying Service commenced operations in June 1962, with partner pilots, Stan Bridcutt and Jim Close. The company was operated by Stan until 1963, when they purchased a Cessna 180 when Jim became an active partner. Jim is a home grown boy and learned to fly in Vancouver in 1957. Stan came to the Yukon in 1946 and has done most of his flying in Y T.

From left brothers Frank and Bob Close on the Watson Lake Flying Service Floatdock. They were about the same age as Scott and they all fished together and explored the lake on those long warm Yukon summer days in the early 70's.

CHAPTER XI
WRANGLING HORSES ON THE
NAHANNI WITH SCOTT

As I flew back to Watson Lake on CPA, I reflected on events of the winter just past: school, meeting new friends, seeing life in the big city. Now I looked forward to a new season of flying the bush, renewing friendships, and, of course, making some money. While at college I was able to draw veteran benefits for the time I had served in the U.S. Navy, but this money was getting a bit low.

The pilots at Watson Lake Flying Service were well paid. We had a substantial base salary, as well as a mileage rate, which doubled after ten thousand miles in any given month. My lifestyle had become unique. Simplicity, simplicity, simplicity would describe it clearly. Since my divorce I had gotten rid of unnecessary things and began a pattern of spring, summer and fall in the north, with winters in the south. It was like what I dreamed about in high school: I would watch those Canada geese fly over, heading north in the spring, and have a yearning to join them; again in the fall would see them heading south. Now I was traveling the same route.

My worldly possessions were quite simple: four boxes, two suitcases, a foamy and a sleeping bag. Fifteen minutes and I could be packed and away. I liked it! My life was more satisfying and happy in proportion to the degree I could make it simple. Things--material possessions--at this time in life were something I just didn't want.

The Boeing 737 stopped at Prince George, Fort St. John, Fort Nelson; now it was on course to Watson Lake, my home in the Yukon Territory. This was my fourth season in this vast land, and, as we got close to our destination, I saw familiar landmarks below: the Alaska Highway, the Liard River, the Rocky Mountains and countless unnamed wilderness lakes.

Flying around the edge of Watson Lake, we turned final. The wheels touched with a solid thump, the brakes caught, and we rapidly slowed on the short runway. Across the lake from the end of the runway lay a World War II bomber in shallow water near shore. It took off on an almost empty tank and ran dry shortly after take-off. The bomber lay in the lake bottom as a lesson to pilots: always check and switch to the fullest gas tank before take-off.

Another rule I followed rigidly was to never, never pilot an airplane after drinking. I always had a night of sleep before piloting an airplane, after even one drink. Alcohol reduces the amount of oxygen'your system has, and as you gain altitude, which also deprives your system of oxygen, the effect can be deadly. Your coordination is off, and your judgement and depth perception are adversely affected.

Sometimes when I was flying Indians to a hunting camp and they were drunk or had one big hangover and started to give me a bad time, I would climb to seven thousand feet or so. The effect of less oxygen at such an altitude, combined with their rich alcohol-soaked blood, would cause them to pass out. When they knew they were going out for the season guiding, they would get drunk at their village and then hide. We would go down, find them, pour them into the company pickup, then pour them into the Beaver. Once out in the bush they were excellent guides, after they had some time to sober up.

One of the pilots I flew with would come to work after an all night drunk, pour himself into the pilot's seat with no sleep, and fly away. I noticed he was very careless; he didn't tie down the forty-five-gallon drums in the airplane to keep them from sliding to the back of the plane. I didn't like to fly the same Beaver he had flown, not knowing what he might have done. He was a poor pilot and a danger to himself and anyone he flew. Another pilot who flew helicopters would take a drink of whiskey before flying, which really surprised me; he was an older man, a man I thought should know better.

As I walked off the plane, the same small terminal building and familiar faces greeted me; it felt good to be back north from "the outside," as we referred to a trip beyond the Yukon.

Between the middle of May and early June, the ice leaves Watson Lake. One year it was about June 15 before the ice left and we could begin flying off the lake. Some of the higher lakes don't shed their ice until July or August, but this June the lakes and rivers in the lower valley were open, and we began our busy season once again. Spring comes quickly to the north. Almost overnight it seems everything is in bloom. Growth is rapid because of the long days of sunlight--it is still daylight at midnight.

Before we actually got the planes on floats and in the water, there was always work to be done scraping floats, fixing leaky compartments, and then painting them. Once the floats were finished and attached to the planes, we hauled them from the airport on a trailer to a nearby launching area close to the airport. We test flew them, then returned for another season at our seaplane base, located on the east end of Watson Lake.

It was good to be flying again, this sunny day of June 5, 1972. I taxied out in our Cessna 185 YIG, prepared to do a few circuits and landings to get back in the swing of things. Run up, full power applied, and the Cessna quickly got on the step and in the air with just the company check pilot and me. A few landings to get the feel once again of a float plane, and I was prepared to begin another season flying prospectors, hunters, guides, canoe parties, and, of course, fire patrol. The season at this time started out slowly, but would soon be in full swing; just getting enough sleep would become a problem.

My first charter flight was in my favorite airplane, the Red Beaver CF-IBP, on

June 8; I flew two passengers to North Lake and logged 2.2 hours.

I obtained a lake lot on Watson Lake from the Yukon government and would be able to obtain title when I put in two thousand dollars in improvements. I purchased a small trailer and set it up on the property, and Scott and I stayed in it. Scott and I ran, spent as much time together as possible, and I took him on as many trips as I could. He spent a lot of time around airplanes and the men of the North—prospectors, hunters, trappers, truckers—and was growing up in a man's world. Sometimes he stayed in the bush for several days at a mining camp and did some serious fishing. His favorite part was the camp cooking; their delicious meals of steak and pie compared most favorably to my pork and beans and cereal.

The mosquitoes were fierce once you stepped outside, but it was nice to have my own place to come home to after a long day flying. Sometimes I canoed from my place to the base, which was about fifteen minutes away.

June 10, I prepared my Beaver for a flight to Skook Davidson's Ranch on the Kechika River in the Rocky Mountain Trench. Skook was a living legend, a symbol of a passing era in this country. His ranch was about 110 miles southeast of Watson Lake in a wilderness area without roads or electricity. He had no neighbors for about a hundred miles, except for a few outfitters during the hunting season.

After fueling IBP and doing a thorough preflight check, I began loading sacks of horse feed. I taxied toward the bay at the south end of the lake, and within thirty seconds we were off the water. Heading south, I soon passed over downtown Watson Lake and continued climbing as the Liard River passed under my wings.

One of Frank Cook's hunting camps on Scoop Lake west of the Kechika River came into sight. Frank was a first-class outfitter and guide—one of my favorites to fly for. He had one of the finest stone sheep areas in the country, and record-class heads were common in his area. Skook's place was twenty miles beyond Frank's.

Soon Skook's ranch and landing site on the Kechika River came into view. I circled, looking for river debris before making my final approach. I landed into the current and was kept busy working the plane against the current toward a tie-up spot nudged into the beach.

Skook waited stoically in a horsedrawn wagon about twenty feet away. He was up in years, maybe close to eighty, but still solidly built. He had arthritis, which had slowed him down some and made walking difficult, so he didn't get off the wagon. I unloaded the horse feed and groceries onto the bank and then carried it to the wagon. Skook said hello but little else as I loaded his wagon. He watched me walk to the Beaver and shove off into the current. I was glad to meet this silent, living legend of the North. I was soon in the air, and Skook and his wagon disappeared behind. It was a privilege to know this man and to be able to fly into his isolated world.

One day I heard that Dennis Ball had crashed in the float-equipped Otter. The story I heard from another pilot, a friend of Dennis's, was the following: Dennis radioed in to B.C. Yukon's flight office that he was following Lafferty Creek, on course to a lake in the Mackenzie Mountains with six forty-five-gallon drums of fuel and one passenger to a mining camp. "I'll just stick my nose in and take a look. If the weather's not good, I'll return to the base camp and do some fishing." That was the last transmission heard. Sid Baird left a short while later to search for Dennis in the jet ranger helicopter. It looked like Dennis took a wrong turn up a blind canyon, tried to make a 180 and then crashed into a mountainside, killing himself and his passenger.

I booked another trip with horse feed, saddles and gas to the Turnagain River, into Earl Boose's hunting camp about 80 miles south. Earl and Marge, his wife, ran a good camp and were well-known in the guiding and outfitting business. The trip was uneventful, except for the final approach and landing on a tricky, shallow river that kept me on my toes, as usual.

One cardinal sin was forgetting the mail. The isolated camps looked forward with a passion to letters from the outside. Pity the poor bush pilot who forgot it--which on occasion had been my bad fortune.

The big game hunting camp was nestled in a beautiful setting on the north side of the river. Coffee and pie were a pleasant treat while the isolated campers asked questions about various events, what people were doing, how Jim and Stan were doing, and world news. They helped by holding the Beaver until it started. Then the guys swung my tail around so I was headed downstream for take-off, as there were obstructions upstream. I had to be careful on the river's series of turns, rocks, and shallow water.

Early in July I prepared for an interesting journey to the South Nahanni River. We had received an emergency call earlier from one of Chuck Hayward's guides. One guide had been swimming his horse across the Nahanni River, when the horse had drowned underneath him. The rawboned cowboy guide, a non-swimmer, was trapped on a sandbar in the middle of the river. The Nahanni was in flood stage and rising. We were asked to send the plane immediately, as the life of the guide was in danger.

Jon Poizer, one of our pilots, left with the Super Cub. He successfully picked up the guide and took him to an island on the river to which the rest of the guides and horses had first swum.

Jim Close said, "Larry, fly up to Little Dal Lake near where Chuck has his main hunting camp. Pick up Chuck and fly him to the group stranded on the island. See what can be done to get the rest of the horses across the river." This was a crucial time for Chuck. He had to have his camp and horses ready for the first Dall Sheep Hunt starting July 15. From where they were stranded it would take two weeks of steady riding to get to camp.

Scott was with me, as I decided it would be a good trip to take him on. We had a light load, and the Beaver climbed quickly north toward Little Dal Lake. With good

126

weather, the trip was 220 miles. As I often did, I let Scott have the controls so that he built up some more co-pilot time.

We flew parallel to the Hyland River and before long could see the landmark high glacier peaks above Glacier Lake. We passed over the South Nahanni River, just north of Glacier Lake, at about eight thousand feet. Little Dal Lake lay about another 80 miles over these rugged Mackenzie Mountains. The valleys and peaks looked so much alike that I always concentrated closely and kept a map handy to make sure I was on course.

"Scott, it looks like we're about there," I said as the blue speck of Little Dal Lake appeared. I flew over Chuck's camp first and then circled the lake in a descending turn. We touched down a few hundred feet from the shore. The Beaver settled into the water after a few bounces, something I tried not to do in front of a client--but such is life. We unloaded a few things for Chuck's camp and readied for the flight to the stranded guides and horses with Chuck on board.

After eighty miles, we spotted some horses on a quarter-mile long island. I circled the raging river, looking for logs and debris and found a spot that appeared clear. We touched down into the current, landing in a westerly direction. The current was swift, and I needed plenty of power just to keep from going backwards. Working into the current, I eased the Beaver toward shore where the guides were standing ready to secure the plane. I was glad for their help to heel the back of the floats onto the beach and securely tie the Beaver to some small trees.

We began constructing a breastwork of logs and driftwood from shore. We hoped we could drive the horses into the river and to the shore on the northside; the horses had other ideas. Because the river was shallow by the island, they walked around the breastwork and back onto the east side of the island. We fired guns and chased horses up and down the island.

Chuck decided to fly in a boat and motor. He hoped to pull the lead horses across the river so that the others would follow. He and I flew to Cantung (Tungsten), a mining town about 50 miles west, for an aluminum boat and motor. We tied it securely and returned to the island.

Chuck and one guide pulled one horse behind the boat stern, into the water. Once in deep water, the horse swam behind the boat through the swollen waters. On the other side, the propeller hit bottom and broke. Since the boat would not make it back on its own power, I pulled it back with the Beaver.

It was late; nothing more could be done, so we prepared to spend the night on the island. We all sat around the campfire, telling stories before turning in for the night. Scott and I slept in the Beaver.

Chuck decided to fly back to Cantung the next morning. A shop there was able to fix the propeller, but we lost another several hours flying to Cantung, fixing the propeller and flying back.

Chuck finally made a couple of successful trips getting horses across the river, and all seemed to be going well. Suddenly, near the other shore, the boat capsized. Chuck and the guide were swept rapidly downstream. A sweeper, a downed tree extending into the swirling waters, saved their lives. After a fierce struggle with the current pulling at them and the weight of their wet clothes, they dragged themselves up the tree and onto shore.

The boat and motor were lost. Once again I cranked up the Beaver and taxied from the island to pick up the two men. The horse they were pulling when the boat capsized made it safely to the far shore.

Darell Nelson, who was in the process of buying Chuck's outfit, was one of the men stranded on the island. "When I saw the Beaver fly over, it was like the angel of deliverance." Darell lost 25 pounds on that trek.

Now that a few of the lead horses were on the other side of the river, the rest of the horses allowed us to drive them into the water and across. After a broken propeller, a sunken boat and a near drowning, the horses and guides were safely across. Scott and I left for home with a new respect for the raging South Nahanni River, which even at this late date was still in flood stage.

It was July 8, and the fire season was upon us again. I had a forest ranger as co-pilot and was flying our Twin Apache CF-KXL on a long patrol. The fire danger was high. It was a treat to fly a Twin once in awhile; it was faster, quieter and handled more like an executive ship. The Beaver was still my favorite, but it was fun to get time in other types. July 16 I flew our Twin Beach 18 into Wasson Lake on a fire.

On another trip a few days later I flew some mining people into Telegraph Creek, an old mining community from the past century's gold rush days. Telegraph Creek sits on a high ridge above the Stikine River. I landed the Beaver above the town on Sawmill Lake.

The store owner, Doug Blanchard, met us at the lake and gave us a ride to this tiny community. He owned one of the two stores; the other was owned by the Hudson's Bay Company. Telegraph Creek was laid-back and peaceful—no hurry, just an easy, slow pace. I was fortunate to stay overnight, so had a chance to walk around and get a feel of Telegraph Creek's rich history. Across the town and up the hill lived the Tahltan Indians in their small houses—some painted blue and red, and some with just weatherbeaten boards. The Indian cemetery nearby still had the little painted spirit houses over the graves, an old Indian custom.

The warm, long, lazy summer days and the slow pace of the locals in Telegraph Creek would, I always thought, make this an ideal place to spend a vacation, to unwind and just enjoy. Telegraph Creek was to become one of my favorite destinations and a place I visited many times in the years ahead.

At an early age I had been an avid reader of stories about the Klondike gold rush and stories of the North--Telegraph Creek, Dawson City, the Yukon River. Robert Service's poems and Jack London's stories were all vivid in my mind. Those boyhood hours of reading made my in-person visits to this land even more enjoyable. The flight back to Watson Lake was pleasant, as I thought of this unique village so rich in history.

Another favorite place of mine, Atlin, British Columbia, was one of my destinations in the Red Beaver CF-IBP. A few days later some mining officials had booked to Atlin, then to Whitehorse with a return to Watson Lake, a flight of just over seven flying hours.

Atlin townsite had the most beautiful setting I had ever seen in my travels up north. It sits on the east side of Atlin Lake. This clean, clear, ninety-mile-long lake is the largest natural lake in British Columbia and is about nine hundred feet deep. Lake herring, whitefish, Arctic grayling, ling cod, and lake trout make their homes in these waters. Glaciers rise above the lake to the west. Birch Mountains, the tallest island mountains in a freshwater lake in the world, jut from Teresa Island

Gold was discovered here in 1898 by Fritz Miller, a German immigrant, and Kerry McLaren, a Nova Scotian. This area is rich in history in its own right, as well as being located along the Klondikers' route to Dawson City.

Any trip to Atlin was a bit of a booze run. Alcohol was cheaper in Atlin, so I always had a standing order to buy booze there and bring it back to Watson Lake.

The flight from Watson Lake to Atlin was about 170 air miles. The course paralleled the Alaska Highway for a while, although it was many miles south and crossed the southern tip of Teslin Lake. It was a nice flight; the weather was good, and Atlin was visible many miles ahead. In the clear air it looked like a sleepy, almost deserted, small town next to the huge lake. We tied up at the dock near the townsite, and my passengers took care of their business.

After lunch we departed for Whitehorse, the capitol of the Yukon, a forty-five-minute flight to the northwest over some spectacular scenery. Whitehorse became the capitol of the Yukon in 1953 after the territorial government was moved from Dawson City. From a village of less then five hundred, it grew to over twenty thousand, as people poured into town to commence building the Alaskan Highway in 1942. It's a regional service center outlet for Yukon communities.

We landed on the fabled Yukon River, behind a dam close to the city. My passengers got a ride into town from the seaplane docks on the river. After fueling, I taxied into the river, flaps, trim, full power. With no load, the Red Beaver seemed to leap on the step. We were in the air in a few short seconds and climbing rapidly on our easterly course to our home base at Watson Lake. The flight course took us by the north end of Marsh Lake and Teslin Lake. The community of Teslin on the east side of the lake began around 1903 with the founding of a trading post serving the nomadic Teslinegit Indians. About four hundred people lived here now.

Soon we were flying over the Cassiar Mountains and over Meister Lake. It was only sixty miles to home, a hot shower, supper and a rest after seven hours with the constant roar of the radial engine numbing my ears and body. After landing it was just nice to get away from the noisy engine and walk along the quiet lakeshore.

It was July 15, and the season was passing quickly as I prepared IBP for a supply and mail run into Broken Bit on the Kechika River for Frank Cook, the outfitter. It was about 110 miles down the Rocky Mountain trench, close to one hour flying time. After landing and unloading I had one side trip before returning to Watson Lake. The trip was routine, with no problem landing on the river, the flight home smooth.

An accident on the Alaska Highway, with some critically injured people, brought a call for a couple of airplanes from our company to fly the injured from Watson Lake to Whitehorse immediately. It was night, and we were not normally allowed to fly floats after dark. Because of the emergency situation, we were allowed to make that trip. It was midsummer, and the days were getting shorter, but in the land of the midnight sun there was still enough light to fly visually.

We loaded one patient and a nurse who would monitor the patient while I flew my Beaver IBP. We were soon on course for Whitehorse. Jim Thibaudeau was flying a couple of injured patients and another nurse in his Beech 18. He too left the lake, heading for Whitehorse. The air was relatively smooth, the flight uneventful. My male patient groaned and seemed to be seriously injured and in much pain. The nurse closely watched and tried to make him as comfortable as possible.

Whitehorse had the only real hospital in the Yukon Territory. Watson Lake had a nursing station, with about seven nurses and a doctor from England by the name of Wigby. The nursing station didn't have the facilities to take care of seriously injured patients, so they were usually flown to Whitehorse by Watson Lake Flying Service.

We arrived over the Yukon River near Whitehorse at about four in the morning, after a flight of 240 miles over a remote wilderness area. A waiting ambulance whisked the patient to the Whitehorse Hospital. I surely hoped he made it.

Jim and I and the two nurses had breakfast at Whitehorse before going back to Watson Lake. I left first in IBP and was flying merrily along when Jim pulled up beside my left wing, in formation for a few minutes, and then passed me. The Beech 18 was a little faster than the Beaver. We arrived back at Waston Lake about eight a.m., ready for another busy day.

One day I was enjoying coffee and conversation with Dr. Wigby. The good doctor had thick grey hair, bushy eyebrows and an ever-present serious look. In spite of appearances, he was a neat guy and very interesting to talk to. One of his favorite topics was flying. Although he had logged seventy hours of dual flying instruction, his solo time was zero. To date no instructor had felt comfortable turning him loose for his first solo, but Dr. Wigby's enthusiasm for flying was still very evident.

A canoe party needed a doctor on the Nahanni River; one of the party had a dislocated shoulder. Dr. Wigby and I left from Watson Lake and located the group after about an hour's flight. We landed on the river. The man with the dislocated shoulder was in pain, and his injured shoulder was at an angle much lower than the other shoulder. Dr. Wigby put his knee in the man's back, his hands on his shoulder and gave a quick hard pull. The shoulder popped into place, and we left for Watson Lake. Dr. Wigby didn't believe in Canada's program of socialized medicine and refused to pay his premiums; he was occasionally jailed for his beliefs. I liked this man!

Early morning flights were a special treat, so often I was one of the first pilots on the lake and in the air. My destination one special day was a flight to a mining camp on Provinger Lake, a few miles south of the Turnagain River. After my preflight check I pointed my craft down the lake, full power, and we were airborne within seconds in the thick, cool air. The light before sunrise had a special quality. The valleys were still dark, without form, with only a faint light to the east over the Rocky Mountains. As I slipped smoothly through the clear air, a special early morning feeling of being the only one in this visible sky, of peace, of oneness with God and his creation, came over me. The steady drone of the engine, with wings attached to my back, made my world secure. Soaring like an eagle, looking down upon this untouched wilderness, gave me a feeling unlike anything else in life. Peaceful, alive, my world was here; it was perfect at this moment.

The advancing dawn brightened the sky, and the valley became alive. Trees, flowing rivers, and meadows revealed themselves; the world below took form. Flying near the Turnagain River at eight thousand feet I began playing a game with the pure white cumulus tops, soaring in and around the valleys and peaks of these early morning giants of the sky. The air was still smooth as we danced with the clouds—alone, at peace with this early morning once-in-a-lifetime place, time and form.

My favorite poem was written by John Magee, an American pilot in the RCAF during World War II shortly before he lost his life in an air battle. It describes something close to what I felt as I soared in around these white mountains of clouds.

HIGH FLIGHT

Oh, I have slipped the surly bonds of earth
And danced the skies on laughter-silvered wings;
Sunward I've climbed, and joined the tumbling mirth
Of sun-split clouds--and done a hundred things
You have not dreamed of--wheeled and soared and swung
High in the sunlit silence. Hovering there
I've chased the shouting wind along, and flung
My eager craft through footless halls of air.
Up, up the long, delirious, burning blue
I've topped the windswept heights with easy grace
Where never lark, or even eagle flew--
And, while with silent, lifting mind I've trod

The high untrespassed sanctity of space,
Put out my hand, and touched the face of God.

This early morning flight and once-in-a-lifetime experience was seared in my mind. In later years I often relived this most special time when I soared my craft in and around the high mountains of white clouds.

Several days later Jim Close told me that I would be flying the body of a man recently killed on the Alaska Highway. Loading a dead man in a body bag onto the Beaver was a strange experience. The front seat next to me was removed, and the body was beside me on the floor. The friend who was not injured in the accident sat in the back of the Red Beaver. It was strange to glance from time to time at the bag on the floor beside me—a bag that carried the remains of a man who until a short time before was alive and driving down the highway. At Whitehorse we were met by a hearse, and two men who helped unload the body. My trip back to Watson Lake gave me a chance to reflect and to appreciate life.

The vastness and beauty of this country continued to excite me as I flew into new areas and experienced firsthand the thrill of landing on a new river or lake. Each trip was different; adventures were many. I recorded many scenes with my camera, in my journal and in my mind.

On the last day of July I prepared IBP for a trip into Glacier Lake, just south of the Nahanni River, at the bottom of some impressive peaks surrounded by glaciers. The tallest peak was called Mt. Sir James MacBrien, at 9,062 feet. My passengers, a group of mountain climbers, were eager to get going. We headed north from Watson Lake on a trip of 145 miles. The steady drone of the engine almost put me to sleep, but after an hour and ten minutes we caught sight of the green spot which was Glacier Lake. I made a lazy circle over the lake.

There was no wind; we had what was called a glassy water condition. Proper depth perception over glassy water is impossible. Many seaplane pilots have ended their careers under such conditions. I began a long approach, with flaps, over the trees at the east end heading west, flying low. I set up the Beaver in a landing attitude with power at about one hundred to two hundred feet per minute descent and continued this until we touched down. Often a pilot under these conditions thinks he is close to the water, rounds out and stalls fifty feet or so above the water with disastrous results. Another technique is to land near some weeds or close to shore, using the shoreline as a reference for depth, but you must always use extreme care.

After unloading the mountain climbers on the northwest shore, we took off toward the south and followed the west side of the mountains closely, getting a nice updraft. As I looked at the glaciers and mountain peaks that I soon surmounted, I wondered what would make these people climb for days to get to the top. The climbers, Glacier Lake, and the ice fields were soon behind as I continued south to Watson Lake.

The rest of the season went rapidly. We flew into Frank Cook's camps, Moodie,

Colt, Scoop and Denetiah Lakes on a fairly regular basis, as well as flights for other outfitters, fishermen, prospectors, and forestry officials.

September 26 I tied up the Red Beaver after my last flight of the season to Whitefish Lake. I said my farewells and ended another season.

I flew down to Vancouver, B.C., and purchased a new 1972 blue four-door Volvo that would log many trips over the Alaska Highway in the coming years. It proved to be a rugged and reliable car and a favorite of mine. I drove to Seattle and rented a home on Lake Sammamish for the winter while I attended school.

I left Seattle on December 23 to visit my son, who was living in Prince George, B.C. We spent the holidays together and watched Ebenezer Scrooge on television in our motel on Christmas Eve, something we talk about from time to time. Scott is the most important person in my life and the best thing that ever happened to me--he's my best friend!

December 26 I headed back to Seattle. As I drove, my thoughts were about my son Scott and how much I was missing watching and just being with him as he grew up. It was difficult to say goodbye, and I missed him terribly.

I continued the running program I had started in the late 1960's while working at Omineca Air Service in B.C. On the last day of 1972, I ran two miles. My journal entry that day read, "Simplicity=key to happiness."

Little Dal Lake N.W. Territories, in the heart of the Mackenzie Mountains where Scott and I picked up the outfitter Chuck Hayward and flew him to the trapped guide and horses on an Island in the South Nahanni River, in the Red Beaver.

Note the boat pulling the horse across the main channel of the South Nahanni river, from the island where I'm taking the picture. We flew the boat in on the outside of the Beaver floats. Just after this picture was taken the boat capsized and was lost. Chuck and a guide were swept downriver.

CHAPTER XII
ALMOST LAKE

On April 8, 1973, after a preflight walk around the airplane, I strapped myself into the 150-horsepower Decathalon and began an aerobatic course with a World War II Air Force fighter pilot as the instructor. John owned the plane, and I figured he wouldn't do anything that was unsafe. However, we both had parachutes just in case. The Decathalon had an inverted system that enabled you to fly upside down without the engine quitting. It was sturdily built for both negative and positive G's.

We headed over Lake Sammamish where I practiced stalls, loops, rolls, spirals and hammerhead stalls for .8 hours, which was about all I wanted for the first lesson. Three more lessons of .8 hours and a final one of 1.2 hours completed the course of barrel rolls, slow rolls, Immelmans, inverted flight, snap rolls, cuban eights, and the ultimate—at least for me—an outside loop.

Rolling over inverted, trying to reach 165 mph before beginning the climb to the top of the loop (And then the fun began!), stick forward, and we were going straight down. Continuous forward pressure on the stick was imperative in order to finish the bottom side of the loop before the speed built up too greatly, causing structural failure. As we continued to go under on the bottom side of the loop to the level inverted position, I rolled the airplane right side up and finished our loop. I'm sure I wouldn't have won a contest, but I did successfully complete an outside loop-- probably the only one I'll ever do. It is really uncomfortable pulling negative G's; you feel like you are going to leave your seat and fly out into space while puking your guts out.

It was interesting to fly upside down and to recover from unusual attitudes. It was a lot of fun to loop and roll through the sky and to open a new dimension of flying! Inverted, all the controls are reversed, and everything is done opposite. To raise the nose, increasing the angle of attack, you use forward pressure.

John told me an interesting story about the German pilots of World War II. He said they all flew gliders first, before flying a power plane. Flying a glider, using the basic stick and rudder, is what he thinks made them exceptional pilots. Many German pilots shot down hundreds of planes. John said whenever a student of his had problems flying a power plane, all he had to do was get him in a glider for some dual, and the problems would be resolved.

May 3 I packed my bags, loaded the car and headed north once again. The next day I stopped at Prince George to pick up Scott, and we went on to Chetwyn, B.C., where we stopped for the night. We spent the next night at Liard Hot Springs, where we soaked in the steaming mineral-laden pools, and arrived May 6 at Watson Lake. It was so nice to have Scott along, even though the next day I had to put him on a plane back to Prince George so he could finish out the school year. I knew he would return in June to spend the summer with me.

The long days of sunshine were back, and it was a beautiful, warm day in May of 1973. We were working daily now on floats, sanding, repairing and painting them in preparation for another busy season. The aspen trees surrounding the lake were clothed in their spring greenery, and the ground was covered with a rich carpet of new growth. Spring came almost overnight, a spectacular transformation.

The frostless growing season in the Yukon is short, but it balances out with almost continuous sunlight during June, July and August. Agriculture is hurt more from lack of moisture than from the frost. Dense forests cover an area in the southeast portion of the Yukon, thinning gradually toward the west and north. The treeline is north of the Arctic Circle in the Yukon; white spruce is the most common tree, together with lodge pole pine, aspen, larch, alpine fir and black spruce. Farther north it's mostly black spruce, shrubs and lichens. Only a small portion of the forests were logged and taken to a part-time sawmill at Watson Lake. Wonderful gardens are grown as far north as Dawson City. The porcupine caribou herd numbers over one hundred thousand, and it migrates between northeastern Alaska and part of the Northwest Territories. The herd's main calving grounds are in the northern Yukon, on the flatlands near the coast.

Flying west some sixty miles near Almost Lake, I occasionally saw small herds of mountain caribou. Polar bears are found along the Beaufort Sea. Black and grizzly bear, timber wolves—including the tundra sub-species found north of the Porcupine River—and the large Alaska wolf are found all over the Yukon, being especially common in the west. Mule deer are found in the southern portion, and moose are plentiful in the interior. Farther north are small groups of woodland caribou. White Dall sheep are found in the north and southwest, and the dark brown stone sheep are located south of the Pelly River. Fannin sheep are also found here; they're white with dark saddles. All three species intermingle.

Birds of prey, such as peregrine falcons, bald and golden eagles, hawks and owls nest here, as do ducks, geese and trumpeter swans. Ptarmigan are one of the few birds that stay north all year long.

Pacific salmon spawn in rivers such as the Yukon tributaries. Trout, whitefish, pike and Arctic grayling abound. Off the coast beluga (white whales), bowhead whales, Pacific whales and bearded seals can be found. The Yukon is a fascinating place, and as the flying season began I was glad to be here once again.

May 16 I loaded our Super Cub with groceries and then fueled it. Hopping into the front seat of the Super Cub, I was soon strapped down.The dependable 150-horsepower Lycoming engine started quickly and sounded smooth. As I taxied to the Watson Lake runway I was really excited; this was my first trip of the season and after all the sanding and painting of the floats, I just wanted to fly and get away to some new adventure.

The flight was into the Shesly Strip, located southeast of the Asbestos town of Cassiar. Being airborne once again for the two-hour trip was refreshing, even if it was in a somewhat cramped airplane. After a circle over the outfitter's camp, I made my final approach at 65 mph for a normal three-point landing. The outfitter Fletcher Day, a handsome, tall Tahltan Indian, wanted me to fly him to Cassiar, which I did. Then I returned to Watson Lake, logging a total of 3.7 hours for the day.

In March, Watson Lake Flying Service purchased the Beaver CF-FLN, which I flew most of the summer. Every Beaver had its own personality, and this one was not a favorite of mine. It didn't perform as well as my favorite Red Beaver IBP, but maybe I was spoiled.

May 18 started a new adventure for me and IBP, as I would be flying it on wheel skis for the first time into Summit Lake, about 160 miles north. The lake was just inside the Yukon border, a few miles west of the Northwest Territories border. Cannex Mining and Exploration Company had chartered us to fly in supplies for a camp they were operating there. The lake was frozen, so they needed a ski-equipped airplane to bring in the supplies.

The wheel ski configuration on a Beaver is operated by means of a hydraulic control unit located on the cockpit floor, to the right of the pilot's seat. To lower the skis, you put the selection lever to the down position, which releases the hydraulic pressure and allows the pneumatic pressure in the upper portion of the activator housing to return the skis to the down position. To raise the skis, you select up position and operate the hand pump until the skis are fully up, as shown by the needle on the indicator and, of course, visually check outside. Approximately one hundred strokes of the hand pump are required to raise the skis fully. Your right arm gets a good workout, like doing curls with a barbell as the bicep gets pumped up. Because the skis trim safely in flight in any position, the pumping may be completed at the pilot's convenience. After getting airborne, the ski position has very little effect on air speed, flight characteristics, or center of gravity and can be left in up or down position, as needed, upon arrival at the landing field.

After loading the Beaver with groceries and camp gear, I cranked her up. Soon the reassuring roar of the Radial Engine drowned out all other sounds. Applying full power and forward pressure on the elevator control, the tail wheel ski lifted and the Beaver flew off the runway at 60 mph in a slight tail down attitude. After reducing the throttle to 30 inches and the prop to 2000 rpm, climb flap was selected, and 95 mph (best rate of climb speed) was used until we reached our cruising altitude of 7500 feet. I followed the Frances River on a northerly heading to the east arm of Frances Lake and then over Tillis Lake and McPherson Lake. Another thirty miles and I see the camp up on the south shore of Summit Lake.

Circling the camp area, I picked out where I would land. I began a descending turn to the left, flaps to land position, skis down and made the final approach at 80 mph. Depth perception was good, and I could see the snow and some tracks clearly in the bright sunshine. On a gray day, unbroken snow is like glassy water, and depth perception can be poor. Today's landing was smooth in the soft snow.

After unloading the supplies, I was soon airborne for Watson Lake. I logged 2.9 hours for the trip. I had several trips scheduled the next day to Summit Lake—trips that were good money makers. I was paid mileage in addition to a very generous base salary from Watson Lake Flying Service.

Max Sanderson, a good friend of Jim and Stan's, flew a helicopter for Cannex and would be flying out of this camp for the season. Max was in his fifties, a real interesting character who kept us all in stitches with his stories and one-liners. A gruff, no-nonsense kind of guy with a heart of gold, Max used to fly a Beaver for Cannex but had switched over to helicopters recently. He took me on my first helicopter ride here at Summit Lake. When we stopped forward speed in the air, I almost expected a stall, but it was a unique experience. Max had a smooth touch that made me feel comfortable. Max shared my low opinion of a de Havilland Otter DHC3, which carried double the payload of a Beaver. His description of a good Otter pilot was someone four feet tall, four feet wide with a small hat size. In an otter you spend much of your time bent over, loading heavy, cumbersome freight within the confines of the five-foot ceiling.

After a supply run to Summit Lake, I headed back to the base. Something I've always wanted to do, but didn't want to try in case I screwed up, was to loop and roll a Beaver. I was flying near Frances Lake at about seven thousand feet. I had recently finished an aerobatic course and decided to give IBP a bit of a workout. Diving to pick up speed, the Beaver seemed eager, and we did a couple good loops. Another slight dive to pick up speed, and I rolled IBP and held it inverted for a few seconds before completing the last half of the roll. A pleasant surprise—they had been hauling hay all winter! Now I had hay and dirt coming out of the cracks and crannies from the floor, settling on the panel, seats, window sills and other places it shoudn't be. I certainly didn't want Jim and Stan to figure out what I'd been doing, so I spent some time brushing the hay and dirt back onto the floor. The Beaver performed like a champ and went through the loops and rolls like a pro. A few days later I told Jim Close what I did, and he just laughed. He had looped a Beaver on several occasions, he said.

The Beaver flies like a big Super Cub and is an excellent STOL airplane; however, you can't expect to crank it around like a Cub. Many Beavers have been stalled in a steep turn at a slow airspeed, often shortly after take-off. It's a large airplane, requires a larger radius to turn, stalls at a higher airspeed than a Cub and has to be flown accordingly. So often too much is asked of any bush plane. There are limits, as wreckages strewn across the northern wilderness bear witness!

At the end of a rather long day, having made three trips into Summit, I logged 8.1

hours. Usually you can figure 8 flight hours requires about 16 hours of loading, unloading, servicing the airplane and waiting for people.

May 25 I logged 4.9 hours in the C-185 on floats; I flew into the Turnagain River and also made some side trips. My next trip was June 3, flying the Cessna 185 CF-YIG into Burnt Rose Lake and Jay Lake, logging a total of seven hours. The 185 was faster than the Beaver, indicating about 130-135 mph, but it doesn't perform as well or haul nearly the pay load. It's quieter than the Beaver and was fun to fly occasionally.

Jim and Lois Close graciously let me stay at their home in downtown Watson Lake for the summer. They had moved out to their lake cabin, which was close to the Seaplane Base. Scott joined me at the end of the school year in June. It was really great to have my son with me once again. I took Scott with me flying as often as I could. He thoroughly enjoyed co-piloting with Dad. He was a big help, pumping the floats, cleaning out the Beaver and helping to load. He was thirteen years old, strong, well built and easy to get along with.

On June 11, I prepared our other Beaver CF-FLN for a trip into Almost Lake. Almost Lake was just that, more like a large pond. With care and a good airplane like the Beaver, we could operate out of it safely for the summer months. Hudson Bay Mining Company had decided to operate out of Almost Lake for the summer. The lake is about 90 miles west of Watson Lake in the Yukon Territory. The company would be prospecting this general area for the summer season.

I flew the tents, camp gear and food in first, along with several men, to get things going as rapidly as possible in this land of short seasons. By the end of the day I had made several trips, and camp was set up. I saw a small herd of caribou south of Almost Lake on a grass knoll, several moose at one end of Meister Lake, and a few more on some other lakes, wading in knee deep water. The rest of the season I would be flying in men, food, mail, horsefeed, etc., and flying out core samples. They had decided to use horses instead of a helicopter to keep costs down. Later they would see which was the most cost effective mode of transportation for getting their crews out and getting the job done.

Mining companies were a substantial part of our business some seasons. They took up the slack until the hunting seasons started, when we begin taking hunters into the various outfitters' camps, shuttling that lasted until October or so.

June 24 I prepared our Beech 18 CF-NCL (a low wing medium twin engine airplane on floats) on a local check-out flight for myself. After fueling up, Jim Thibaudeau, our chief pilot and the one who flew the Beech most of the time, climbed in with me. I sat in the left hand pilot's seat with Jim in the co-pilot's seat.

The Beech had two Pratt & Whitney R-985 engines (the same engine that the Beaver uses). It was fun to fly a twin, especially with NCL on floats.

After pushing away from the dock I started first one engine, then the other, and taxied to the south end of the lake. Runup took a little longer, as I now had two engines to check. Everything was normal, and I applied full power. The Beech responded quickly because of the light load; with the 900 horses roaring, we left the water quickly. One hour of air work and landing, and we were back at the dock.

Most seaplanes won't get on the step if they're heavily loaded and conditions are bad. The Beech 18 gets on the step quickly and will get in the air under adverse conditions and heavy loads, but because of the high speedwing sometimes doesn't want to climb. Occasionally on hot days the engines start to overheat, and the pilot has to return to the lake to either unload some of the gear or wait for cooler weather.

On June 26 I flew NCL into Quartz Lake several times on a freight haul for a mining camp, with Jim sitting in the right-hand seat. Although the Beech was an interesting machine to fly, I decided the Beaver was my favorite, and I preferred it over all others.

Near the end of June I loaded the Beaver FLN with supplies for Hudson Bay Mining Company to be taken into Almost and Erwin lakes, which are in the same area. Scott helped with the loading. He was going to stay in the camp at Almost Lake for a few days to do some fishing. Scott, like most boys at thirteen, loved to put away the grub. The camp had excellent chow; steaks and roast were normal daily fare, with potatoes, gravy and freshly made pie.

Scott climbed aboard the Beaver and sat in the co-pilot seat while I pushed off the dock and climbed into the pilot's seat. Climbing over the lake with a gentle turn to the left I flew a westerly heading to put us on course to Almost Lake. I let Scott have the controls, as I often did; he was a good co-pilot and enjoyed flying.

The country was fairly flat for about forty miles before we began flying through the Cassiar Mountains with several peaks at nearly seven thousand feet. We were following the Little Moose River and were lower than the peaks. After flying over a pass at the headwater of the Moose River, we picked up Irvin Creek and could see Irvin Lake sparkling in the distance. We caught a glimpse of some moose near the lake in a meadow. We landed, unloaded supplies and departed for Almost Lake a few miles away.

Almost Lake came into view as we flew over a mountain range. I checked the wind on the lake surface and saw it was from the southwest. We made a descending turn over the north side of the lake and approached into the wind, touching down close to the northeastern shore. The lake was small, and I did not want to overshoot. Once the floats touched, I brought power back to idle; we slowed down rapidly, settling into the water like a heavy duck.

Men came from camp as we taxied toward shore. We tied the Beaver and made a human chain to unload the supplies. Mostly the men were interested in the mail, something eagerly sought in isolated camps.

The cook's tent had a plywood floor and wood stove. We enjoyed coffee and some home-cooked rolls. Scott met Dan, the cook, and the other men who would be his mates at this camp for the next several days. His likeable nature soon made him fit into his temporary home.

After coffee and a good conversation I slowly walked down to the White Beaver CF-FLN. I breathed the fresh air, viewed this remote valley and the mountains above and was thankful for my flying job and the opportunity to see this vast country and to play my many roles as a pilot.

The other ways I've made a living pale in comparison to this unique job. This is partly because flying is a respectable, necessary and rewarding career, but mostly for me it is because flying had been such a love of mine since my youth.

The fascination of actually piloting an airplane, the take-off, flying through the mountains and landing in these wilderness lakes was a breath-taking experience. Big troubles in life shrink into proper perspective. The changing conditions of weather and country, the challenge of increasing my knowledge and skill of piloting, and the satisfaction of a job well done all contributed to a fullfilling means of making a living and of satisfying my inner man. I especially enjoyed sharing the north country with my clients. Not all flights were smooth; sometimes passengers and pilot got grey hairs. Winds, short and treacherous strips, lakes, river landings, bad weather and pilot fatigue can contribute to an uncomfortable ride. But by the next day, the discomfort is only a memory, and I'm ready to crank up the Beaver for another adventure. One thing I've noticed: if a smooth landing can be pulled off, people usually consider it a good flight, maybe because it was the last thing they remember. So I always try to make a good approach and gentle touchdown, although I don't always succeed.

The trip back to Watson Lake from Almost Lake was a pleasant flight. I logged 3.9 hours for the day and made a trip to the Signpost Bar for a few drinks. Some of the pilots from Watson Lake Flying Service showed up and were soon feeling no pain. I left somewhat later than I planned. Because it was light at midnight, it was difficult to go to bed. During the summer months sleep was a short commodity.

It was June 29 when Jim Close informed me, "Larry, you have a flight to Godlin Lakes in the Northwest Territory. Then you will fly up to Norman Wells to pick up more supplies and return to Godlin." An outfitter had chartered the Beaver. It would be a money maker for me, with interesting company and an interesting trip into a new area. It was 255 miles one way into Godlin Lakes and another 125 miles from there to Norman Wells, close to 800 miles total.

Godlin Lakes consists of three lakes near the headwaters of the Godlin River in a valley that runs north and south. The lakes are due north of Watson, and I calculated the flying time at just around two hours. Once again I'd be flying into the rugged Mackenzie Mountains. The course would parallel the Hyland River, cross the South Nahanni River, over O'Grady Lake, June Lake and over the Elwi River. Just a few miles north of there lay my destination—Godlin Lakes.

After fueling up and doing my walk around, I put some extra fuel in. I would be able to fuel up at Norman Wells; there was an oil refinery there. Norman Wells gas was considerably cheaper than at Watson Lake, but I might need extra fuel. It was always wise to leave some extra ten-gallon cans at this camp as a reserve for later trips. The Beaver carried about three hours of fuel and the reserve, so we often had to carry extra gas on the longer trips.

The flight up was smooth as I climbed to eight thousand feet and had a wonderful view of the country. I landed in the middle lake, unloaded the supplies and then headed for Norman Wells. There groceries and camp gear were quickly loaded, and I was soon heading back to Godlin Lakes. After unloading again at the middle lake, I had a quick coffee break and headed back to home base.

July 2 I flew into Tootsi Lake, about sixty miles southwest of Watson Lake. The trip was uneventful except for the gusty condition on the lake surface. One nice thing about flying into a lake is that by reading the marks it makes on the water surface, you can tell if the wind is gusty, if it's coming from several different directions, or if it changes direction part way down. Surface gusts caused a hairy landing approach and an up-and-down ride. But we finally landed, taxied to shore, and unloaded gear and supplies for prospectors.

A couple of days later I flew into Daughney and Erwin Lake for Hudson Bay Mining Company, then picked up Scott at Almost Lake. Scott had caught some nice trout, eaten a lot better food than he got at home, and had made some new friends.

On July 21, I flew my favorite Beaver IBP into Swan Lake, ninety miles from Watson Lake. I was flying for Mr. MacCaully, who had a guiding territory in this area. He was someone for whom I would do a lot of flying later in the season. Swan Lake adjoins the Alaska Highway on its northern shore; MacCaully guided moose hunts close by, as well as trips for other game, such as caribou, sheep and bear at other lakes near here, lakes accessible only by float plane or horseback. After a few more flights for other outfitters and for Cannex, July was history.

August started out fairly busy; we flew mail and supplies into various outfitters' camps, since the hunting season was underway. The most sought-after trophy was the stone sheep. Frank Cooke seemed to have one of the best areas, both in number of sheep taken and also for size, although I had noticed in all the areas the size of the horns seemed to decrease over the past several years, partly due to the heavy hunting pressure, I thought.

After work one night and before bed Scott said "Dad, what do you think about buying a taildragger?"

"Well son, maybe a Super Cub someday or a Citabria would be a fun airplane," I replied.

Scott was an avid airplane buff, and our conversation usually got around to flying.

The alarm went off at five a.m.; I had a six a.m. flight in the Beaver. After a nourishing "stick to your ribs" breakfast of oatmeal, we jumped into the Volvo and drove to the seaplane base.

FLIGHT OF THE RED BEAVER

After gassing the plane and checking the oil, I did a visual inspection of the airplane, checking to see if the elevators and ailerons were working properly, looking at the float fittings, nuts, bolts, cables, and checking the prop for nicks. When taxiing down wind, the water often causes nicks, which we file down from time to time. Sometimes I took the round blade of a screwdriver and ran it over the nicks to smooth the prop down a bit. Care in taxiing was essential to keep the nicks to a minimum. We flew to Frank Cooke's camp at Scoop Lake.

We overnighted at Scoop Lake and after sundown went skinny-dipping in the lake. We were sweaty, and it was very smokey because of many forest fires. After the sunset I said, "Scott, look at the setting and remember it in later years. See the old log cabin and the pole-covered fence and the lake in the background." We still talk about that from time to time, sharing our memories of that special place and time.

After a short sleep in a tent on the sandy beach of Scoop Lake, we left at about 5:00 a.m. and flew to Colt Lake, a tiny lake high in the mountains twenty miles southwest of here. We had groceries and camp supplies to freight in and were kept busy flying, loading and unloading for several hours before returning to Watson Lake.

One day near Bluesheep Lake, I flew low over a peak and started down the other side, which was fairly open. A large grizzly stood on his hind legs, angry at my invasion of his space, and swatted at the Beaver as though it were a pesky fly.

I logged the most hours I've ever flown in a single day on August 10. After trips up to the South Nahanni in the Northwest Territories and trips down to Moodie Lake and other lakes for Frank Cook, I had put in 12.8 hours of flying time. I was flying lots of long days—total hours for the month of August, 1973, were 193 hours, probably the most I've ever flown in a single month. About half of that was double mileage, as anything over ten thousand miles in a single month pays double. It was an exhausting month.

To pick up some geologists I made a trip into a small river east of Watson Lake that runs into the Liard River. Landing on the Liard, I taxied up the small river, heading north. It was clear and looked about five feet deep. About one-half mile upstream I saw the men on the east bank of the river.

The water was very swift and clear as I nudged up to the bank, holding the front right float to the bank and had to leave the engine running, with lots of power. The men jumped aboard; a couple crawled in the back door and sat down. One man who had a bad foot climbed up in the copilot's seat and caught the door with his bad foot. The door flipped off the hinge and sank to the bottom of the raging river.

I taxied out from shore and turned downstream toward the Liard. Once I reached the Liard, I headed upstream, trying to locate the door. Sure enough, we could see it coming downstream, bouncing on the bottom. A couple of the men tried to catch it and almost fell in. I yelled, "Forget it!" It was gone. "Let's get out of here before someone falls in." My nervous passenger sitting next to the doorless opening in the side of the Beaver leaned toward me all the way back to Watson Lake as the wind whistled around him.

Back at Watson Lake, Wally fixed a makeshift solid plywood door cover. I flew the plane that way until a replacement arrived.

On September 21 I flew into a lake for Murd MacCaully, the outfitter. My destination was Goodwin Lake about 130 miles southwest of Watson Lake in northern B.C. and just a few miles west of the south end of Teslin Lake.

I had some hunters going in and some coming out. After about an hour of flight we flew over the camp, which was on the east shore; the lake runs north and south. Sure enough I could see the wind from four different directions and a wind shear about where the camp was. The wind went north and south from that point. I saw severe gusts all over the lake, which looked like someone had thrown splotches of ink on the surface.

"Hang on!" I told my passengers as I made another hairy approach. I made my approach faster than normal to compensate for the gusts, wind shear and cross-winds. I wanted a little extra air speed for a cushion. Until the Beaver was on the water and off the step, anything could happen and often did. That knowledge kept me alert, my knuckles white and my body a bit tense. This was one of those lakes I would rather not fly to, money or no money, but it was part of my job and had to be done.

As I neared the surface, the Beaver began a fight with an unseen foe. First up, then down, the wind blew us sideways to the left, then the right, and hammered us relentlessly in all directions.

Finally there seemed to be a bit of a let-up, and I touched down. "Ah, we're home free!" I thought. But a gust picked us up again. We had to make a couple more touch- downs before I could pull the power and settle into the water. It was nice to be safely on the water, although we were still being buffeted with gusts.

Taxiing to the camp, I shut FLN down and glided into a makeshift pole dock. I needed a cup of coffee to settle my nerves and a few minutes on firm ground before I was ready to think of leaving.

After loading up the returning hunters with their sheep trophies and gear, we taxied out to the south end. We had a tail wind as I began the take-off run. The Beaver got on the step okay, but as we reached flying speed, the wind started to do crazy things. It hit us from many different directions. I wanted an excess of speed on the step before I flew off, because I was sure we would hit one or more wind shears, and I didn't want to be dumped hard back into the lake. Finally I pulled it off with excess airspeed, holding the plane close to the water until a safe airspeed was reached. Then I began a gentle climb. We were buffeted from many directions, and I was busy trying to keep the Beaver in the air to gain some altitude. Soon the north end of the lake slipped below, and I turned to the east, down a valley toward

Teslin Lake and some smooth air, I hoped. As I crossed Teslin Lake, the air was smoother, and I could relax, watching the country slip by. I still dislike that lake with a passion.

Scott caught a flight on CPA to Prince George and returned to school once again. He had a few stories to tell his mom and his schoolmates. It was always a sad time, as we said our goodbyes. However, I would see my son next month when the flying season was over.

Occasionally, Terry Cooke would fly to town in their float-equipped Cessna 185 and sometimes bring along his brothers. We would do some serious partying. Mostly I partied with Terry, and we had some memorable times.

One night Terry and I were having a party at the Signpost Bar. We were just getting into the program when Terry told me he was going out front with a young helicopter pilot for a fight. I followed Terry and the pilot out by some cars. Just before they got into their fight, a big man happened to walk by and asked, "What's going on?" The helicopter pilot claimed that Terry was going to beat him up. The stranger said, "Oh, I don't know about that!" Terry made one quick blow to the stranger's chin. The stranger slid down the side of a car door and hit the gound, knocked out cold. In the meantime, the helicopter pilot went back inside, untouched. The stranger learned a lesson he would not soon forget.

On another occasion we received a report that one of the Indian guides at Denetiah Lake had gone berserk after getting into some cooking alcohol. He had threatened some hunters with a knife. I flew Terry into the camp. He walked up to the crazed Indian, knocked him out with a quick blow and restored order to camp.

One native with a hangover and a grumpy demeanor was sitting on a box of groceries as we flew into a hunting camp in northern B.C. He was squirming around, and all of a sudden smoke filled the airplane. I've never seen an Indian sober up so fast. He began digging in the box to put out the fire while I dove the airplane toward a lake, as fire is the most dreaded event for a pilot. It turned out to be wooden matches that caught fire because of his squirming. The rest of the flight went well.

Another night Terry and I were whooping it up at the Signpost Bar again. We did a bit of a war dance near the stage. I drank seven poose capays, seven Singapore Slings and two creme de menthes; Terry drank as much. Shortly after our performance, I think Terry slipped, as I noticed he was lying on the floor near the bar. The bouncer, a mean-looking cuss who was Mac Sanderson's definition of a good Otter pilot, jumped on Terry before he could get to his feet and started flailing away. I shoved the bouncer back, and Terry was able to get up. Although the bouncer could have probably made short work of both of us since we had trouble standing and focusing our eyes, he backed off and indicated that he didn't want to fight. John Brink, the owner and a nice guy, stepped in and asked us if we would please leave. We reluctantly did, wanting to continue the party.

ALMOST LAKE

Terry was about six foot, lean and wiry, but very quick with his fists. All the Cooke boys were good with their fists and enjoyed a good scrap. They were hard-working and excellent guides, and when they came to town, they loved to have a good time.

Two men from New Jersey were in one of Frank's camps, and I picked them up in the Beaver and flew them back to Watson Lake. I'm not sure why, but maybe it's because they were from a highly populated area with lots of pressure, that they started griping the minute I landed to pick them up. They didn't like something about the hunt, they didn't like the flying service, and they were teed off at me because I was a little late due to weather problems. I guess I took it personally. After they paid their bill, they went to a bar. Later in the day, I happened to go into the same bar. The one who did most of the complaining was there, and we got into a bit of a scuffle.

During the time I was in Watson Lake, I was involved in only a few scraps. There were some mean, tough guys around who loved to fight. They couldn't care less if they got hurt, and once they got a man down, they put the boots to him, kicking the stuffing out of any poor devil lying on the floor.

Most of the hunters were real gentlemen. The few who were complainers seemed to come from big city areas. The hunters from Texas were good old boys—they brought their booze, told tall tales and just had a great time. In fact, most hunters from down South seemed to enjoy themselves and were nice to be around.

The Cooke boys followed the rodeo circuit when they weren't guiding. Terry flew them to the various towns in their Cessna 185. Terry was a good bronc rider, and Frankie, the oldest son, a well-built young man with strong legs, was a very good bull rider.

One day Frankie was involved in a fight with a third-degree black belt karate instructor. Shortly he knocked the instructor out. While at the Signpost Bar one evening, I saw young Mac nail a man at the bar with the same quickness and accuracy that his brother Terry displayed on several occasions.

Jack O'Conner, who was the outdoor editor for *Outdoor Life,* was a renowned hunter who hunted over most of the world, including Africa for lions and other game. He was an expert on rifles and ballistics. He came to Watson Lake to hunt, and on two occasions I flew him out to different camps. I flew him into Colt Lake in the early 1970's and he shot a nice stone sheep, which was his last ram.

Jack, who was in his seventies then and reminded me a great deal of my grandfather, lived in Lewiston, Idaho. It was very interesting for me to sit and listen to his stories about his hunts and to discuss rifles while we were in Frank's camp.

He was a bit of a white knuckle flier, and the weather wasn't very good when I flew him to Colt Lake. There was rain, fog and low clouds, but it was flyable, although we had to do some dodging through low clouds in order to arrive at Colt Lake. Jack was glad to get his feet back on solid ground.

Later I corresponded with Jack. He died a few year ago. I read Jack's stories from the time I was a boy and felt privileged to have met him and to fly this man who was a legend in the hunting fraternity. The guide on that last sheep hunt said Jack was still an excellent shot. A picture of Jack O'Conner, me and another hunter on the trip to Colt Lake hangs on my office wall.

At an earlier date in the late sixties, Jack O'Conner and his wife came to Smithers, B.C., and one of my fellow pilots at Omineca Air Service flew them out to a camp where they went on a trail ride into a wilderness area of northern British Columbia with an outfitter for a week or so.

Jack shot a stone sheep on each of the two hunts I flew him on. Colt Lake is a puddle at about four thousand feet in elevation, dammed up on the west end by a beaver dam. There is a cache on stilts at the northeast end of the lake, and we had to be careful when landing or taking off in that direction so we didn't hit it. The tent camp was located near the cache. Colt Lake was ideal, since at four thousand feet, the hunters didn't have to climb much higher to be in the middle of excellent stone sheep country...probably the best area of North America for this species.

At this time, there wasn't any limit on the number of sheep that could be taken out of a guide's area. Now, each guiding area has only a limited number of permits issued for each season by the Game Department.

One late evening in September, just before dark, I managed to fly into Colt Lake to spend the night. I knew there were some young ladies in camp who were excellent cooks. Besides a good meal and fresh pie, I knew I could spend a few hours talking to these attractive young ladies. Frank's camps were known for their good food, and I always tried to fly in, if possible, around dinner time, so it was no accident that I lighted here on this particular evening. I had been flying for Gary Moore, near Skook's old ranch south of here.

After a good feed, the boys, Frank Jr. and some other guides started to tell what I thought were tall tales. They spoke of flying saucers and swore they visited the camp after dark, flying nearby. I listened tongue-in-cheek, trying not to laugh, and told them, "Oh sure, what else is new?" As it got dark, the stars stood out sharply in the clean mountain air, and sure enough, up high overhead, I could see moving objects which I was sure were satellites. But in a short time, a pinpoint of light many miles east of the Kechika River and beyond the distant Rocky Mountains appeared. Within a few seconds the light became a rather large pulsating object, hovering over the Kechika River. It must have gone fifty miles in a couple of seconds. The hunters in camp were looking through a spotting scope on a stand which I also used, and we saw a pulsating light beam emitted from this stationary object, hovering maybe a mile high and seven miles away. It soon disappeared in a few seconds to the east over the Rocky Mountains, then a little later reappeared the same way, at the same terrific speed! I was stone sober and have no explanation for what we saw. It was a strange experience—unreal, but I was there and experienced this happening.

One day after landing at Moodie Lake, which at the time was Frank Cooke's main headquarters, I was instructed by Frank to fly a young lady by the name of Dee Dee and her baby to another camp of Frank's. Dee Dee was a cook and a relative of Frank's. I applied full power and, after getting on the step in the Beaver, the oil cap, which is visible and below the panel, came off and hot oil sprayed all over us. I immediately shut the engine off, and we came to a quick stop, dead in the water.

Frank couldn't figure out what was going on and came out in the boat to see what the problem was. He then helped us clean up the mess. After putting more oil in and securing the cap, I again applied full power and we were soon in the air, this time making a safe flight to Frank's camp at Colt Lake.

A unique phenomenon happens during the fall. The northern lights are at times spectacular. Sometimes it's like you're in a round room, and they are all about; other times it's like a moving curtain on a stage, with the curtain waving, changing form and color. It adds mystery to the North and is one of the special events that became part of my life.

One afternoon when I was in Scoop Lake on a charter for Frank, I took a short flight just south of the lake and counted about three hundred moose. It was like a large cattle ranch. There is a lot of marsh and feed here for the moose, and horses can be wintered here as well, living off the land as the grass is abundant and the winters are relatively mild. Frank and Skook left their horses here over the winter months.

The outfitters have been known to start fires here. After the ground is burned, the new growth makes excellent moose feed. The forest service frowns a bit on this practice, but it was carried out successfully, and, as far as I know, they never caught anyone. But I am sure they knew who the fire bugs were.

The many flights for Frank and his sons will always remain as some of my most cherished and memorable times in the North, as I flew over some of the most beautiful wilderness areas in North America with the magnificent, rugged Rocky Mountains (my favorite mountains) visible just a few miles to the east. I also had the best fishing in my life at Denetiah Lake. Denetiah Lake is in Frank's hunting area. I heard George Dalziel planted those Rainbow trout years ago, as he did in numerous other lakes in this country.

Jim Close's accountant had purchased an Aztec, which was a piper twin engine wheel plane. He was going to lease it back to Watson Lake Flying Service. Because I was the only one in the company to have flown an Aztec (the one in Seattle that I used to obtain my ATP), I was elected to pick it up in Calgary, Alberta.

I caught a connecting flight to Calgary and did a circuit at the airport with a pilot before departing for Dawson Creek. The flight from Calgary to Dawson took 2.7 hours flying time.

This plane performed exceptionally well. The normal 260-horsepower engines had been replaced with 290-horsepower fuel-injected Lycoming engines, and it made a real performer out of it. After flying at 120 in the Beaver all summer, it was nice to cruise along at about 200, and it was fun to have two engines to play with! It kept me on my toes, and it was just a lot more interesting. The seats were cushy, like a comfortable reclining arm chair.

After fueling up at Dawson Creek the next leg took me to Fort Nelson, where I landed and fueled up again before the final leg to Watson Lake.

I made my first trip on October 11 in our new Aztec CF-HIA with paying customers. I flew them into Fort Liard, in the Northwest Territories, 190 miles one way. The trip was smooth and took only about two hours flying time. After refueling, I tried to start the engines. However, when they're hot and you try to restart them, sometimes they get a vapor lock, and then I would let them set for a time. These fuel-injected engines were much more temperamental than an engine with a carburetor. After letting them cool down, I once again hit the starter and got first one engine started and then the other one. After a while I learned the necessary tricks to starting these engines and had few problems after that.

The trip back was pleasant, as the air was fairly smooth and I was beginning to feel more comfortable flying a twin again. It was a nice change; however, the Beaver was still my favorite. This was like a sportscar, a fun airplane to fly, but the Beaver was still the workhorse of the North, as far as I was concerned.

The next day Frank Cook booked the Aztec HIA to fly into Scoop Lake, where he now had a landing strip and several new cabins for hunters. One building had toilets and showers and was a big change from the old days of an outhouse and a wash basin. However, this was only at the main camp; once the hunters left here, it was horseback and walking, and using the Johnson bar or a trip behind a bush to take care of nature's call.

AT 200 mph, the trips in HIA were noticeably shorter. Over the next few days I flew into Dease Lake, Skook's ranch at Terminus Mountain, and Frank's camp at Scoop Lake.

My last flight of 1973 was in the Beaver FLN. I flew to Teslin, Burnt Rose Lake, which was just north of the Turnagain River, then back to Watson Lake, logging 4.0 hours.

Jim Close certified my log book from May 16, 1973, through October 20, 1973, for a total of 638.4 hours, the most I've flown in a season. This was also the longest season I'd flown in the Yukon. The days had been long, time off almost non-existent. Fortunately, there had been no accidents, although there were some close calls, a few grey hairs started and maybe a few hairs lost. But it had been a good season, I had new adventures, flew some new airplanes and had an enjoyable time for the most part.

Attending the Annual Fireman's Ball, I got thoroughly smashed and had a great time celebrating with most of the town.

Octoer 21, 1973--Last day for Watson Flying Service, and I wrote in the journal I had started a few years ago, "No accidents. Feel worn out!"

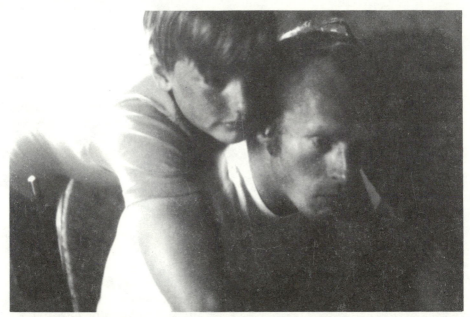

Scott and Larry at Watson Lake, summer of 1973.

Two geologists at Hudson Bay Mining exploration tent camp at Almost Lake, where Scott spent several days fishing and eating good food. Note the horses in the background that they used, in the place of helicopters, to compare costs of the modes of transportation.

CHAPTER XIII
HOWARD'S PASS—
WHITE KNUCKLE STRIP

Today was the day to head north for another flying season at Watson Lake. April 20, 1974, I climbed into my reliable 1972 blue Volvo, departing the Seattle area on course for Watson Lake via the Alaskan Highway. It took three days of driving to reach Watson Lake.

For the next several days I hibernated in my home on the shore of Watson Lake. I had bought a trailer the year before and had it on my lake lot, just across the bay from Watson Lake Flying Service seaplane base. Sometimes I canoed to work. It was nice to be alone to collect my thoughts, review the past winter and plot a course for my future.

The previous year I had met a nice school teacher in Seattle and, after a brief courtship, we married. She didn't like Watson Lake and missed her friends in Seattle, and I missed my freedom. We were divorced after a very brief marriage.

Last December my son Scott spent some time with me in Seattle, and then we drove to Spokane for the Christmas holidays with my parents and relatives, having a good, warm visit with all. In Seattle, Scott picked up some bamboo poles to use in the construction of a hang glider that he intended to build. Fortunately he decided not to proceed, much to my relief. We toured the underground city that lies beneath the present city of Seattle and had a wonderful time.

On March 23, I had departed Seattle for Hawaii to visit a high school buddy, Gary Johnson. We joined the naval reserves together while in high school. Gary made a career out of the Navy and was now a Lieutenant J.G., stationed at Pearl Harbor. I took advantage of the free champagnes on the way over, and when I got off the plane I wasn't feeling any pain. Gary met me at the airport; I stayed the first night with him and then stayed at the Coco Palms for ten dollars a night. It was about one block from the beach and had a kitchen, so I was able to fix some of my meals there. I flew to Maui the next day for a couple days there. The trip to Hawaii, which lasted a week, was a relaxing time; it was good to see my old high school buddy again. It was nice to relax in the sun and body surf. When Gary and I were in Honolulu in the mid '50's it was a quiet, sleepy town with very few buildings over a couple stories. Now it looked like a big eastern city with many tall buildings and packed with people.

But it was great to be back to the land I loved, on my own place—which was now paid for—and to enjoy the freedom of spirit that I felt in this great land called the Yukon.

Again I was spending my days working in the hangar, repairing floats and sanding and painting, so all would be ready when the float season got underway. The Master Painter touched the quaking Aspen along the lake with a light green, and seemingly overnight the meadows came alive with new growth; spring was upon us here in the Yukon. A glorious time, a new season had begun.

I had my first flight of the season in my favorite Beaver CF-IBP on May 28 and made a short local flight. It was really great to be back in the air and flying over the country I loved. May 29 I had my first flight booked to Howard's Pass in IBP on wheel skis, for Hudson Bay Mining Company. Russ MacIntosh was in charge of the camp, located in the mountains just a few miles north of Summit Lake, 160 air miles from Watson Lake, close to the Northwest Territories border. There were still several feet of snow at this camp. This was an exploration camp, and a lot of drilling had been done. Because the core samples looked good, there was a good chance the site would become a mine.

The Beaver was loaded with a lot of canned goods, some staples and various mining equipment. Climbing into IBP brought back many memories, most of adventures on floats: now flying wheel skis would create new ones.

Taxiing to the end of the paved strip at the Watson Lake airport, which was run by the Department of Transportation, I did a runup, then called air radio and let them know I was ready for departure and checked to see if any airplanes were in the area. "None reported," he said. I acknowledged and stated that I was departing for Howard's Pass, filed a flight note with him and then lined up with the center of the runway. Full power was applied, the skis were up, and I was using the wheels since the snow was gone at the airport.

The air was cool, and the Beaver responded quickly. In a slight tail down attitude I let the Beaver fly off at about 60 mph and then reduced the throttle to 30 inches (mp), the prop to 2000 rpm, and pumped up the flaps to the climb position. We were indicating 95 mph—our best rate of climb speed.

Once I reached an altitude of about seven thousand feet, I pumped the flaps up and reduced the throttle to 28 inches of manifold pressure and the prop to 1800 rpm. The airspeed indicated about 120 mph. As soon as the engine had time to cool a bit, I leaned the mixture setting until the engine lost a little power, then enriched the mixture a bit until the engine smoothed out. I set my trim and enjoyed the scenery, which was mostly dark forest, blanketed on the ground by snow.

The reliability of this engine was comforting to me, as I had never had a Beaver engine quit yet; I trusted it with my life. On many occasions, an engine failure on take-off would probably buy me the farm.

The Beaver engine was changed every one thousand hours, and a rebuilt R985 was put in. This was a mandatory regulation from the Canadian Department of

Transportation for Canadian planes. In Alaska planes are not restricted to the one thousand hours but can fly much longer. After flying on the Alaska coast in an engine that was clapped out, I really appreciated the strict Canadian regulations. In some cases, such as during bad fire seasons when the plane was needed urgently, the Department of Transportation would give a one-hundred-hour extension if the compression check was okay.

Flying north along the Frances River I wondered what the snow condition would be this late in the season. The airstrip was about 5,000 ASL feet; the snow strip was about fifteen hundred feet long, which left not a lot of room, with the high altitude. Even with the supercharged engine, the performance would be considerably less than at Watson Lake.

Frances Lake appeared below and soon slipped behind—about sixty miles to go. Summit Lake was now visible. As I flew up a valley northeast of Summit Lake, the camp came into view. As I circled the camp, I took a good look and noticed the strip ran east and west. I made the final approach toward the east at about 80 mph with landing flaps. As I got near the snow strip, I slowed down to about 70 mph and rounded out, touching down about one hundred feet from the end of the strip. The snow was soft and granulated; it slowed the Beaver rapidly. I used power to get to the other end of the strip where there was lots of help to unload. Then the help and I headed to the cook tent for coffee.

The large cook tent was at the eastern end of the camp and on the north side of the strip. Near the cook tent was a radio shack with wire antennas strung to nearby trees and posts. The rest of the camp lay toward the west. Each tent had a plywood floor and a stove inside and would accommodate four bunks comfortably. Just above camp on a mountain pass there was a rough airstrip built with a dogleg in the middle. After the sun melted the snow strip, I would fly the Beaver on wheels into this strip. Near the far west end of camp was a diesel generator that supplied electric power to the camp.

After about twenty minutes of good conversation, strong coffee and fresh baked pastries, I headed back to the Beaver with some outgoing mail and a couple of passengers. Because the snow was soft, it took a little while before we picked up much speed. About three-fourths of the way down the strip we finally lifted off; I had wondered if I would run off the strip before getting airborne. The trip went well, but I could see the strip was deteriorating rapidly, and it wouldn't be long before the ski season ended at Howard's Pass. I made almost daily flights from Watson Lake into Howard's Pass until June 14, which was the last trip I felt could be made safely. The snow strip had broken up badly; the Beaver broke through in several places, and I almost got stuck.

In my journal, I wrote the following: "This was a grey hair run as the snow strip was breaking up. Getting off this short fifteen hundred foot strip at five thousand feet elevation was a nervous proposition—especially when hauling equipment and men!" I logged 62.1 hours on wheel skis into Howard's Pass from May 29 to June 14—not bad, since June was usually a slow period.

June 18 I purchased Scott's ticket on CPA from Prince George to Watson Lake and talked to the foreman at the local sawmill, hoping to get employment for Scott there; he said there were no openings at present.

I had been continuing my running program, and on the evening of June 21 I ran three miles. Running gave me a real high, and I had been doing it for five years. It helped keep my weight below two hundred pounds most of the time. I was in good shape, as I also lifted an assortment of weights. I wrote in my journal, "This run was very invigorating; the fragrance of the flowers and greenery filled my lungs with sweetness. I felt like the wind and ran effortlessly!" At least that was what the journal said!

Scott arrived at the airport for the summer on June 24 and settled in at my lake place. After a good night's sleep, Scott and I headed for the seaplane base. I was getting a checkout on our Beech 18 CF-NCL from Jim Thibaudeau, our chief pilot.

One and a half hours of circuits and bumps (landings) and some air work with Jim constituted my checkout. The following day I flew the Beech one hour solo.

Gordon Scott, an apprentice engineer, hopped aboard with me in our Beaver IBP, and we flew into the Hudson Bay Mining Camp at Almost Lake. Gordon was an easy-going guy and did a good job for us doing checks and maintenance on the various planes.

It was now July 4, Independence Day in the U.S.A. but not up here, and Scott was doing some fishing. Scott and I headed to the Texaco service station in town where Scott landed his first job, at $3.00/hour. I was really proud and felt confident he would do okay. The station fueled most of the trucks that came along the Alaska Highway, and Scott would be pumping lots of diesel, as well as changing flat truck tires weighing about two hundred pounds. Scott was husky and strong for his fourteen years.

July 7 I fueled the Beech 18 CF-NCL and loaded gear for a trip into Dal Lake, Northwest Territories, for Lori Bliss, who had a guiding territory in that area. The flight into Dal Lake took about two hours, part of it over the rugged Mackenzie Mountains. The trip was without problems. This was my first real trip with the Beech on a freight haul, and I would be gone several days on a new adventure.

After landing at Dal Lake I flew over to Wrigley along the Mackenzie River in the Northwest Territories, about half way between Fort Simpson and Fort Norman. After landing I taxied to a dock and began loading freight in the Beech for the trip back to Dal Lake. To save money, Lori had horsefeed and camping gear barged into Wrigley earlier; I would be making shuttle flights for a few days from here to Dal Lake.

It was getting late, so I decided to call it a day and overnight at Wrigley. It was a small community on the east bank of the mighty Mackenzie River. It was quiet and peaceful there, as if the clock had stopped years ago and time had stood still. It didn't get dark at that time of year, but I finally managed to get to bed around midnight. I slept well, but morning came too quickly. After a bite to eat, I walked down to the river to ready the Beech for the day's first flight to Dal Lake.

As I tried to start the engines, I discovered the battery was dead. It took a few hours to remove and recharge the battery. After the delay, the one hundred mile flight to Dal Lake took less than an hour. Several of Lori's guides helped me unload, and I was soon off to Wrigley for another load. By the end of the day I'd logged 5.7 flying hours. Because of the battery trouble, it had been a long and frustrating day, considering the amount of time I had actually flown. Overnighting again at Wrigley, I reviewed the day's events and felt some frustration with the Beech. Once again the Beaver, which was so trouble-free, stood head and shoulders above the Beech and the single engine Otter. I was spoiled!

The new day was clear and warm, with very little breeze here on the Mackenzie River. After breakfast I wandered down to the Beech and discovered the battery was dead. I had to have it charged once again. Frustration soon set in, and I felt jinxed. I wished I could trade this plane off for my reliable Beaver IBP, which I really missed now. One flight from Wrigley to Hook Lake and back was all I had time for because of the trouble with the battery.

July 9 I logged 5.6 hours on three round trips to Hook Lake. July 10 I made one trip to Hook Lake from Wrigley and then the welcome trip back to Watson Lake.

Howard's Pass was my destination on a hot twelfth of July. I was taking the Beaver FLN on wheels into the strip. The muddy strip had about one thousand usable feet. It lay on a fifty-five-hundred-foot pass with very tricky winds and had a dogleg curve in the middle, sloping into a draw on the east side.

The usual crosswind was coming down from the mountain from the west side of the north-south strip, blowing directly across the runway into the draw. Approaching from the south, the strip looked something like an aircraft carrier. The edge on the south side dropped about straight down, and I usually experienced a down draft. Today was no different; one quarter to a half mile out an invisible hand pushed me down below the level of the runway. I had to increase power substantially to get back on the proper approach altitude. As I got close to the end of the strip, I had to cut all power, because the down draft quit and I could over-shoot.

Touchdown! Mud was flying through the prop and solidly filling my windscreen. Meanwhile I kept the left wing down with left aileron to compensate for the crosswind. I skidded around the left dogleg, trying to keep from getting sucked into the draw, something which would certainly have wrecked the airplane and probably ended by career.

The Beaver finally slid to a stop in the mud. Even sitting in the middle of a mud hole I felt relief at being safe. I unloaded and took off to the south, trying to get up enough speed in the mud to get airborne before going off the south end of the strip. That end dropped off at about a sixty-degree slope. If I was not airborne, I would have a wild ride bouncing down the mountain side. Lucky Day! I was airborne about one hundrd feet before the drop-off. What a relief it was every time I made a successful landing and take-off and flew back to Watson Lake in one piece!

This was probably the toughest, hairiest strip that I'd ever operated off, and every trip kept me on the edge. However, there was always a tremendous high after pulling out of any tight, risky situation. Living on the edge, with my life on the line, and getting away with it was hard to describe. It had its own reward and made me feel I'd done something worthwile.

One of our pilots refused to fly into strip anymore, because he once didn't get airborne by the time he passed the south end of the runway. He bounced down the mountain side before getting enough airspeed to fly. I heard the story from one of the Hudson Bay Mining Camp geologists at the airstrip. It just gave me something else to worry about, since I could easily visualize it happening, especially when the strip was muddy and it took so much longer to get up to flying speed. One day I made an "aircraft carrier" landing, right on the end of the strip with a payload of canned food. I hit solidly—too solidly. The impact bent a bulkhead just in front of the tail wheel. The skin was wrinkled, but I was able to take off safely. After I made the hard landing, one of the mining men at the strip said, "Wow! That was sure a good landing; you put it down right on the end of the strip." His comment didn't make me feel superior as I viewed the damage to the aircraft. Later, landing on the long, wide, paved Watson Lake strip was pure joy. It took Jim Close one day to fix the wrinkle, having to replace some skin and beef up and straighten the bulkhead.

I wrote in my journal the next few days, "Have obtained a twenty-six foot Corsair trailer, self-contained, and have it on my property at the lake. Nice location, but we don't have water or electricity yet. The hungry mosquitoes wait outside the door to jump Scott and me when we had to do nature's bidding over a Johnson bar." I previously owned a smaller trailer on the property.

On July 21 I passed the nine thousand mile mark in flying for the month. After ten thousand miles I will get paid double mileage. I flew to Ross River twice, then to Howard's Pass and on to Cantung and returned to Watson Lake. My son's smiling face greeted me at the dock.

I wrapped up July with several more trips into Howard's Pass for Hudson Bay Mining Company, some flights into Irwin and Doughney Lake for the same company, a trip into Hook Lake, and then a trip into Tuya Lake (Frank Stewart's hunting camp) and Netson Lake on the thirty-first.

August started out well; I logged 9.6 hours on the first flying into Provinger and Scoop Lake with my favorite Beaver CF-IBP. I made two trips into Howard's Pass in the wheel Beaver FLN over the next couple of days, then made a trip into the Cadillac Strip just northwest of Deadman's Valley for a mining company. On August

6 I flew the Red Beaver into Flat and Glacier Lake and to Summit Lake the next day.

It was a beautiful day August 8, as I taxied IBP out into Watson Lake. I had a trip into Provinger Lake, which was located about 130 miles south in northern B.C. Huge boulders of jade, weighing several tons, lie along this lake and in the surrounding areas keeping several companies and individual prospectors busy working during the short summer months. Jade is extremely hard and had to be sawed with a diamond blade into eighty pound chunks that could be flown out in the Beaver. It was a slow process, but when they had a load ready, they gave us a call and we picked it up.

Larry Barr was overseeing the jade operation in Provinger Lake. Two brothers, Andy and Paul Jenson, were avid prospectors and had some good property on nearby lakes. They were in the process of striking an arrangement with some Chinese businssmen who wanted some of their jade for the commercial market. Jerry Davis, a good friend of Jim and Stan's and a super guy, had some good jade property in the area on Boulder Lake close to the Turnagain River. Jerry and his wife, two of the nicest people I met in the bush, spent the summer working their property. Jerry flew his own green Super Cub and was an excellent pilot. Another prospector close to Jerry from Mount Vernon, Washington, gave me a gold nugget in a plastic paper weight which I keep on my desk.

I had propane, groceries and some mining gear, and of course the mail to fly in and would be flying some men and gear back to Watson Lake. After runup and about a forty-second run on the lake, IBP flew off the water, gently climbed and turned to the left toward the south. I relaxed and continued the climb to seven thousand feet; it was a clear day and I enjoyed the safety of altitude.

Flying over the Dease River and coming up to the west side of the Horse Ranch Range, I got a nice updraft. Soon Cry Lake took form, and we flew east of the north end, paralleling the Turnagain River for a few miles. Provinger Lake appeared. The camp was visible on the south end, and I circled as we descended to make the final approach to the south into the wind. After touching down I taxied on the step until we were a few hundred feet from shore, reducing power to idle, in order to slip slowly into the makeshift pole dock. Helping hands quickly and efficiently unloaded the Beaver, and we reloaded it with the gear to be flown back to Watson Lake.

I heard the sound of perking coffee as I walked into the cook tent. No cook as such was here, but the storebought cookies dunked in my coffee tasted just fine. I am a Swede, raised from a child on my great-grandmother's coffee bread and coffee; I became a dunker for life.

After a quick five minutes of dunking, two men and I climbed into the Beaver. The men were feeling bushed after a season away from civilization and were delighted to get out of camp. Tonight a real shower, restaurant food, clean sheets, and, of course, a good roaring drunk were in order. We made a downwind take-off and had a pleasant flight back to Watson Lake.

HOWARD'S PASS—WHITE KNUCKLE STRIP

On August 11, 12, and 13, I made several trips from Cantung into Howard's Pass, flying fuel for the helicopters and assorted camping gear into that miserable Howard's Pass strip. After collecting some more grey hairs, it was nice to prepare the Beaver FLN for a flight into Scatter River airstrip for Dempsey Collison, who had a guiding territory there. In the winter Dempsey, a handsome, single young man, went south and evidently met a lot of good-looking young women. When I flew a hunting party in to his camp, usually a young lady went along as a cook or camp helper with each change of hunters.

After unloading horsefeed, Dempsey and I flew to Fort Nelson and back to Scatter River strip with some more supplies, after which I returned to Watson Lake.

The Snow Birds, the Canadian acrobatic jet team, flew into Watson Lake one day to put on a show. It was a nice day and one of the pilots from the other company that flew out of Watson Lake put on a little air show of his own in a Stearman Bi-wing plane.

Down the runway and into the air went this trusty, open cockpit antique airplane, putting on quite a show. A few seconds after touchdown, and in front of a watching crowd, the Stearman suddenly flipped over on its back. The crowd was silent, not knowing what to expect. A figure wriggled down to the ground from the upside-down position and silently walked away, never lifting his eyes from the ground.

The Stearman was nose-heavy. After the acrobatic performance, the pilot probably had his feet on the top of the rudder peddles, which were the brakes on the ground, and that would cause the ship to flip over quite suddenly. The Snow Birds put on a marvelous show of breathtaking precision acrobatics as they swooped and climbed in formation!

August 18 Scott was with me in IBP as several mining people were on their way to Smithers, B.C. It was a beautiful flight. We stopped at Provinger Lake, Germanson Landing, Delcluz Lake and then Smithers. We landed at McClure Lake, where my flying career had began. I had forgotten how beautiful the country was in the Bulkley Valley. The valley was a rich, deep green, and the day was warm. I felt the same peaceful feeling this place first gave me when we arrived in 1964.

We caught a cab to town, and then another cab drove us to our former log house in Driftwood. The log house was as I remembered it—no noticeable changes except for a large window and a fence. A quiet, beautiful, peaceful setting among the pine and spruce trees. This was my first trip back, and I was glad to see it with my own eyes and to feel as I did. I didn't want to go back: the past was gone.

Scott worked Sunday through Friday, six days a week from one p.m. to ten p.m. He was well liked and did an excellent job. Grant Taylor, the owner and his boss, said he was the best help they had ever hired.

Scott repaired two hundred pound truck tires, serviced trucks and cars and cashed out at night. I disliked the stubborn diesel smell that clung to his clothes when he got home. We often went to the Watson Lake Hotel and used their shower.

FLIGHT OF THE RED BEAVER

I flew into Telegraph Creek in our Aztec CF-HIA on August 29. The mighty Stikine River flows just below the town of Telegraph Creek, B.C. The town was named by the Collins Overland Telegraph Company. Their line to Asia was to cross the Stikine River at this location. The Tahltan Indians had a village near the townsite. About four miles east the Stikine River flows for sixty miles through the Grand Canyon of the Stikine, a truly remarkable and awesome area to fly through.

HIA was back from a repair shop in Calgary, repaired to the tune of about $30,000. One of the pilots had evidently retracted the wheels before the Aztec was airborne. He nicked a prop. Instead of going around and landing, not knowing if the props and engine was badly damaged, he bellied it in, which was the wisest thing to do.

After a nice flight to Cassiar and Telegraph Creek with Scott and school officials, Scott and I sat down for breakfast at a cafe in Telegraph Creek. We talked about many things: the history of the town, our feelings. We then walked through the Indian graveyard and saw some Indian bones lying in the open. There were small spirit houses over most of the graves. We left, wondering deeply about who these people were and what their life had been like.

I also wondered to myself about being alone, without a family--sad feelings indeed.

On our trip back toward Eddontenajon, the door in HIA flew open, and it felt as though the plane would shake itself apart and fall from the sky. The passengers held on as tightly as possible to the door but were not able to close it. We landed safely in the Indian village of Iskut and shut the door. However, the day was hot. The cranky fuel injected 290-horsepower Lycoming engines acted up when they were hot, and it was one hour before I could start them. We returned to Cassiar with the school officials and then flew to Watson Lake. Gordon Scott, our apprentice engineer, worked on the faulty door lock and told me it was okay, or so it seemed at the time.

My journal entry for August 30 reads, "Almost wrecked the Aztec. Today was another grey hair day, one of my most nerve-racking. I flew to Macmillan Pass with my son Scott to pick up a load of mining gear. The strip was fifteen hundred to two thousand feet long and forty-five hundred feet above sea level. Fortunately, after putting in a heavy payload, I had the sense to unload a few heavy items. This was after warming up, taxiing for take-off and then deciding not to take an unnecessary risk. Good thinking for me this day! It no doubt saved a wrecked airplane and possibly our lives! After unloading the heavy items that were on top, I taxied to the far end of the north end of the gravel strip. I applied full power, released the brakes and picked up speed rapidly as the two powerful engines propelled me toward the end of the strip. Just as I began to rotate past the point of no return, the door popped open. Not having room to stop, and knowing I would go off the end of the strip if we didn't become airborne, I somehow managed to lift the plane into the air. The flight manual says if the door comes open in a situation like this, the outcome is "doubtful" or words to that effect. We staggered into the air and down the valley. Bringing up the landing gear helped somewhat, but we struggled down the valley for many miles until I got some altitude and could breathe regularly. Scott was holding onto the door for dear life, pulling it as far shut as he could, but the air pressure kept it from closing completely.The airplane continued to buck and complain all the way home. I was angry because I was told the door had been fixed earlier. Having been very close to death, I vented my anger when we returned. A bolt-type sliding lock similar to an outhouse lock was installed, and it solved the problem."

Fall came quickly and early to Watson Lake. The trees and meadows were suddenly splashed with golds and red overnight; the season was rapidly drawing to a close. Winter would soon come...in fact, much sooner than we expected.

September 7, 9 and 10, I made fuel hauls into Howard's Pass in the Aztec HIA without too much difficulty; the strip was dry by then. Because of altitude and the heavy loads I was carrying, I noticed 85 mph was as slow as I could approach on final. Approaching slower than that resulted in buffeting, a warning that the airplane was approaching a stall.

September 10 I flew IBP into Rex Logan's Hunting Camp on the Keel River. Rex was a well-known and respected old-timer and one of the best big game outfitters and wranglers in this country. I flew new hunters and groceries in and other hunters out.

The trip in was about 240 miles one way, a good money maker. But it was over the rugged Mackenzie Mountains, and it was worth every penny I made. The river landing was a bit tricky, and a mishap could occur easily on this stretch of the river. When you are a long way from civilization, special care is a must.

September 18 I made another trip to Rex Logan's camp. The season was about over, as winter could come any time and the freeze up was drawing close. I flew several hunters out. Rex and his guides trailed the horses out to a road—about a two- week trip.

I wrote in my journal on October 5, that the weather the past ten days had turned to snow and cold in the higher elevations. I tried unsuccessfully to get into Plateau Lake, and those hunters were picked up later by a helicopter! This lake was thinly frozen, so I was unable to land there. I flew skis into the Scatter River airstrip, 20 miles distant. I was also able to fly into a small lake on floats in IBP to pick up some German hunters. A small bay was unfrozen. I told them to leave all their belongings, including toothbrushes. My Red Beaver IBP performed superbly, and we were off the water and into the air before we hit the ice. One of the Germans who was a pilot pounded my back and said "Good, good!" It had been four months exactly since I had made the last trip on skis—a short summer.

There were constant reminders that we really were "braving the untamed wilderness." This fall a hunter I flew in earlier to a hunting camp got lost and was never found. He went ahead of the guide on the trail and said he could find his own way back. Another man, a prospector, was also lost and never found. A pilot dropped him off at Divide Lake, and two months later I flew in the Royal Canadian Mounted Police in the Beaver on floats. We flew low, but no trace was found, and fresh snow and ice on the lake prevented our landing. We found his neatly set up camp, but no prospector. The scene was stark and etched deeply in my mind. We recognized the tragic end to this man's dream. In 1983 his thick glasses, some tattered clothing and wristwatch were found near Divide Lake. Darrell Nelson, who outfitted in that area, said the watch began ticking. He thought that a grizzly bear might have killed the prospector, but no one will ever know for sure. A guide and a camp helper from two separate camps lost their lives that fall in accidents, as well.

This was a season of tough flying for me; I felt very fortunate and lucky that I experienced no accidents and still had my hide.

On a typical trip into the "white knuckle strip" at Howard's Pass, I was carrying explosives on the Beaver. As usual, a crosswind was coming down the mountain, tending to push me off the strip into a draw. As I bounced around the curve, the wind and centrifugal force and the sloping strip pushed me toward the draw. I bounced to the very edge and rode the ridge along the drop-off! Full left aileron, left rudder, and we somehow stayed on the edge until the plane slowed. At that time, I got it back on the main strip, but I mentally expected a wreck and an explosion at any moment. I once made four passes at that strip before landing.

Flying late in the fall when it was snowing made navigation very difficult. In a snowstorm if you followed a river that was open, you had a dark object to fly over and to help keep your horizon in perspective. If the river was frozen and everything was white, it got very hazardous. Then you were at risk of a whiteout condition, when you lose all visual contact. We flew VFR (visual flight rules) in our operations; the airplanes were not equipped for instrument flight. Jim Thibaudeau and I had instrument ratings, but without navigation equipment in the airplanes we are unable to make instrument approaches. He and I often talked about getting out of flying; we felt we were close to being burnt out and were pushing our luck. The seasons of long hours without days off and the many close calls we had in this type of flying caused us to think about another kind of work before long. Jim had opened a sporting goods store and was also going to work with Ron Holly, putting water and sewer lines into new homes.

As the season drew to an end after many flights into Howard's Pass and some other rather hazardous trips, I felt ready to give it up, at least part of the time. However, I still had a love for flying, so there was a conflict. Of course, after a long and busy season with your last few trips in winter-like snow conditions, you get superstitious and hope your luck and good fortune holds until the last trip is completed.

HOWARD'S PASS—WHITE KNUCKLE STRIP

Jim Close signed my log book October 2, 1974: "Time logged to date certified," and he put the Watson Lake Flying Service stamp above his signature.

I left Watson Lake and began the long drive down the Alaska Highway. It was a demanding season, and I felt as though this might be my last season of flying the bush. I was drained and looking forward to a long rest, away from flying.

The mighty Mackenzie Mountains, N.W. Territories, in the early 1970's. Note the unusual layers of rock.

From left, Jim Close owner of Watson Lake Flying Service. Middle Arnold a prospector and Jim Dodge, a geologist, and the Red Beaver. They were great guys to fly for and good companions over the years as we flew into the remote lakes of the far north looking for that pot of gold.

CHAPTER XIV
THE YUKON SEASON ENDS

On December 20, 1974, I picked up Scott at Vancouver International Airport and drove to Seattle and Bellevue, where I had rented for the winter a four-bedroom house with a nice view on Lake Sammamish.

Scott began gliding lessons near here on a grass strip and soloed on the third day of flying lessons. The instructor and I watched Scott make his solo approach to the small grass strip to land, but, because of other traffic in the pattern, he had to circle first. Because there was no engine we were concerned that he might not have enough altitude left to make the field, and we both tried to put on a good face, as though there was no problem.

Scott handled the situation like a pro. He made an extra circle but stayed close enough to the field to make the landing without a problem. He made a good landing, but because one wing was a bit low on landing, the instructor said, "Scott, you're part Chinese, One Wing Lo." Scott was all smiles, and I was one proud father. Scott was fourteen years old, which was the minimum age to solo in a glider. Minimum to solo in a power plane was sixteen. He made twenty-four flights in all and paid for them with the money he made working for Grant Taylor's truck stop and service station in Watson Lake.

After Scott finished his glider flying, we headed for Spokane to spend the holidays with relatives. Scott had to return to Prince George in early January, but I had a trip planned to visit him in mid-February.

After I picked Scott up for my visit, we found a motel and stayed up late watching TV and catching up, then slept late the next morning. We spent the afternoon at Prince George Airport and looked at a sharp DC-3 used by Northern Thunderbird for hauling passengers to Penticton. We also watched some cross-country skiers and discussed world problems but reached no real solutions. Scott had a mature insight into life and raised some interesting thoughts. Over breakfast the next day, we discussed Luscomb Silvars and the possibility of purchasing one and installing a 150-horsepower Lycoming engine, flaps, and floats. I so enjoyed making plans with him—it was hard to leave for Seattle.

I made a trip south to spend a week in the Arizona sun. After visiting Yuma, Tucson, and Phoenix, I went to Las Vegas, where I lost thirty dollars. Good thing I had only a little money on me. Then it was back to Seattle. I bought a leather flight jacket, pilot's log book, maps and other items for my position as a pilot in Sitka, Alaska, where I had been offered a position. March 9 I caught an Alaska Airlines flight for Sitka. I spent a nice day, but somehow didn't feel comfortable about the job, and I decided to return to Seattle. The flying in the area was usually marginal at best, due to bad weather along the coast, and it just didn't feel right. Turning it down was the right decision.

I spent my thirty-seventh birthday in Spokane, Washington on April 2, 1975. I was most happy, contented and at peace with myself and the world. My life was rich beyond my hopes of earlier years. My Canadian dream had become a reality. I became a bush pilot flying into wilderness areas and seeing those places I had read about as a child. About two years of college were behind me, and I had this wonderful freedom, with unlimited possibilities. My son was soaring to great heights, literally, with twenty-four glider flights under his belt, and figuratively speaking, as he was an excellent student and got along well with others.

Near the end of April, I began packing personal belongings and, of course, my blue down-filled sleeping bag that I had bought many years ago from Tommy Walker, which was always part of my survival gear in the red Beaver, and left for Watson Lake. After three long days and nights driving and sleeping along the Alaska Highway, I arrived safely at Watson Lake for another season of flying for Watson Lake Flying Service.

On May 20, 1975, the Mercedes-Benz people arrived. The owner of the Mercedes Corporation would arrive later for a hunt into Frank Cooke's area. These people were going to be making several flights into the camp to make sure it was set up the way their boss wanted it. They chartered the Aztec CF-HIA to fly into Frank Cooke's main camp at Scoop Lake.

The trip to Scoop Lake took forty minutes one way. I did almost all of the flying in the Aztec, which I really enjoyed. Leaving the Beaver and climbing into the Aztec was like getting out of a truck and into a Cadillac with cushy seats and almost 200 mph cruise. It was interesting to have two engines to play with instead of one. The flight back to Watson Lake was pleasant; the days were getting long, and the weather was sunny and mild.

I flew them back into Scoop again on May 22 and 23 with the Aztec before they were satisfied all was okay. Later on, the son of the family that owned Mercedes-Benz arrived in Scoop Lake. He told Frank he wanted a certain tame goose Frank had for dinner. Frank replied, "It's not for sale."

"I'll give you five hundred dollars for that goose."

"It's still not for sale!" The goose went on to live its pampered lifestyle.

"White Knuckle Strip," Howard's Pass, came back into my life on May 25 and again on May 27. I safely flew the Red Beaver on wheels into the pass with a load of groceries, camp supplies, and mail.

Gary Moore, the new owner of Skook's ranch and hunting area, chartered me to fly into the ranch at Terminus Mountain. It was not a great strip, but the Aztec got in and out without any problem. Gary was an interesting man. He had done well for himself in the lumbering business. At this time he was in his thirties and really enjoyed the guiding business. He had a Cessna 185 on floats that he flew into some of the lakes in his guiding area.

Mitchell B-25's in Watson Lake? Yes indeed! Two flew into the airport, to be on call for the Forest Service in the event of forest fires. They had been converted to water bombers. Since they were a co-pilot short, they offered me the position. They assured me it would be only while they were in the area and it should not interfere with my charter flying. They would check me out, give me an endorsement on my license, and provide free meals if I acted as co-pilot on a B-25 with a shark's grin painted on the nose. This B-25, CF-MWC, which I flew reminded me of Chinault's Flying Tigers.

Of course, I agreed and started logging time on this type of airplane. The B-25 was the first plane to bomb Tokyo. This mission was handled off carriers under the leadership of Jimmy Doolittle.

I logged 2.2 hours on the B-25 June 9, 2.3 hours in two separate flights June 11, and 2 hours on June 15. My log book entry for June 15, 1975, read, "Time for North Americn B-25: Certified Correct. L. Harrold, North Western Air Lease Ltd. (Chief Pilot)." The Department of Transportation put an endorsement on my commercial license for the B-25.

The engines were rated at eighteen hundred horsepower each, and when they idled, they gave you a good shaking. It was a beautiful airplane to fly, honest and forgiving. The B-25 had a good, high lift wing and gets off quickly with a full load and climbs well. In the stall it's honest, and I couldn't detect any bad characteristics when I did stalls, steep turns, landings and take-offs. It was a fun airplane.

The B-25 pilots from back East, what I called the flat lands, were not used to flying in the mountains and did not know this area. We were notified by the Department of Transportation that a large helicopter was lost. They asked if we would help in the search and agreed to furnish free gas if we would.

Because I knew the country and was used to flying in the mountains, the captain in my B-25 let me do the flying. I flew as I always did in the mountains. I tucked one wing up close to the mountain, where there was some lift on one side of the valley, so if I needed to I could make a 180-degree turn safely. The captain eyed the side of the mountain and me with a quizzical look, but said nothing. We logged many hours, but were unable to find the helicopter; as far as I know, it was never located.

Because the pilot and copilot of the B-25's didn't have float endorsements, we let them fly our Super Cub. I gave them several hours of dual instructions and endorsed their log books for float flying when I thought they could handle the seaplane safely.

In Canada any commercial pilot with a float endorsement can give a float endorsement to another pilot. I had an instructor rating but didn't really need it to legally give them their float ratings. They enjoyed the float flying, and I was thrilled to get a free endorsement and several hours in a B-25. When I was flying the B-25 through the mountain, I went back in time and pretended I was in World War II on a bombing mission.

We practiced and demonstrated water bombing at the airport on June 20 for thirty minutes. It was exciting to drop on a target and pull up and away, light now that the hold was empty. It must have been impressive from the ground because of the size and noise of these wonderful birds from another age.

One day they were called to another location, and that was the last I saw of the planes or pilots. The memories are still vivid: climbing up into the belly of the B-25 in a chin up configuration, cranking up the engines and roaring off into the wild blue yonder with a tremendous noise.

I made two trips safely into Howard's Pass with the red Beaver on June 15, two trips on June 17, two trips on June 21, and one on June 23. On June 24 Scott and I prepared for a most interesting trip in the Aztec.

Some mining people wanted us to pick them up at Cantung (Tungsten) in the Northwest Territories and fly them first to Faro, and then Dawson City, where we would overnight. On the following day we would fly to another mining camp for a few hours, then drop the men off at Whitehorse before returning to Watson Lake. It was a nice trip, a good money maker, and I would be able to take my son along.

The flight to Cantung was 130 air miles. We picked up the Hyland River near Stewart Lake and followed it most of the way. The gravel road to Cantung intercepted the Hyland River about twenty-two miles north of Stewart Lake, and we followed it into Cantung. Besides being a good landmark to follow it could be used as an emergency airstrip if we developed engine trouble or had weather problems.

Flying in this country without floats made me feel somewhat naked. There were so few places to land a wheel plane. With floats there are countless lakes or rivers; even a meadow is okay and can be used without much of a problem on floats, because you have a large surface with the float bottoms and are not as likely to flip over as you would with a wheel plane.

Thinking of Dawson City, I went back to my childhood days when I read Jack London's *Call of the Wild*, listened on the radio to "Sergeant Preston of the Northwest Mounted Police" and his wonder dog King, and stories of my grandfather's uncle who left his store and headed for the gold fields in the last century.

Dawson City sat at the junction of the Klondike and Yukon Rivers. In 1975 it was a town of about eight hundred people, but it had once numbered over twenty-five thousand when the klondikers came between 1897 and 1905. Silent buildings are about all that remain of a once lively, riproaring town, where saloons and gambling casinos kept busy and where the motto was "Never refuse a man a drink or kick a dog". A few buildings were still in use and some had been renovated. The original post office was still in use, as was Diamond Tooth Gertie's, a gambling hall that offered roulette, black jack, can-can girls and bingo. As far as I knew, it was the only place in Canada that allowed legalized gambling.

Gold was discovered ten miles southeast of here on Bonanza Creek, a tributary of the Klondike River, in 1896 by George Carmack, Skookum Jim and Tagish Charlie. Word of the gold reached the outside in 1897, and the Klondike Stampede began.

We approached the town of Cantung from the south. The gravel airstrip, just south of town was clearly visible as I came through the pass, following the road. Rounding out near the end of the strip, we were soon down and taxiing to the pickup truck that waited for us with the mining officials who would be our companions for the next couple of days.

The two gentlemen climbed aboard. We taxied to the north end of the strip and accelerated down the runway. Because we had twice the weight and a little higher altitude, it took longer to get airborne, and we used about fifteen hundred feet of the strip before we were airborne.

Out first destination was Faro, 170 miles due west. Soon Pelly Lakes in the Yukon Territory slipped under our wings, and then we crossed the old Canal Road and picked up the Campbell Highway west of there and followed it into Faro, where we landed on a good gravel strip near town.

After fueling and waiting a few hours for our clients to take care of their business there, we were once again airborne, our destination Dawson City. This was Scott's first trip to Dawson, and he was excited. I once flew the Beaver on floats there, landing on the mighty Yukon River.

We followed the Pelly River on a northwest course, cross country flying over this wilderness. North of Pelly Crossing we picked up the gravel Klondike Highway and had a road under us to Dawson City. Flying over Dawson City, we circled the gravel strip and soon were on final, landing into the wind from the southwest. We touched down on the fairly soft surface, a good ending for this day's flying.

After tying down HIA, we managed to catch a ride to town, where we had a room booked in the motel. But guess what--somehow they had us booked for the next day, and they had no available rooms. It was at the peak of the tourist season and we couldn't seem to find a room anywhere. Someone suggested Black Mike's place, an old, tall, skinny two-story gold rush original, from the 1800's era. It was out of town and a good mile's walk.

The building looked like something from another time zone, but we were glad to get a room. They even had inside plumbing down the hall. We had a large room for the four of us, with three beds. Scott and I agreed to share the double bed.

It was light outside all night, and we didn't feel like going to bed yet, so we walked back to town and hit some of the bars. We walked to Robert Service's log cabin, the old hospital, and saw many of the original buildings.

Scott and I went to the Gaslight Follies Theater, which had been restored to its original condition. We watched a play about the Klondike days. Because we were in Dawson City, and the buildings were the genuine originals, we were able to feel that special time of long ago. The acting was superb, and the audience was soon into the play. Laughter seemed to shake the building, bringing life from that era into the theater. Romance, life and death were acted out in a light comedy of the far North.

Scott decided to go back to the hotel at around midnight, but the rest of us were just starting to feel a bit of a glow. We had a few more drinks and made it back to Black Mike's at about three in the morning, only to face yet another unexpected setback. Scott had locked the door, and he had the only key. We banged on the door to try to arouse him from a deep sleep, but finally gave up. One of the men climbed into the bathtub to try to get some sleep, and the other stretched out on the floor. I told them that someday we'd recall this event and laugh about it, but of course we were dead tired and didn't see any humor in it just yet.

Finally I decided to go outside and see if I could get up to the outside window and maybe wake Scott. I found a ladder and was able to get to the window, which was close to the bed that Scott was sleeping in. Scott broke an eardrum in a swimming accident and didn't hear well in one ear, and of course he was sleeping on his good ear. I banged on the window for awhile, and Scott finally woke up and let us in. It was about 4:00 a.m. by now, and we got about three hours of sleep before getting up, eating breakfast and departing for the mining town of Clinton Creek about forty-five miles northwest. There we spent a few hours and had a good meal before departing for Whitehorse.

Flying on a southeast heading we picked up the Klondike Highway at Minto and followed it, flying over Yukon Crossing, Carmacks—passing just west of Lake Labarge, where the cremation of Sam McGee took place, the event immortalized in one of Robert Service's poems—and on into the Whitehorse airport.

After unloading their gear, we hopped in, and I cranked up both engines and taxied out near the end of the runway to do my preflight take-off check list. I got clearence from the tower to take off. We accelerated rapidly, because we were lightly loaded, and soared into the clear Yukon sky. Shortly after take-off, the door popped open, since the sliding bolt lock wasn't completel closed, and the regular handle door lock never did work properly. I quickly opened a vent to equalize the pressure, and we were able to lock it. The flight back was pleasant, and the weather was sunny and warm, so we relaxed, cherishing this adventure that we shared. I let Scott take control on the co-pilot's side, and he flew part of the way home with a smile on his face.

On July 1, I flew the Beaver FLN to Little Dal Lake, then to the Nahanni River for Darell Nelson's South Nahanni Outfitters.

It was July 12, and I was waiting at the float base office for the weather to improve. A system of bad weather had us grounded here at the lake, but it was moving north and had improved a bit. I had a trip booked into Macmillan Pass with the Beaver to fly some camp supplies in for a mining camp. Sometimes waiting for the weather to clear was one of the hardest things for me. The trips continued to pile up, and the pressures built as the various camps needed food and supplies. The camps did not always understand why we couldn't fly in when the weather at their locations was good.

Some of the camps were one hundred to three hundred miles away, and the weather between us was often unflyable. We did our best, however, to keep the supplies and people moving into the various camps as close to the scheduled flights as possible. We called this weather a whisky front and often headed for the bar and told tall tales of our life in the clouds over some strong spirits. It was not a lot of fun to sit at some isolated place and wait out the weather. It was much better to wait at the base and go another day.

By late afternoon the worst of the storm seemed to have passed through, and I decided to head north to see if I could get to Macmillan Pass. I followed the Frances River north, flying close to the Campbell Highway until I reached the west side of Frances Lake, and then headed on a northeast course cross country in a fairly direct line to the Canal Road and Macmillan Pass.

On wheels instead of floats, I felt naked. The many lakes and swamps made a good emergency landing easy with floats, but with wheels the prospects were poor for a safe landing in most areas along this route.

Visibility was okay, although the ceiling was still low. I could see the canal road ahead and was soon flying parallel to it, following it to the airstrip. I relaxed somewhat, as I had a road that could be used as an emergency strip if I had to set it down.

Up ahead and under my port wing the strip at Macmillan Pass came into view, running north and south. The wind was from the south, so my downwind leg was parallel to the strip in a northerly heading, and final was into the wind on the south runway.

I quickly unloaded the Beaver, as I wanted to get back before the weather deteriorated again. It was about 150 miles home to Watson Lake, and the weather looked black and threatening to the south and was beginning to lower again. Flying over Frances Lake, seventy miles from home, the clouds and the ground met a few miles south of the lake over the Frances River. Having no other choice, I made a steep turn and did a quick 180. The weather behind me, where I had been minutes before, formed a solid barrier to the ground, and I had to fly over the east arm of the lake.

I was restricted to a small area, and all I could do was circle and circle. My situation was becoming critical. The gas gauges all showed empty, the needles bouncing off the E mark on the three belly tanks, and the darkness descended to envelop my small craft. I prepared to crash. There was a couple who lived in a cabin below, and I planned to set down in the trees or water, thinking they would help me get out of the plane if I was injured.

Circling up the side of one mountain on the east side of the lake, I was hoping to get a better view of the mountains to the west where I could find a hole and land on the road beyond. My airspeed dropped to a dangerously low forty-five miles per hour, but I happened to glance down before a stall occurred and quickly lowered the nose to resume the seventy miles per hour slow flight speed that I was flying with partial flaps. In bad weather, slowing down and using flaps gives you more time and also enables you to turn in a smaller radius, if the situation requires.

To the west I could see a little light above the mountain ridge where there was a saddle. Skimming over the tree tops, I was able to get through and slip down the other side of the mountain, fly over the west arm of the lake and to the road beyond. A straight stretch of road appeared, and I flew parallel to it as I descended, giving it a close look. The road ran north-south just west of the lake. I was flying south, to the right side of the road, intending to land in a northerly direction. Slowing down, I started lowering the flaps and began a 180-degree steep, descending turn to the left, approaching the landing site with full flaps and an airspeed of about sixty miles per hour. Complete concentration was necessary, as this was probably the only chance I would get. It was a moonless night, the gauges showed empty, and the road was extremely narrow. Touchdown was smooth, and the Beaver rolled to a stop up a small incline. The wheels almost touched each edge of the road. Had we been off the center slightly or touched the brakes, the Beaver probably would have been wrecked, as the road bank was steep and there was a good drop-off to the bottom.

The airplane was safe, and I was alive. The relief was overwhelming, and I didn't care whether I ever flew another plane. Using the landing light, I taxied north on the road for about two miles until I found a place wide enough to park the Beaver off the road for the night.

I stretched out my sleeping bag behind the pilot's seat and soon fell into an exhausted and very much appreciated sleep.

Jim Thibaudeau was close to my location here on this road. He was down on Frances Lake in the Beech 18, flying freight into Lorrie Bliss's area in the Northwest Territories, but had been holding for weather. I knew Jim would have gas, so I walked down to the lake at the end of a dirt road. Jim and the other people there were surprised to see me. We loaded up a forty-five gallon drum on a pickup. After I had breakfast with some people from Watson Lake who were camping here, I left with Jim and one other man who guided for Lorrie Bliss, at about 0900.

After I fueled up the Beaver, Jim walked in one direction, and the guide walked in the other direction to stop any traffic while I took off in the Red Beaver. I warmed up the Beaver, went through my checklist, and then applied full power. IBP, being light, lifted quickly off the narrow dirt road, and I headed south to Watson Lake, about one hundred miles away. The weather was good, and the bosses, curious as to why I was a day late, were glad to know I was okay. Add another to the list of close calls that almost ended my flying career.

The very next day I had a trip to Howard's Pass. Two days later, on July 15, I made my last wheel flight in the Red Beaver to Howard's Pass and returned to Watson Lake safely. On July 19 I began flying this Beaver on floats, as we took the wheels off due to the demand for another float plane. The hunting season was approaching, and the hunters would soon be arriving and would have to be flown on floats to the various lakes in B.C., the Yukon, and Northwest Territories.

Over the next few days I flew into Burnt Rose Lake, Mayfield Lake, and Wolverine Lake, and made a trip in the Aztec to move a camp from the Liard Airstrip. I flew through a flock of small birds upon landing, but no damage to the plane was done. I made several more trips in HIA to Howard's Pass and several in the Red Beaver to places like Summit Lake and Terminus Mountain on the Ketchika River, Misty Lake, and Sandpile Lake. A long day for Frank Cooke, mostly with the Red Beaver to Scoop and Denetiah Lakes, finished out the month of July. I logged 8.5 hours in the Red Beaver.

In August I flew into Tobally, Misty, Tom, Hyland, Provinger, Sandpile, Deadwood, Stone Axe, Ervin, Flat, Mink, Junion, Daughny, Muncho, Brown, Mayfield, Tootsi, Meeting, Plateau, Crooked, Colt, Scoop, Island, Forsburg, Moodie, and Boulder lakes. As usual there were trips to Howard's Pass, Terminus Mountain, and other airstrip camps and small towns. September followed much the same routine.

The next couple of days I flew into Plateau, Sandpile, Dease, and Glacier Lakes. From the sixth through the twenty-first, I flew the Red Beaver, mostly for outfitters as the hunting season was drawing to a close, into dozens of lakes: Junkers, Netson, Mink, Goodwin, Swan, Ice, McCaully, Daughney, Marker, Provinger, Ogden, Scoop, Colt, Sandpile, Misty, Brown, Whitefish, Pike, Meeting and more.

On September 22, I flew the Aztec to Stewart, B.C., located at the head of the Portland Canal, three hundred miles southeast of Watson Lake. I was only a few minutes' flying time north of Alice Arm, B.C., the destination of my first commercial trip with a paying passenger in 1967 when I started flying for Omineca Sir Services, nine years ago.

Glaciers tower over Stewart, and it was quite a drop as I flew direct and came over the mountains. Then the town appeared far below. I was just a short distance west of Stevens Lake, where I once flew out the world record grizzly bear in Omineca Air Service's Cessna 185, CF-OXE. Rex Handcock shot that bear with a bow and arrow in 1978, at the headwater of the Kispiox River, which was the river we lived on when we first moved to Canada. Memories flooded back: that seemed like a long time ago, a distant life, and it seemed so strange the way that time and events had flown.

On September 25, I flew the Aztec to Frank Cooke's Scoop Lake airstrip and on to Terminus Mountain airstrip at Skook's old ranch and returned to Watson Lake, logging 1.5 hours. Another trip of 1.7 hours the same day became the last flight I logged in my favorite airplane of all time, that beautiful *"Red Beaver"!*

On the twenty-sixth I flew again into Frank Cooke's camp at Scoop Lake in the Aztec, and later in the day I flew the same airplane to the Titina airstrip.

My last day of flying for Watson Lake Flying Service was September 27, 1975. I flew the Aztec HIA to the Titina airstrip, logging 1.2 hours. On these last trips of the season I became superstitious. It was this time of year when the weather got bad. Snow storms and icing conditions prevailed and made for hazardous flying. I was tired after a busy flying season and was flying on the edge of my seat, hoping for a safe ending.

Goodbyes were said. I told the pilots I flew with and my employers that this was my final season; I was planning to get into another line of work. I felt it was time to make a change. I was burned out after the close calls I had flying into Howard's Pass and Macmillan Pass this past summer. I was looking forward to going south and to beginning a new career.

After packing my 1972 blue Volvo, I left Watson Lake on the journey south and new adventures. I felt fortunate and relieved to have the flying season safely behind me.

The trip down the Alaska Highway was wet and the road muddy, due to heavy fall rains. The Yukon slipped away, and a new season in my life began.

Max Sanderson, helicopter pilot for Placer Development. Max was a bush pilot who once flew Beavers and he gave me my first and only helicopter ride.

Canoe party that Larry let off at the headwaters of the South Nahanni River and later picked them up at Nahanni Butte and flew them back to Watson Lake. Larry and the school teacher from Nahanni Butte are on the far right.

173

Frank Cooke and his sister in a sled at Ft. St. James 1936, standing by Grant McConachie's Waco airplane. Grant started Canadian Pacific Airlines from this Bush operation. (Photo Frank Cooke)

Ft. St. James about 1935. Russ Baker's Junkers airplane. Russ obtained the first Beaver #1, and later started Pacific Western Airlines from this Bush operation. (Photo Frank Cooke)

From left, Frank Cooke, his wife Hatti, his son Terry Cooke, and Larry at their hunting camp at Moodie Lake, standing on the floats of the Red Beaver. This is the camp where 5 grizzly bears charged thru.

Larry and Gary Moore at one of Gary's hunting camps in Northern British Columbia. Gary bought out Skook Davidson's territory in the early 70's.

Frank Cooke Jr. with a near record 45½″ stone sheep taken in Northern British Columbia.

THE YUKON SEASON ENDS

Darell Nelson's hunters with a 45½" Dall Sheep, Mackenzie Mountains.

Larry's favorite blue 1972 Volvo, that logged many years on the Alaska Highway and in the Yukon. Note the Yukon plates.

The Red Beaver with the plywood door Wally made after Larry lost the door in a river and had to fly back in a somewhat drafty airplane.

The Red Beaver with a boat tied to the floats, a common practice in the Bush.

THE YUKON SEASON ENDS

Larry Schnig and a fisherman at Larry's fishing camp at Tobally Lake with a 36½ lb. lake trout.

Larry Schnig's trapping cabin at Tobally Lake. Larry guides fisherman during the summer and spends about 4 isolated months in the winter trapping.

Larry Schnig at Tobally Lakes, Yukon with a nice catch of Pike.

DC-3 unloading freight at Frank Cooke's main hunting camp at Scoop Lake, British Columbia, where I met that grizzly bear face to face.

Scott on his first solo in a glider, east of Bellevue, Wash. at age 14. He learned the use of stick and rudder well in this glider and the J-3 CUB he later soloed in.

My son Scott is all smiles after his first solo flight in a glider, winter of 1974. He saved up his summer wages at Watson Lake and paid for his glider lessons.

THE YUKON SEASON ENDS

Largest recorded Moose taken in Canada, by Dr. Peterson, Natla River. Mackenzie Mountains N.W. Territories.

Don Taylor, center, at his fish camp at Stewart Lake, with some happy fishermen.

Northern, British Columbia 1962. Sheep hunter Johnny Caputo on the left with a nice stone sheep with Skook Davidson an old time packer and legend of the north who was his guide. I flew Johnny into a hunting camp in the 70's.

183

Skook Davidson as I knew him. Skook would meet me at the Kechika River, B.C. in his wagon and I would unload the Beaver on the bank. His beloved Diamond J Ranch was close by.

Our crew at Watson Lake Flying Service about 1974, in front of the Company Beeche 18 float plane. From the left, Dave, Jim Thibaudeau, Stan Britcut, Larry Whitesitt, Jim Close and John Poizer. Our engineer Wally Waulkonan is kneeling in front.

Frank Cooke's Stone Sheep hunting camp at Colt Lake, B.C. It's a small mountain lake at about 4,000' ASL

Left, Jack O'Conner, the outdoor editor for Outdoor Life Magazine, center Larry and another hunter. This was Jack's last sheep hunt and he bagged a nice stone sheep. We corresponded and kept in touch after the hunt. Jack reminded me of my grandfather.

185

The Red Beaver. Loading up some hunters to fly out of Colt Lake, B.C. about 1973. The lake was small and light loads and care were used to get off this 4000' lake.

Scott and Larry on the South Nahanni River with the Red Beaver, about 1973. We're about 2,000 feet upstream from Virginia Falls, N.W. Territories.

Larry in front of the B-25 that he flew as co-pilot, at the Watson Lake Airport in the summer of 1975. Note the shark's grin. This B-25 was used for water bombing fires and it was a great ship to fly; an honest and exceptionally good performer with a high lift wing and lots of horses. (1800 HP engines)

Larry at the top of Virginia Falls, N.W. Territories about 1973.

Beautiful, Coldfish Lake, in Northern British Columbia, one of my favorite places.

Wilbur O'Brian a fellow Yukon pilot by the Jet Ranger he flew. He managed the base at Dease Lake, B.C. for Frontier Helicopters and recently said, "those were the best years of my life." Wilbur now manages ERA Helicopters in Anchorage, Alaska.

Sid Baird the manager and one of the owners of Frontier Helicopters at Watson Lake, Yukon. He now works for ERA Helicopters in California.

189

Flying the Red Beaver over the Island at Watson Lake. Watson Lake Flying Service Seaplane base is around that point in the background.

Park Officials, Scott and Larry upstream a short ways above Virginia Falls, N.W. Territories about 1973. This was in the proposed Nahanni National Park area and they were mapping out future campsites. It did become a National Park.

Virginia Falls, N.W. Territories, about 1974. These falls are about twice as high as Niagra Falls and it's in a pristine wilderness area.

THE YUKON SEASON ENDS

Larry flying the Red Beaver north of Watson Lake, in the Yukon Territory. Note the mountain lake in the center.

Larry flying the Red Beaver over the beautiful lakes and mountains, of that magic land, called "THE YUKON."

CHAPTER XV
RETURN TO THE YUKON

Lonely, haunting voices from the past drift across the still waters of this far northern lake. For the first time in over a decade, this beautiful melody, the soft hooting call of a Loon and its mate's contented reply, fills my world.

The peace and quiet of these surroundings bring back memories of a time long since past, when this was my home.

These elusive, magnificent black and white birds have once again returned to Watson Lake in the Yukon Territory. Both the male and female loon look identical, with piercing red eyes and a dark green head and neck. Long bodies of 3 feet and a wingspan of 5 feet give them a majestic appearance on the lake as they glide over the surface or dive to a depth of 200 feet catching fish. I've seen them underwater chasing fish, close to the seaplane dock, just a streak of black and white!

RETURN TO THE YUKON

Each year a pair of loons will lay one or two eggs. The young chicks often ride on the backs of their parents for protection from large Pike below or silent eagles soaring overhead.

Usually only one pair of loons nest on the lake, as they are a solitary bird and very territorial. Their life span can be 20 years or more.

At midnight the piercing, clear Yukon sky is still light, and dawn is not far off as I gaze across the lake from Jim's cabin nestled in the trees above the seaplane base. The buzzing and ferocious appetite of dozens of mosquitos brings me quickly back to reality, but that's a part of the North.

The seaplanes, looking like giant birds with huge wings, rock gently beside the seaplane dock. Tomorrow the largest, a de Havilland Otter, has a trip to Virginia Falls on the south Nahanni River; the smaller bird, a Cessna 185, has a trip to Clark Lake in the Northwest Territories. But for now they are resting until it's their time to soar into the Yukon sky and accomplish the tasks they were created for.

Having flown in Alaska, I can really appreciate this more remote and far less densely populated wilderness area and much prefer flying in the Yukon and Northwest Territories. Being somewhat of a loner, I appreciate the space.

Some of the mosquitos had followed me into the cabin and joined their indoor relatives for a midnight snack on my exposed skin. It didn't matter, though, and my exhausted body soon fell into a deep sleep, in my old past surroundings.

Seaplanes passed by as my feet splashed through the water of the partially submerged dock. The sights and smells were familiar as the warm afternoon sun penetrated my skin.

The dock looks tired and worn, as the waters of the lake gently wash over its surface. Hopes and dreams of many from all walks of life begin here as they climb aboard a float plane and depart Watson Lake for that special place on some wilderness lake or river. Some visitors disappeared and were never found. Some found their dreams; others didn't. But most were rewarded, their life enhanced with a unique experience and an appreciation for this vast land called the Yukon.

Two young Germans and their gear arrived at the seaplane base, as they had chartered the Cessna 185 CF-YIG to fly them into Clark Lake in the Northwest Territories.

There was a book called, *Two Against the Wilderness*, which was later made into a movie, about two Germans that built a log cabin at Clark Lake (which is about 140 miles northeast of Watson Lake in a wilderness area, far removed from civilization), where they lived off the land and did some trapping.

These passengers had two very heavy packs that included a life raft. They planned to raft from the outlet at Clark Lake, down the Caribou River, to the Nahanni, then float to Nahanni Butte.

It was a warm July day in 1987 as we loaded the gear into the airplane. The Germans, who spoke broken English, climbed aboard as we taxied out into Watson

FLIGHT OF THE RED BEAVER

Lake toward a small bay, around a point from the base, near the old B.C. Yukon Air Service seaplane base which is now used by the Forest Service.

This was the first trip I've made since departing Watson Lake in late September of 1975. It felt good to be back in a seaplane I once flew as a bush pilot, over a decade ago.

I listened to the familiar sound of the 300-horsepower fuel-injected engine's steady drone, as we completed the runup near the end of the small bay. Take-off flaps, trim, and as we turned into the wind, the water rudders were lifted, full power was applied and the airplane quickly climbed on the step.

I was surprised, as YIG performs like a different airplane and is soon airborne. I found out it had a Horton STOL Kit, which has made a real performer out of this formerly sluggish 185. The kit consists of some minor changes to the wing surface that lowers the stall speed, enabling it to get off the water in a shorter distance.

As we made a climbing left turn, keeping the lake underneath us, we headed south to gain altitude and then headed northeast over the Hyland River. It was strange flying in the right seat as a passenger. Paul Stahnke was the pilot, and I was going along as extra baggage, courtesy of Jim Close, my old boss, who with Stan Britcut still runs Watson Lake Flying Service, the oldest flying company in the Yukon still owned by the original owners.

For many years I've wanted to return to Watson Lake and fly once again in the bush, to relive those feelings.

Those years as a bush pilot were the most exciting period of my life. They helped influence my thinking and my appreciation of nature, flying, and life, probably more than any other events in my life.

Climbing to 7,000 feet, the steady roar of the engine lulled me into a relaxed state of mind. As I looked up the Hyland River at the surrounding mountains and valleys, they looked so familiar and yet so strange. I then realized what this strange, almost out-of-body experience was! For years this scene and picture had been repeated in a recurring dream, and now I wasn't sure if it was another dream or reality. However, I was taking pictures, and that wasn't part of my dream, so maybe this was reality. Yes, a long aching feeling, deep inside my bones, was being satisfied as I was back and fulfilling a dream. I was like a kid again, excited, wide awake, and enjoying an exciting new adventure. Although it's the country I once flew over, this was a different time, and it's not really the same.

Many years have elapsed, but the same feeling and thoughts I had when I used to fly over this wilderness area were similar, yet somehow different, as if I've been in a time capsule for over a decade. The beauty of this country, far removed from the civilized world I now live in, is a refreshing experience and something I had needed for a long time. The country looked much the same. The same warm feelings were within as I scan the wilderness, as if I were back home!

After leaving Watson Lake in the fall of 1975, I ended up in Lake Havasu,

RETURN TO THE YUKON

Arizona, for part of the winter. I then returned to Spokane, Washington, in 1976. A short marriage with a beautiful woman and three children lasted about one year, and I returned to a quiet single life once again.

I made a couple trips flying charters in this area and in Alaska, but my heart wasn't in it. One memorable trip was with Bill Brooks, who owns and operates Brooks Seaplane Service at Coeur d'Alene Lake. We flew to Fortress Lake, B.C., which is on the west side of the Rocky Mountains in Southern B.C. We each flew a Cessna 185 and landed on Fortress Lake in a snowstorm. A few minutes before landing, Bill advised me to veer to the left, as the valley to the right was a box canyon. We stayed in a small cabin by this isolated, roadless, pristine wilderness lake. We caught two- and three-pound fat Eastern Brook trout and had a marvelous time in my favorite mountains. Bill is one of the most experienced and capable seaplane pilots I've met. He began flying the flying boats during the war and has a wealth of experience. Bill's son Grant flies for his dad and has the same smooth touch with a seaplane. It's a pleasure to watch this close-knit father and son team as they pursue their love of flying off beautiful Lake Coeur d'Alene.

The long hours and close calls as a bush pilot sent a message to my innermost being: it was time to make a change, and I knew it. The question was, after an exciting experience getting paid to do something I loved to do (flying an airplane), what could I possibly find to replace it? At age 37, with an aviation career behind me, what else could I qualify for? My father was in real estate, and I decided to give it a 2-year trial. I have been in it since.

My son and I have made several flights together in the float-equipped Cessna 185 N8367Q that I rent, flying out of its Newman Lake base.

On a beautiful sky-blue day in July of 1986, Scott and I arrived at Newman Lake and began preparing the Cessna 185 for a flight. Scott once again got to pump the floats, as in the old bush pilot days in the Yukon. He didn't complain, and, like me, was excited to be able to spend the day flying in this beautiful lake country of northern Washington and Idaho.

Scott spent two summers in Alaska—one of which was at Angoon, an Indian Village on Admirally Island, when he built a triplex for the government school teachers. He fished, hunted with the natives there and had a fabulous summer. Another summer he and two others bought a boat and crossed some treacherous seas to an island in southeast Alaska to finish a construction job. They encountered numerous grizzly bears and had many tales to tell of their northern wilderness experience. I went with Scott on one trip, and we visited our cabin on the Kispiox, then caught a ferry at Prince Rupert. We got off at Juneau, and I flew to Skagway while he went off to another adventure.

After a thorough Whitesitt preflight check (Once years ago I found loose bolts connecting the floats to the airplane.), pumping the floats, and checking for fuel contamination and quantity, oil level, control surfaces and satisfying ourselves that all was shipshape, we pushed away from the dock. Switches on, starter engaged, and after a few cranks, the engine coughed and roared into life. We turned to the north end of the lake. After the runup I turned the aircraft into the wind, lifting the water rudders and applied full throttle. With just the two of us, the seaplane climbed to the surface quickly, and we were rapidly picking up speed on the step. Back pressure on the elevator control and we flew off into the blue, sunny skies and began a lazy, climbing turn to the left on a northerly heading.

It's nice to have my son Scott, a young man of 26 years old, with me again in a seaplane. Scott built homes before graduating from Washington State University in architecture. He was 7 years old when he first flew with me in a Cessna 185 on floats, when I worked for Omineco Air Service in British Columbia.

As we flew toward Mt. Spokane, we had time to just sit back and enjoy the beautiful scenery of mountains, meadows and deep blue lakes. Twin Lakes and Spirit Lake were visible under our starboard wing. I turned the controls over to Scott and let him fly to the Furlott's. He has a good feel for the airplane; training on a glider and then on the J-3 taildragger has given him a good basic foundation on the use of the stick and rudder.

In a few minutes a blue, winding sliver of water could be seen to the north, as Pend Oreille River took form. Newport was visible in the distance, along the southern bank of the river. We were on a northwest course to the Furlott's summer place, which is located on the northern side of the river, nine miles downstream from Newport.

Memories are many as I think of those years as a bush pilot, flying seaplanes much as I'm doing now, and it feels soooo good! When I was 29, only a few years older than Scott is now, I started flying in the north country for Omineca Air Service out of Maclure Lake, near Smithers, B.C.

The old feelings came back, the marvel of flight—especially being in a seaplane once again, which is my favorite kind of flying because it's so free! You can land on rivers or lakes and don't have to hassle with busy airports, the last kind of free flight!

The Furlott's place popped into view. There were several families, all relatives, looking up as we flew over and made a descending turn into the wind. We flew over an island in the river and touched down just upstream from their place, then taxied up to the neighbor's dock. After coffee I began taking my family members for rides, three at a time. Nancy Furlott is my sister, and her husband's name is Doug. They have two sons, Jon and Andy. My mother and father were there and, after a bit of coaching, we were able to persuade Mom to go for a short flight. After a good meal, Scott and I departed for Liberty Lake, as I promised the County Park Ranger, Dan Miller, and his wife a seaplane ride.

I hike almost daily up a mountain that overlooks Liberty Lake, or I go up the Liberty Creek Trail that starts at the lake and goes south for many miles. These daily hikes along this trail, following a mountain stream that has many small waterfalls, is usually the highlight of my day, unless, of course, I go flying. This is a unique ecosystem. By the lake the trees are mostly pine. As you hike up the trail the valley narrows, more rain falls, and fir trees become visible. Farther up the trail a mile or so, cedar trees appear and then nice stands of cedars grow, which reminds me of the coast and the Olympic National Forest that I love. So often I'm filled with memories of long ago when Jim Goerz and I were 15 years old and began our dream of going north and becoming mountain men. Deer are abundant, Canada geese, ducks of various kinds, hawks, pheasant and other wildlife, as well as fish, make their home here. I have dreamed for years of flying over the county park and landing in a bay near the marsh that I often hike along. Now, the vision of the approach and lowering over the marsh and into the lake just down from Dan's house is reality, and it's really satisfying. We fly along the mountainside to the east of Liberty Lake, losing altitude, one notch of flap, slowing to 90 knots. Turning base over the south end of the marsh, another notch of flaps and turning final, we use three notches of flaps and slow to 75-80 knots on final and touch down about 500 feet from the beach, as there are boats and swimmers close to shore.

Because the lake is small, I left Scott on the shore. Dan and his wife climbed aboard, and we were soon airborne. I decided to fly to Harrison, Idaho, on beautiful Lake Coeur d'Alene, just across from my grandfather's cabin, where I spent my boyhood days and began my dreams of the north, 40 years before.

This was the first time I'd flown a plane to Harrison, and we flew along the west shore of the lake toward Spokane Point. As we neared Harrison, I could see Grandpa's cabin. The Millers and I were enjoying this beautiful view. Lake Coeur d'Alene is one of the five most beautiful lakes in the world, according to the encyclopedia.

Circling over the town of Harrison—which I love, mainly because it looks like it did in the forties and I have a hard time with change, and I always feel comfortable here—I checked the water for logs and deadheads, which are common on this lake. Letting down to the east, I flew over the bridge that spans the Coeur d'Alene River and flew low over the marsh near the lake, touching down a few hundred feet north of the Harrison Marina. We tied up to the dock and ,although there were some fancy yachts, we had the only craft that could fly, and I wouldn't trade it for any boat. We made a quick tour of the town and then headed back to Liberty Lake as darkness was fast approaching.

After landing at Liberty Lake, a very friendly and quite inebriated young woman came up and put her arms around me. She was vaguely familiar, but I couldn't place her. She finally told us who she was, and I know her husband well. They wanted a ride, but I had decided that because the night was fast approaching, Scott and I had to leave immediately and fly back to Newman Lake, as we didn't want to make a night landing.

FLIGHT OF THE RED BEAVER

We taxied out, applied full power and the 300-horsepower engine wrapped up, pulling us upon the step and with a little back pressure we lifted off. Ten minutes later we were tying up to the dock on Newman Lake where the owners of the plane, Mr. and Mrs. Babkirk, have a cabin. They teach school in Spokane and both love to fly their seaplane. They are a very friendly, open couple and nice to be around.

It was a super fun day. The nice thing about flying floats now is that I can pick sunny, good weather to fly in. It takes the pressure off and is much more enjoyable than when I was so busy flying up north, fighting weather and trying to keep up with all the charters. My love affair with flying continues, and it's so good to be back in a seaplane with Scott.

My high school buddy and long-time friend Gary Johnson, now retired from the Navy, stopped in Spokane and introduced me to his wife. He operates a service club for the Navy overseas. His attractive wife Anna, is from the Philippines.

One day a friend of mine, Jack Hammond, who is originally from Kalispel, Montana, and I were discussing our desire to go back in the sticks and get away from the hassle of people and things, during one of our fairly frequent lunches. I said, "Jack, I'm going up North this summer for sure. I need to see Watson Lake again and just get away." Jack's dream is to get a secluded place on a river, with a log cabin, and just sit and watch the river go by. My long-time friend Pete Anest (who checked me out in my Chief, in 1965) and I got together occasionally and talked about our first love, flying. Pete (Mr. Aviation) has almost 30,000 hours, some 7 years in the air. We made plans to do some flying in his airplane into Moose Creek, a wilderness strip in the mountains of Idaho.

The maps of B.C., the Yukon and the Northwest Territories that hang on my wall cause my mind to wander and relive those days when I was a bush pilot flying into those wilderness lakes. I begin to plan a trip and draw lines and measure distances. For many years I have planned trips back and several times had people lined up to go with me. I was going to rent a plane, but something always seemed to happen, preventing me from going, which was usually my friends canceling out.

I decided to rent a plane this summer and fly up, but the weather was bad the first week of July, 1987, and it was questionable whether I could get all the way up, as the weather system was over much of British Columbia.

Finally on July 6th, 1987, I purchased a ticket and decided to take the commercial airlines, departing the next morning. My mind travels to the North, and I go back to 1975, when I last lived in the Yukon.

At 5:46 a.m. on July 7th, 1987, I drove to the Spokane International Airport, on course to Watson Lake. A breakfast of oatmeal, whole wheat toast and coffee was soon finished, and the excitement of this trip, after all these years, made my juices flow with anticipation. I have pictures in my suitcase of the Red Beaver CF IBP to give to Jim Close. Maybe I will get to fly IBP once again; who knows?

AT 6:51 a.m. I boarded flight 1051, 16A window, port side, behind the wing. I

199

always try to get a seat in the back of the airplane. In case of a crash, that's the place farthest from impact and statistically the safest. We pilots make the worst passengers.

I wondered how Watson Lake looked. Would the log Watson Hotel be standing and in use? I would know in a few hours. I was a bit tired, as I could only get a catnap or two during the night. The flight was only a third full on this warm, sunny morning. Taxiing to the runway for departure, we lifted off at 7:10 a.m. Quilted fields and ponds and doll-size houses slipped under the wings as we rapidly made a climbing turn to the west on course to Seattle.

We were over the Cascade Mountain Range at 7:34 a.m., descending toward Seattle and SeaTac Airport. Majestic Mt. Rainier was off the port side, and it was overcast ahead, with glaciers visible on some of the mountains.

Descending now through the overcast, clouds were covering the airplane like soup; however, I could just see Lake Washington below, the floating bridge, and Bellevue. We were on final, and, even with the rotten weather, made a good safe landing.

While waiting for a ten o'clock departure at the terminal, I watched the Iran contra hearings. Colonel Oliver North was being quizzed, and he gave his answers. Obviously he is not dumb, admitting to some falsehoods he perpetrated. I withheld judgment until I learned more. I should sleep well tonight. I would get a room in Watson Lake and crash.

The sun was out, a good omen, and I had a window seat on the jet to Vancouver, B.C. We were about 3/4 full, as full power was applied. Take-off run took 34 seconds, and we made a left climbing turn in the soup, with a vapor trail visible off the wing tip. As we broke through the overcast, sky-blue sunshine and smooth air were noticeable at cruise altitude. Soon the pilot brought the power back and descended through the overcast. The ocean was visible off the port wing, almost in Canada.

Flaps were down as we made our final approach over the bay, and we were soon over the grass off the end of the approaching runway, then touching down at Vancouver International Airport. After lunch I boarded a Boeing 737 for Fort St. John in northern B.C. It was raining, and the ceiling was low. The weather was socked in from Vancouver most of the way to Fort St. John.

Puffy cotton-like clouds were visible, as they were over a decade ago on an early morning flight in the Beaver over the Turnagain River. Then I had soared in and around the top of the clouds—just me, the Red Beaver and the cloud tops. What a great memory! The weather was much better at Fort Nelson, and we made a good landing. I was told by a passenger that the Belvedere Hotel in Watson Lake burned down.

At almost 5:00 that evening, I was aboard another Boeing 737, taxiing for take-off. It is a 20-minute flight from Fort Nelson to Watson Lake. We were off after a ground run of 27 seconds and made a sharp turn, which felt like bush flying. Now the wonderful sun popped out, and a yellow seaplane was visible on a small lake far below and off the port wing. It's amazing what sunshine does to my spirits.

We began our let-down to Watson Lake at 5:17 p.m. The day had finally arrived, and I was excited. This was something I had to do, and I am thankful for the opportunity. At last, after about 12 years, I was back! Bright blue sky here above the clouds, and I could see another jet, south and higher up, leaving a contrail. The Liard River was visible below, and I could see the bridge over it as we were on final. The weather was good, but snow could be seen on the mountains over by the trench. This is familiar country. We touched down at 5:34 p.m. at Watson Lake Airport.

After leaving the airplane, I walked into the terminal where people were milling around, and only one face was familiar.

I rented a white Ford Taurus and drove to the seaplane dock where B.C. Yukon was based, but found out it belongs to the Forest Service and is no longer a flying operation. B.C. Yukon Air Service had abandoned Watson Lake and now operated out of Dease Lake, B.C.

Stan Britcut and Jim Close, owners of Watson Lake Flying Service, are the only ones with a seaplane operation at Watson Lake. I then drove south along Watson Lake, turned right off the main road, and drove into Watson Lake Flying Service seaplane base. As I walked into the office, Jim Close got up, and I put the overalls down on the counter that I brought from the states. "Hi Jim, here are the overalls I said I would bring." We shook hands and exchanged greetings, and at last I was back where so much of my past began. The map on the wall, the surrounding area and the other things in the room were like it was before, no visible change. The dock where the seaplanes are tied up was the same, only more weathered and almost under water. I noticed the Cessna 185 CF-YIG had been recently repainted. Jim told me that one of the pilots was on final last winter for the Watson Lake runway when the crankshaft broke. He wasn't able to make the runway, but set down short, and the plane flipped over. Fortunately no one was hurt, but that was the reason for the new paint job. It was sent south to be repaired, and repainted.

Jim said, "Lois is down in southern B.C. where we have a lake home, and you are welcome to stay with me. In fact, Lois has the spare bed made up, clean sheets and all." We talked until three in the morning, and Jim filled me in on the various outfitters and people I knew and what they had been doing the past 12 years.

Once again the cry of the loons drifted softly across the night waters of Watson Lake, and that was the only sound except for the many mosquitoes in Jim's lake home that were buzzing around my head when they weren't feeding off my exposed skin. But I was so tired that they weren't that much of a bother; after awhile I let them feed.

Jim and I spent many hours catching up on events that had happened in the past

12 years or so since I made my last flight here. The topic turned toward pilots that were killed in the area since I left. Coin Collison, a guide, was killed while piloting his own Super Cub. Murd McCaully, another outfitter I flew for, was killed near Fort St. John in bad weather. Matt, a young man from Switzerland who had flown the Super Cub on floats while I worked there, was killed in a glider crash in Switzerland. Jim showed me a letter his mother had sent Jim telling about the accident. Shortly after I left Watson Lake, on October 9th, 1975, Jim Thibaudeau and two hunters he was flying back to the base were killed in the Beech 18. Jim described the events to me: "They left Burnt Rose Lake, which is about 80 miles south of Watson Lake, but had to stop at Solitaire Lake, just a few miles north of there because of bad weather. When they departed for home, they suddenly ran into severe icing conditions, and the plane was rapidly covered with heavy ice. Not able to maintain altitude because of the accumulation of ice, Jim Thibaudeau tried to make an emergency landing in an open meadow (the throttles were wide open and the props at full RPM) and he almost made it before hitting a tree with one wing. This caused the airplane to roll and then crash inverted, about 40 miles south of Watson Lake." Jim Close thought that the ice on the wing that hit the tree was knocked off, and that was possibly the reason it rolled.

Jim Thibaudeau was well liked and respected in the community, as he was in the flying fraternity. He was an experienced bush pilot and knew the country well after his many years of flying out of Watson Lake. Late fall is a hazardous time, as there are hunters still to be flown out from the last hunts, and snow and icing conditions can occur at any moment.

In the early '70's while I was flying for Watson Lake Flying Services, Frank Stewart, an outfitter who was flying with a hunter, in the hunters own Super Cub, disappeared shortly after leaving Frank's base camp at Tuya Lake. Three days later the hard-to-spot, burnt wreckage and bodies were found on the slope of a mountain on the west side of Tuya Lake.

We were up at 6:00 a.m., because Jim is an early riser. We had coffee and headed down the hill to the seaplane base about 200 feet away, where Jim starts his usual busy day. Calls were made to various camps that have the base's frequency, and another day began.

I caught a ride to town with a man I knew from the old days and purchased post cards to send back home to relations and friends. I sat on the porch of the Watson Lake Hotel and watched the clouds breaking, with a blue sky showing through. A Loon was flying very low past the hotel, heading north toward the lake, and he gave out that lonely call. It was the first time I had heard a loon call while it was flying. I got up from the porch at the log hotel and headed past Dalziel's old log house, which is the oldest building in Watson Lake. Dal and his wife passed away several years ago, and his home is a museum now. His trophies can be viewed during the day. The second largest and fifth largest stone sheep ever taken are here in full mount, as well as a tiger and various North American and African trophies.

As I walked through town and past houses that I once lived in or where parties were held, it all seemed strange. Those people have gone, it's another time, many years removed from those old flying days.

Watson Lake seemed quieter, more subdued. It was not the wild frontier town I remembered of over a decade before, where a couple of drunken prospectors had a shoot-out on main street; of course, they couldn't hit anything they shot at, and both survived unhurt.

I stopped and visited with Wally Waulkonan, who was the airplane engineer for B.C. Yukon and then for Watson Lake Flying Service while I worked there. We had a good visit, and it was nice to see him and catch up. I then visited his wife Marge, who works for the Tourist Bureau. She gave me a tour and we had a nice visit, but, because she was working, it was too short. The town looked about the same, except that the Belvedere Hotel had burned down. It kind of reminds me of Harrison, Idaho, that I return to, with little changes; in fact, fewer people live there now than did years ago.

After a time, I began the drive back toward the airport, turning right at the Watson Lake Hotel and continued around the scenic lake road to the airport. I parked in front of Watson Lake Flying Services hangar. My favorite airplane, the Red Beaver CF-IBP was in the hangar with no engine. They were in the process of putting a rebuilt Pratt and Whitney R-985 engine into it. Jim Close said, "IBP has about 18,000 hours total time now, and with the new engine will soon be logging more." I sat in the cockpit, and it felt like old times, an old friend that never let me down. She's my favorite airplane of all time, and I'll never forget her!

When I asked Paul Stahnke, (one of Jim's pilots) about his flying in the Yukon and what he might have learned here, as opposed to the flying he did commercially on the coast of British Columbia, he replied: "When I flew for Stan and Jimmy, I learned a few important things. Only one of these seemed to be about flying. I learned to handle myself with river work. That is something we don't have on the coast. The main example set is the value of people." For example, he gave an illustration of a client of theirs that didn't have any money; they just kept flying for him, even though his bill was quite high. Paul said, "They consider it almost a duty to operate this way, and the trappers and other customers in the bush, without money, are treated in the same manner. It's like they're an institution, and maybe because they're business-men second, in the North, they outlasted everyone else. Sometimes nice guys finish first, but then they earned it!"

We also talked about the Beaver. The Canadian Prime Minister, Brian Mulroney, kicked off that country's Engineering Centennial year by presenting de Havilland of Canada President William B. Boggs with a trophy and certificate to commemo-rate the selection of the DHC-2 Beaver as one of the country's ten best engineering achievements of the last 100 years. The rugged Beaver first flew in 1947, spanning a 20-year production run of 1631. Worldwide 1,000 Beavers are still flying. Canada is home to more than 400 of the aircraft. After listening to Paul, I remembered quite clearly many, many people Jim and Stan flew for on credit and helped out when they were down on their luck.

That afternoon I departed with Paul Stahnke and the two Germans to Clark Lake in the Cessna 185. After take-off we flew over the Hyland River on a northeast course. I was thinking how fortunate I was to have flown here those many years, which was the end of a special era. Paul had a sure, smooth touch, and I relaxed.

The country is untouched; Clark Lake is isolated, and, as we flew over it, we could see a cow moose and calf. We touched down by another moose, but it just stared at us and seemed to say, "Who are you and what's up?" Not excited, just curious at the big bird landing on its lake. Taxiing toward the cabin at the west end, we saw two grown moose and glided near them until they seemed to fill up my camera lens before I clicked the shutter and hoped it would turn out. The cow was in good shape, and the bull was in magnificent condition. As they trotted away 30 yards or so, the fat rippled along his flank and then rolled as he picked up speed to his trotting gait. Moose have a deceptive trot that is actually much faster than it appears, probably due to their great size.

The cabin on Clark Lake was built by two Germans who lived and trapped here until the Game Department shut them down. We took pictures, and the two young German adventurers were let out. The stillness was complete, and a blanket of silence seemed so strange after coming here from a world of cars, trains and human voices.

After getting back into the Cessna we took off, climbing quickly to 6,000 feet, on course to Stewart Lake to see an old acquaintance. Don Taylor, a former representative for Watson Lake in the Yukon Legislature for 26 years, has a nice fishing lodge and cabin overlooking the lake. We landed in front of the lodge, and Don met us at the beach.

A loon was swimming out front and spread its wings, showing its beautiful coloring and sticking its chest out. "Hey, this is my lake," he seemed to say as he swam by on a westerly course.

Coffee and home-made peanut butter cookies were served by Don. We talked about the lodge, bookings and other topics. I noticed a picture on his wall of the Red Beaver CF-IBP on floats, flying next to some clouds. I thought, "I would sure like to have that same picture." Don later sent me the negative, and I had a large picture made that now hangs in my office. Don showed us around the various cabins. It's an excellent set up. The main lodge where Don lives, by himself, is comfortable, yet rustic, and blends in well with the wilderness and has a magnificent view of the lake. The prices are very reasonable, and the fishing is great. Our visit was too short, and we climbed back into our ship.

Full power and YIG quickly climbed to the surface, performing remarkably well with the new Horton STOL Kit. Slight back pressure on the elevator control and we became airborne. Once again the freedom of flight was mine, and I soon began a shallow climbing turn to the left, on a southerly heading. After reaching a safe cruising altitude, lively YIG was trimmed for level flight and I relaxed, enjoying the vast wilderness and my love of flying.

Plans began forming as pictures in my mind of future summers piloting a seaplane, hopefully my own, north of here up to the Arctic Ocean, to explore the northern Yukon Territory. A new dream begins! Caribou steak, wine and thick flying stories will be ours tonight as Paul and I are dining at Jim's place.

We began our descending, straight-in approach about five miles north. I eased the throttle back and put the flaps down. The scene was familiar, as the ribbon of water changed from a distant pond to a beautiful lake, and a slight ripple from a south wind took form. Leveling off several feet above the water, I continued back pressure on the elevator control, raising the nose to the landing attitude. Soon the floats touched the water gently, and we came off the step near the point of land that's just west of the seaplane base.

This was a special time, and I knew it! I was at peace with my world, and a special dream was fulfilled. I was back where my far northern adventure began, almost two decades ago, to a land called "The Yukon."

Scott's solo on his 16th birthday in this Piper J-3 Cub at Henley Areodrome, northern Idaho.

Larry and Bill Brooks in front of Bill's Cessna 185 Float Plane. Bill operates Brooks Seaplane base here on beautiful Lake Coeur d'Alene and also operates a Beaver float plane. The Coeur d'Alene Hotel is in the background.

Scott, Lake Sammamish, Bellevue, Wash. in the background. Scott graduated from nearby Lake Sammamish High School where he still holds the discus record.

Scott with a nice King Salmon in Alaska. After high school Scott and I bought a home in Greenacres, Wash. While attending Washington State University, he built homes during the summer in Alaska. Photo taken in the Angoon Alaska area.

My cousin Danny McDaniel and his bride Jackie, making a quick get away from a church in Spokane to the Coeur d'Alene Hotel on Lake Coeur d'Alene for their honeymoon.

My special sister Nancy with her son Andy and husband Doug Furlotte. They just purchased their dream land, on beautiful Pend Oreille River near Newport, Wash. where they plan on building their dream house.

The Cessna 185 float plane that Larry flew into the Furlott place on the Pend Oreille River. Nancy and her son Andy Furlott standing by the plane.

Jon Furlott, my nephew, on his first flight ever (in the Cessna 185), with Larry on Upper Priest Lake in northern Idaho, 1988.

Larry standing by N8367Q, the C-185 he flew to Spirit Lake, northern Idaho for lunch and a swim with a friend.

Scott's wedding to Stacy Hanson. Stacy's parents Dan and Rita are on the left, Scott's parents Kathy and Larry are on the right. January 18, 1987 Scott's wedding.

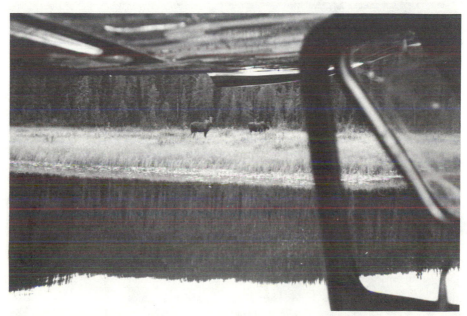

After a flight into Clark Lake N.W. Territories and while taxiing to the dock in the Cessna 185 float plane CF-YIG I was able to get this picture of a fat cow and bull moose. July 1987.

Watson Lake Flying Service pilot Paul Stahnke on the left and Larry with the C-185 on Clark Lake, N.W. Territories. July 1987.

Darell Nelson's rainbow spike camp in the heart of the Mackenzie Mountains near Divide Lake, N.W. Territories. Photo - Darell Nelson.

Darell and Rose Nelson, Northwest Territory Outfitters, at one of their hunting camps. Darell was named the Outstanding Outfitter of 1989 at the Spokane Bighorn Sportsman Show.

White wolf near Keel River, N.W. Territories. (Darell Nelson photo)

Frank Cooke's charted Beaver, that crashed at his sheep camp at Colt Lake, B.C.

Darell Nelson's hunting camp on Divide Lake, in the Mackenzie Mountains, N.W. Territories. This is the lake where we dropped off a prospector in the early 1970's that disappeared. I flew the Royal Canadian Mounted Police in, but we could not find him. His watch, glasses and tattored clothing were found in the 80's, perhaps he was the victim of a grizzly bear.

Curious 2 year old grizzly bears, near the Keel River, N.W. Territories.

213

Large Caribou on a glacier near Divide Lake, N.W. Territories. Photo courtesy of Darell Nelson.

CHAPTER XVI
FLIGHT TO THE ARCTIC

Lake Quinault Lodge sits peacefully in a natural clearing, with a splendid view of the quiet lake below, and blends well with the surrounding rain forest. The spirit of this fine old wood structure, built by artisans and craftsmen in 1926, is one of peace, and you feel protected from the outside world.

As Scott and I walked through the tall entry doors, escaping the damp outside world, my eyes were drawn to the heart of the lodge on the opposite wall: the massive but warm and friendly stone fireplace. Large logs burn for hours, and guests read, play chess, or take naps on one of the the old original wicker chairs as the fireplace crackles and gives off that special campfire glow.

People from many walks of life have entered these doors. President Franklin Roosevelt visited here in 1937, and that visit inspired the creation of Olympic National Park in 1938, the year I was born.

Scott came here with me for the first time when he was about fourteen years old, and we hiked in the nearby forest. I shared with him my love of this old place. When I was fifteen, I experienced this place for the first time and backpacked on nearby trails with my buddy Jim Goerz. In 1988 I hiked on a nearby trail and visited the lodge, celebrating the park's fiftieth anniversary, while I questioned my half century of life. It went so fast! Scott brought his wife Stacy here about a year ago, on their second wedding anniversay: looks like it's going to be a family tradition for generations to come.

We could hear the gently falling spring rain through the open window of our room as we unwound from our busy jobs, stretched lazily across our beds. Scott lay propped up on one elbow reading a book. I thought how much I appreciated our time together. This was the first time we had really been alone since his marriage over two years ago.

The sun peeked out, and we decided to take a hike on a nearby trail south of the lodge. The towering giants of spruce, fir, and cedar blocked out most of the brief sunlight, and the moss hung down from the trees much like in the bayous of the deep South. As we walked deeper into the old growth rain forest, we heard a roaring noise. The land dropped abruptly off to our left, and at the bottom a crystal clear, cascading stream tumbled over a series of large rocks to create beautiful waterfalls as it hurried on its journey to Lake Quinault and then to the nearby ocean. It felt good to have the companionship of my son on the trail, and I stopped to give him a hug and tell him how I felt.

215

As we left the thick canopy of trees, we met an older gentleman and a younger man loading timbers on a mechanical cart for a new trail they are working on that requires a bridge. The older man was a packer and was frustrated because the Park Service won't let him pack these timbers in, on his mules, which he assured us would be much quicker. He's like the old-time packers and outfitters I knew in the far North—honest, hard working men, with a love for the outdoors and a simpler way of life that's rapidly passing. We enjoyed listening to him talk about his mules, as one might talk about a special lady. "Well," he said with a twinkle in his eye, "this work keeps me out of trouble and off the streets."

We walked back to the lodge, where our biggest decision was when to go to the dining room and what to eat. Later we relaxed by the massive fireplace, and in the evening we played two games of chess, each winning a game. We didn't finish the last one until the early hours of the following morning.

After sleeping in and eating a breakfast of oatmeal, we drove around the east end of Lake Quinault and saw about twenty-five elk in excellent condition and a plump bobcat scurrying across the road and up a steep bank, obviously surprised by intruders. Driving along the coastal highway, we found a beach about one mile north of the Indian village of Lapush that was similar to the Oregon coast, with high rugged rock outcroppings along the shore and in the ocean. The beach had stretches of fine sand, small pebbles and larger rocks. Driftwood, including uprooted trees, was flung along the high tide mark next to the forest.

We chased the waves back into the ocean and then ran up the beach when another mighty wave came towering over us. We tried to outrun these monsters of the vast Pacific and managed on a few occasions to get soaked. We were like kids again as we climbed on rocks, discovering tide pools with starfish, crabs and interesting plant life of various kinds. We were drenched by the surf and the steady rain, but kept warm by running along the beach. I found a unique piece of driftwood that reminded me of the mythical thunderbird and carried it home.

We shared our thoughts about flying and perhaps one day buying another airplane. Scott mentioned the play we saw at the Gaslight Follies in Dawson City, the day we flew the twin Aztec CF-HIA there and then overnighted at Black Mike's. We talked about our goals and dreams in life. Scott hoped he and Stacy would return to Spokane in a few years and build a home on Lake Coeur d'Alene, and he wanted to open up his own architectural firm.

"Dad, let's backpack from this side and hike through the Olympic Mountains to the east end of the park with Stacy," Scott suggested.

"I'd enjoy that, Son, and we could hike through Enchanted Valley where there's an old hunting lodge, surrounded by several magnificent waterfalls. Jim and I overnighted there during that year when our dreams of becoming mountain men going north and living off the land began."

Jim Goerz now lives in the country east of Yakima and owns a home on a few acres with a peaceful creek running through the property. We keep in touch and talk about our days up North and our children.

After driving back to Renton, Washington, where Scott lives, we said our goodbyes, and I drove back to Spokane.

Summer arrived and passed swiftly as I was extremely busy, often working seven days a week. Preparations began in earnest to leave in July or by mid-August on my flight to the Arctic, but work and weather conditions delayed the departure.

The early morning sky was blood red, and it brought to mind my days as a sailor on a ship in the South Pacific and a saying we had: "Red skies at night, sailors' delight; red skies in the morning, sailors take warning." Was this ominous sky a warning, or was it just because I was tired from only two hours' sleep, with a delayed flight due to the weather a couple of days ago, that I felt superstitious at this moment?

After parking in front of the old concrete terminal building at Felts Field, I walked up the stairs to the second floor and through the door at the west end of the building to the Flight Service Station (FSS). "The weather looks good on your route; however, it's still down over the Rocky Mountains near Cranbrook," the young man said, after reading the latest hourly aviation report. I'd revised my intended route, and planned to fly to Penticton, Quesnel, and points north of there in British Columbia. I had planned to fly over the Rocky Mountains northeast of Cranbrook, but now elected to stay on the west side of my favorite mountains and hopefully cross the Continental Divide in north central British Columbia.

After filing a flight plan, I left the FSS, my boyhood juices flowing as I anticipated the departure for my long-awaited flight to the Arctic.

This old, solid building from my past felt good, like an old friend. Walking down the cement steps, sliding my hand over the iron hand rail, I sensed spirits of the past, memories. Many beginnings took place here at this special place called Felts Field in Spokane, Washington. I experienced my first flight on this field and later the first flying lesson from Russ Swanson on March 5, 1959, in an Aeronca Champ N84886. My first airplane, a J-3 Piper Cub N42200, was purchased here and tied down at the west end of the field. One spring day a mighty wind lifted up my bird, breaking the tiedown ropes, and deposited it at the far east end of the field, undamaged except for a small dent in the cowling. My private license was obtained here and my first flight with passengers began here. Later I obtained my multi-engine rating in a light twin-engine Piper Apache on this field.

Old pictures of early bi-wing airplanes hung on the lobby walls. Across the lobby on the west wall, a door opened into the cafe where pilots drank coffee and told tall tales of their exploits in the heavens. Old steam heaters lined the outside walls by the large framed windows that had thirty-two panes each. Sitting at a window table on the north side, you could see Beacon Hill and watch planes land and take off on the twin parallel runways that ran in easterly and westerly directions.

FLIGHT TO THE ARCTIC

When I was a boy, I rode my bike here with my good friend Bob Johnson, and we collected decals for our bikes from the flying school and watched in fascination as small trainers landed and took off. This was shortly after the war, when returning veterans were using their GI bills to obtain their pilots' licenses.

Wooden propellers hung over a doorway and an archway on the east side of the restaurant. An old advertisement from the Piper Aircraft Company that hung near the archway featured their new airplane, a Piper J-3, the same type my son soloed in on his sixteenth birthday.

"Piper leadership in the training of flyers has for years been an established fact. Hundreds of today's airline pilots, military pilots, and Army, Navy and civilian flight instructors secured their initial training in Piper planes. In the U.S. civilian pilot training progam, these dependable ships outnumber all other makes combined," the brochure read, and it showed a picture of a Cub flying off a runway.

A picture of Jack Fancher in a military flight uniform in France during World War I hung on the west wall with a picture of Lieutenant J.B. Felts in a leather helmet and flying goggles, this one taken about 1928. A couple of pictures of Charles Lindbergh hung on another wall, taken after some of his exploits.

Outside, just west of here, a stone marker about thirty feet high with clocks on three sides has a metal plaque that reads: "In memory of Lieutenant N.B. Nick Mamer, veteran flyer of the World War. Founder of Northwest Transcontinental Airways. Born January 28, 1889, died January 10, 1938." These men were all noted airmen from the Spokane area, from a time long past when aviation was in its infancy. When I was a boy about three years old I watched an air show here.

The airplane I rented from Felts Field aviation was a four-place Cessna 172, N734UW. It had a nose wheel (tricycle landing gear) and a steering wheel type control column. The familiar loading began: light gear in the baggage compartment in the rear of the cabin and the heavier gear toward the front, up against the back of the two front seats, to keep the CG (center of gravity) within safe operating limits.

The survival gear included a rifle, shells, fishing pole, lures, axe, hunting knife, dried food, bread, jam, honey, canned chicken, nuts, granola, eating utensils, downfilled parka, felt-lined boots, several changes of clothing and—on top—my link with the past, the blue downfilled sleeping bag that I purchased from the outfitter Tommy Walker; it was always part of my survival gear.

After unloading, I parked my favorite car, the blue 1978 Buick LaSabre that I purchased new and recently restored after some 250,000 miles, in a nearby parking lot. This car was a lot like the old Beaver: they're not made that way anymore. After walking back from the parking lot, I made a thorough check of my airplane. The white Cessna 172, with its orange trim speed line down each side of the fuselage, was a Sky Hawk II, an all-metal highwing airplane powered by a four-cyclinder Lycoming engine that develops 160-horsepower at 2700 rpm. The fuselage is twenty-six feet long, and the wing span is thirty-five feet. Its two wing tanks each hold twenty-one and one-half gallons for a total of forty-three gallons. However, only forty gallons are useable. I calculated that it would burn eight gallons per hour.

The empty weight is fourteen hundred pounds. The weight of full fuel, oil, pilot and baggage, which is called the useful load, is approximately 740 pounds, making our total take-off weight approximately twenty-two hundred pounds. The maximum take-off weight for this airplane, according to the flight manual, is twenty-three hundred pounds.

During my walk around, I checked each gas tank to make sure it was filled to the top (tanks topped). While checking the tires, I noticed one was low. The line boy added some air; I would need to keep an eye on it.

After satisfying myself the ship was safe, I climbed aboard through the left door and prepared to crank up the engine and head north.

Mixture rich, carb heat off, master switch on, four shots of prime, throttle cracked open. "Prop clear," I yelled out the window to advise anyone in the vicinity that the engine was starting and to stay clear of the prop. I turned the ignition to the far right, the starter kicked over, and the engine sputtered, coughed, and after a few seconds, settled down to a reassuring smooth roar. I glanced down at the oil pressure gauge to see that it was okay. Turning the radio on, I switched to Felts Ground Control on 121.7.

"Felts ground, this is Cessna seven three four uniform whiskey by Felts Field Aviation, requesting taxi instructions."

"Seven three four uniform whiskey, taxi to runway three left, cleared to cross extended center line of runway three right, wind calm," he replied.

"Roger, cleared to taxi runway three left," and I pushed the throttle in, pulling out of the parking area, turning left onto the taxiway heading west. Pulling off the taxiway near runway three left onto an asphalt apron, I began my own pre-take-off check list: (CIGFTPR) controls, instruments, gas, flaps, trim, prop, and run-up, in conjunction with the items on the printed check list in the plane--fasten safety belt, flight controls free and clear, flight instruments set, fuel valve (both), mixture rich below three thousand feet (Felts is less than two thousand.), flaps (check to make sure they work!), elevator trim (take-off position), throttle 1700 rpm, mag check for no more than 100 rpm, drop in each mag, and fifty rpm max difference between mags. All checked okay. Throttling back to one thousand rpm, I taxied to the edge of runway three left, short of a painted hold line. Normally on this airplane take-off is with no flaps, so the flaps were up.

Changing to the tower frequency of 119.0, I looked to the west for any aircraft on final for runway three left. "Felts tower, this is seven three four uniform whiskey, ready for take-off runway three left."

"Seven three four uniform whiskey, you are cleared for take-off on runway three left. Altimeter 3004, winds calm."

"Roger, cleared for take-off, three left, seven three four uniform whiskey," I acknowledged and once again looked to the west to make sure no one was on final as I increased throttle, taxiing to the center of the runway, and applied full power smoothly. My ship began moving slowly, sluggishly, but quickly picked up speed as I worked the rudder peddles to keep us centered down the runway. At fifty-five knots, with slight back pressure on the elevator control, the nose lifted skyward, and the main gear quickly followed, allowing me to enter another world as the earth slipped away beneath my wings. It was just the two of us, me and my sturdy ship. We were beginning to feel comfortable together in the air.

"Felts tower, seven three four uniform whiskey is airborne. Please open my flight plan at this time."

"Seven three four uniform whiskey, your flight plan is open. Do you wish to make a lefthand departure?"

"Roger, lefthand departure. Good day, sir," I replied as I begin a lazy, shallow, climbing lefthand turn to the north, crossing the Spokane River toward the heading of 305 degrees that would take me to Penticton, British Columbia, where I would clear customs and close my flight plan.

My flight journal began in the air: *"The time is 0740, September 1, 1989, as I leave Spokane, Washington behind and begin recording my feelings. Smoooooth air!"*

The long-awaited dream of flying to an Eskimo village in the far northwest corner of the Canadian Northwest Territories, Tuktoyaktuk, and then west to the village of Old Crow in the Yukon on the banks of the Porcupine River, was here before my eyes. If all went well, I would get my first sip of the Arctic Sea, as I planned to take a swallow.

My ear plugs drowned out some of the roaring engine noise and relieved some of the fatigue that's inherent in flying. The skies looked fairly clear to the west and northwest in the direction of Penticton, my destination.

The Cessna 172 has the best safety record of any airplane built, and I felt comfortable in my cockpit world, as if it was where I was supposed to be at this time in my life. After reaching cruising altitude I leaned the mixture, trimmed the airplane and relaxed.

"Passing over a lookout sixty-five miles out, I get my first view of Lake Roosevelt," That large body of water backed up behind the massive Grand Coulee Dam southwest of here. A few minutes later, *"The Indian town of Inchelium on the west shores of the lake slips beneath my wings at 0821."* At eighty-five hundred feet ASL (above sea level), we indicated one hundred knots with a power setting of 2375 rpm.

Once past the Kettle River Mountain Range, the town of Republic, Washington, appeared far below, directly ahead, telling me I was right on course.

"At 0837 Republic slips under my wings, in the silky smooth air." The valley running north of Republic was socked in with ground fog, but it was clear on my

course.

My mind went back in time some twenty-four years when I flew my newly purchased Aeronca Chief from Felts Field to Penticton, where I had to have it licensed for Canada and then flew it to Wookey's airstrip, south of our cabin on the Kispiox River. Scott was about five years old then; now he's twenty-nine and has his own family. Where does time go? What does it mean, this time and space phenomenon?

We have shared many flights together. The first one was shortly after I obtained my private pilot license when Scott was about three years old. We flew as a family in a Cessna 150 to an airstrip near Radium Hot Springs and soaked for a couple of days in the warm mineral springs.

At eighty-five hundred feet: *"It's great to be flying, and I feel confident, like I am in control. The skies are peaceful and smooth as we head northwest on our heading of 305 degrees."*

My feelings about this trip the past month had been mixed. My work, the weather and all the seemingly endless preparations, the survival gear, all the required maps, fuel stops, the avialability of gas, the vast wilderness I would fly over, hundreds of miles from airports--all that weighed heavy in my decision making and at times seemed overwhelming. My rational self said, "Larry, stay home, be practical. Why take unnecessary risks?"

Thankfully, my adventurous spirit won out and said, "Go for it!" One of the saddest things I can imagine for myself would be sitting in a rocking chair at an advanced age and saying to myself, "I wish I had flown to the Arctic when I had the opportunity. I wish I had taken the risk." The journey I've taken through life has been a marvelous adventure; I haven't missed much, and I didn't want to miss an Arctic experience.

Besides, it was time to take a break. Several of us who had worked together the past eight years or so had started a new company in March. So far the bills were being paid; the outlook was good. I'd worked long hours, often seven days a week, and a flying trip was a good change of pace.

Charles Lindbergh is a favorite hero of mine. After he became the first man to fly solo across the Atlantic, he and his wife Ann pioneered new air routes over the wilderness and the vast Pacific Ocean in an open cockpit seaplane. He said that if he could live as a pilot through ten years of flying (at a time when a pilot's life was very short), it would be worth far more than a long life of doing anything else.

Amelia Earhart lost her life in the vast Pacific Ocean trying to fly around the world when navigational aids were very primitive. She was doing what she obviously loved, *flying an airplane.*

About twenty percent of the pilots I flew with or knew, including the big game guides who flew their own planes, were killed in the far North. They loved to fly; it was their life, and they accepted the risk. Pilots had the most dangerous white collar jobs, and loggers had the most dangerous blue collar jobs, according to a recent study I read.

Flying high, heading north, gave me an incredible sense of freedom and anticipation.

Oliver passed under my port wing a few miles west, and Okanogan Lake lay directly ahead as we began descending and made preparations to land at the Penticton Airport. On 118.5 I call the tower, "Penticton Tower, this is Cessna seven three four uniform whiskey, ten miles south landing Penticton."

"Cessna November seven three four uniform whiskey, you're cleared to make a straight in approach, runway three four, altimeter three zero one two, winds from the north at three five zero, at ten knots."

Winds are given in knots and magnetic headings, as are the runways. The compass points to magnetic north, not true north. The true north heading from Felts to Penticton was 325 degrees. The easterly variation on my route was 20 degrees. To convert true to magnetic, you subtract easterly variation, giving me a magnetic heading of 305 degrees. The heading of 305 degrees took us on direct course to Penticton. Of course, if you have cross-winds, you have to adjust your heading to stay on your intended course.

"Roger, seven three four uniform whiskey, cleared for straight in approach runway three four," as I concentrated on making a good approach and, if fortune smiled, a smooth landing. I watched for other traffic. You're always responsible for your own ship and expected to fly in a safe manner. A tower or controller may tell you to do something, but you make the final decision whether it's safe or not. Controllers are only human; they make mistakes.

Flying over the lake south of the runway, we descended at five hundred feet a minute. As I flew over a paved road, I began to raise the nose with back pressure on the elevator control, rounding out to level flight several feet above the runway. Continuing the back pressure, I raised the nose to the landing attitude, and the "urk, squeal" of the main tires could be heard; they had to start rolling at forty-five knots or so as soon as they touched the runway.

'0912: Good approach--good landing--no bounce--safe flight. Cleared customs, nice man, ordered fuel. Weather is good, looks okay to Quesnel."

The flight was one and one-half hours. The Cessna 172 is an easy airplane to land, but it felt good to make a decent landing on the first Canadian airport I touched down upon.

"1022. Off Penticton O/C Quesnel," I noted in my journal as the airport faded away. My course followed the lake for twenty miles as we steered a heading of 315 degrees. Whiterock Mountain at 6130 feet stood below off my starboard wings. Douglas dropped away ten miles or so off my port wing.

"1100, estimated position, 16 miles south of Kamloops." At eighty-five hundred feet, my cruising altitude, I found myself above scattered to broken clouds with tops

at sixty-seven hundred feet. The air was smooth, and I relaxed and took in the vast surrounding sky, occasionally looking down through an opening at the earth far below. I glimpsed an occasional lake or mountain peak, but mostly my world was soft, fluffy, white clouds below and clear skies ahead above the tops.

The broken cloud cover turned to a solid overcast as far as I could see ahead and on either side. Having been caught in a similar situation when I was flying from Maclure Lake to the coast, I wanted no part of this and made a 180-degree turn. Within a few minutes we spiraled downward through an opening in the clouds and once again headed on our course to Quesnel, staying in visual contact with the earth below.

We were flying VFR (Visual Flight Rules), and I wanted to maintain eye contact with the ground as I was supposed to while flying in Canada. This airplane was not really equipped for instrument flying, and, even if it were, the Canadian regulations forbid single-engine airplanes to fly IFR (Instrument Flight Rules) in Canada. In the U.S., it's okay to fly single-engine IFR, and it's done on a regular basis by many pilots.

Passing over Kamloops, I pressed the mike button. "Kamloops radio, this is Cessna seven three four uniform whiskey, passing over the airport at this time."

They acknowledged my transmission report but called me several minutes later with a special Williams Lake Airport weather report. It didn't sound good, but Quesnel was north of Williams Lake and the present weather was okay, so I decided to continue.

"Roger, seven three four uniform whiskey," I replied. With some two hours sleep, fatigue was starting to catch up with me. The cups of coffee I had at the Penticton Airport were wearing off.

After passing Kamloops on a new course, the weather dropped lower and lower. I began dodging scud, although I kept heading on a west, northwest heading. My WAC chart didn't help much. The sectional chart was behind the seats in a sack, and I couldn't locate it even after I found the stack of maps, but I found it later. Small lakes a few hundred feet below were under my wings. I was back: just like old times, the same feelings, danger—yet the feeling I was in control as the pilot in command. I could crash, could lose it, but I was in the cockpit, and it was life. There were some roads, and "I could land on them if I had to," I said to myself.

I flew by an airport, figured out it was One Hundred Mile House, then flew north on towards Williams Lake. I flew over the town but didn't see the airport. The visibility was low in that direction, and the airport was at a higher altitude than the town. I landed at Quesnel, fueled up and filed a flight plan to Dawson Creek, where I wanted to see my friend and outfitter, Frank Cooke, so we could talk about old times.

Mother Earth felt good under my feet. But as always, after a bad weather trip passed and became a memory, the love of flying and the excitement of getting

FLIGHT TO THE ARCTIC

airborne on another adventure took over my senses. Flying out of Spokane, mostly on floats, I flew only when the weather was good and when I felt like flying. I'm a fair weather pilot. However, on this trip I felt that I might have some weather problems, especially at this time of year. I was willing to take that risk.

I crossed over the Frazer River by Sinclair Mills just before the Frazer makes a loop, changing course from a northwest direction to a southerly direction on its winding course to the Pacific Ocean. Looking toward the distant horizon, I picked out a course between two peaks on my heading. The Rocky Mountains slowly surrounded us on two sides, and a massive glacier appeared off my starboard wing at about eight thousand feet. I saw a woman's figure, made of glacier snow and ice, flying west, with her hair blowing eastward. I crossed the Continental Divide at 7,500 feet; now the creeks drained northeasterly into the Peace River that flows into the Arctic Ocean, my destination.

Flying through the Rockies I thought of my planned visit with my friend Frank Cooke. I had called Frank a while back and asked, "How are you feeling, Frank?"

"Well, I feel like I could hang a licking on any of the young fellows around here. Of course I can't, but I feel like I could." One day Frank was in a bar, and evidently someone called the Mounties about a disturbance. When two Mounties came through the front door, Frank went out the back door, with the Mounties in hot pursuit! The first Mounty out the door got into it with Frank and was knocked out. When his partner asked what happened, Frank replied, "Oh, I guess he stepped on his spurs."

In the late seventies Frank leased a rebuilt float-equipped Beaver and pilot from Vancouver, B.C., to haul hunters and supplies to his various camps. Frank described what happened:

"He took off from Colt Lake flying east toward the Kechika, with one passenger and his belongings. When he popped around the corner on that little lake to the edge of the main valley, he ran into a bank of fog. He banked her around in a real tight turn, and she stalled on him. They went into the rocks about a hundred yards from the camp. They weren't killed, but they were sure in bad shape. They couldn't get out on the radio at Colt Lake. Frankie helped carry them into the camp on a stretcher and had the guides and cook take care of them. He rode all night in the dark for forty miles to get to Scoop Lake and tell me what happened. It rained and snowed all night long as he was riding through those high mountains, and it took him twelve hours in the dark to get to Scoop Lake. When he got there, he was soaking wet and cold." Terry flew to Watson Lake, and help arrived by helicopter; the injured were successfully flown to a hospital and survived.

"I think about how tough my son Frankie really was and what a bushman. I think it's a crime he's gone. I loved him dearly." Young Frankie recently passed away.

We passed over the West Kiskatinaw River after leaving the eastern edge of the Rockies, some thirty-five to forty miles from my destination, Dawson Creek. The sky grew darker and darker, and the air began to buffet my ship. Daggers with jagged edges of white, searing streaks lit up the black void ahead; the air shook my cockpit world.

Flashbacks to the thunderstorm I entered early in my pilot career near Coldfish Lake warned me to turn away. I peeled off on a northwesterly heading to clearer, calmer air and headed for Fort Saint John, now my safe port in a storm even though it lay some fifty miles away. Fatigue once again set in; fighting weather was taking its toll on my tired body, and my thoughts were focused on a safe landing with a safe place to crash for the night.

"Fort Saint John radio, this is Cessna seven three four uniform whiskey, ten miles south, landing the airport," I called on 126.7.

"Cessna, November seven three four uniform whiskey, this is Fort Saint John radio. Contact the tower on 118.5."

Turning the frequency from 126.7 to 118.5 (as I only had one radio), I called the tower. Silence was my answer. Turning back to 126.7 I called, "Fort Saint John radio, this is uniform whiskey. Unable to raise the tower on 118.5."

"Roger, try again. Roger, try again," came the request as I kept changing channels, getting madder and madder. Those juicy, fat, long runways were below me a few miles away--*safety!* If they didn't quit fooling around with this very tired pilot, I would just peel off and land without permission from the tower! "There's no reported traffic; what a bunch of nerds," I thought to myself.

Finally the air radio operator informed me, "The tower will change to frequency 126.7."

"Finally, someone is making some sense and doing something constructive," I said to myself.

"Cessna seven three four uniform whiskey, this is the tower. You are cleared to land on runway one zero. What's your position?" a booming voice from the tower asked.

"Fort Saint John tower, seven three four uniform whiskey is five miles east. I'll make a lefthand base for runway one zero," I replied, relieved to finally get the okay to land.

The strain of only a few hours sleep, fighting weather and flying to an airport I hadn't planned on visiting, preferring to stay away from controlled, busy airports, was starting to wear me down physically and mentally.

After making a rather long base leg, I contacted the tower. "Fort Saint John tower, seven three four uniform whiskey turning final, runway one zero."

"Roger, check November seven three four uniform whiskey turning final on runway one zero." The Canadian radio operators always seemed to use the full number, including the "N" in transmissions.

I set up a short field approach, as my tired body wanted to get back to Mother Earth and rest as quickly as possible. Approaching at fifty-five knots and thirty degree flaps, we touched down by the numbers, 10 and made a respectable, shortfield landing.

"Seven three four uniform whiskey is on the ground. Please close my flight plan," my relieved, relaxed voice called into the mike.

"Roger, your flight plan is closed. You can refuel at Shell or Esso pumps, your choice," the tower replied.

Taxiing to the closest pumps at the Shell station, I pulled the mixture lean. The faithful airplane that I was becoming so fond of died, and silence enveloped pilot and airplane. Life was sweet once again. The feeling of letting it all hang out, relaxed and safe, was overwhelming. After on older gentleman topped my tanks, I gratefully tied the ship down securely.

Flying reminded me of my years as a sailor in the South Pacific. You couldn't really appreciate the beautiful sunrises and sunsets on a quiet sea until you had been through a few typhoons and experience the unleased fury of nature from the skies above, and had to strap youself into your bunk to keep from being thrown out of bed by the angry seas.

My tired mind and body said, "Larry, what are you doing? Go back to Spokane; be sensible. Why fight weather and head north at this late season when you could be in a nice, comfortable, safe place? Look at the money you would save." I seriously considered chucking the trip and flying home in the morning.

The ride to downtown Fort Saint John with a talkative truck driver, who was driving a cab so he could eat, was an interesting experience. It was his second day on the job; he was from another town and didn't know the location of the Cedar Lodge. After a search and a wrong turn, we found it. It was a clean room and cost only thirty-five dollars.

At 6:00 in the evening I lay down on the bed with my clothes on, since I wanted just a few minutes' rest before supper. At three the following morning my eyes opened. I realized that I had missed supper and had not experienced that kind of exhaustion since the days I flew long hours as a bush pilot out of Watson Lake.

Rousing lazily, but feeling rested, I climbed off the bed, sat on the floor and plotted my course to Fort Simpson in the Northwest Territories. Provided the weather was good, this would be my first leg this morning. At 5:15 a.m. I showered and shaved and left the motel in search of a place to have breakfast quickly before an early departure. After my good sleep, thoughts of turning back were gone, and I was looking forward to this new day.

A passing motorist on a street corner pointed out the Pioneer Inn, where I enjoyed a delicous breakfast of oatmeal with bananas, toast, bacon and good strong coffee. That started by boyhood juices flowing. I felt ready for a new adventure and eagerly anticipated the next leg of my journey north.

It was a strange world here at six in the morning--quiet streets, clouds moving toward the east, a light wind evident as I gazed out the restaurant window. A native man picked up aluminum cans from the nearby parking lot.

FLIGHT OF THE RED BEAVER

The North is a tough country, but the people are a hearty, optimistic lot and take it in stride. The language is strange—lots of "a's," Canadian accents, Canadian expressions. However, a real warmth and friendliness showed when I asked a question or entered into a conversation with a stranger.

Flying alone yesterday over my favorite Rocky Mountains was extremely satisfying, as was flying on the edge of that black, fierce lightning storm and successfully finding a safe haven for my ship. Satisfying, that is, once I was safely on the ground and had my ship securely tied down for the night. While others back home were doing normal, mundane things, I was flying across the skies on a fantastic adventure.

I caught a ride to the airport, where I walked into the flight service station and checked the weather on my intended route—Fort Simpson, Norman Wells, Inuvik and Tuktoyaktuk. The weather wasn't very good between here and Fort Nelson, so I waited another hour until 9:00 a.m. when it looked good on that course and into Fort Simpson, where I would refuel.

I took a preflight walk around, unsnapped the tiedown chains and crawled into my cockpit world and cranked up the engine. The tower gave me clearance to depart runway two zero, and in a few minutes I was airborne at 9:04 a.m., the time the tower activated my flight plan.

At 9:20, I called, "Fort Saint John radio, this is seven three four uniform whiskey, at sixty-five hundred feet, twenty miles north of the airport, O/C Fort Simpson."

"Roger, November seven three four uniform whiskey, thanks," a voice replied through my speaker.

I continued writing in my journal. *"Smooth air, some scattered rain storms, looks dark toward Fort Nelson which is northwest of my course. Can feel a few bumps as I get close to a rain shower.*

"Looks good ahead, it was great to be in the air again, alone with my ship, and look at God's wonderful creation below and the sky and clouds surrounding my cockpit world. Patchwork like farm fields abound in this Peace River country far below; it was fairly flat country.

"Indicating 100 knots airspeed, getting to know the airplane better. Nice bird. Some fog over the mighty Peace River, some rain (virga) falling out of a cloud off my port wing, a few bumps, O/C 300 degrees looks like smooth sailing ahead."

"Thoughts about quitting, going home after yesterday's weather and fatigue left, and I decided to go for it, grab on to life."

At 10:16 I wrote, *"6700 feet--rugged Rockies off my port wing parallel to my course. Haven't seen houses or people for some time. Isolation, peace, tranquility."*

Something strange! "What's that road doing crossing under my craft?" I asked myself. Whoops! I goofed! My intended heading should be 330 degrees. I'd even marked it on my map next to the line drawn from Fort Saint John to Fort Simpson. But for some reason, my brain said to follow a heading of 300 degrees. I was now

FLIGHT TO THE ARCTIC

several miles west of my intended course and promptly changed my heading, feeling foolish and dumbfounded. It didn't create a problem this time; the weather was good, and I had plenty of fuel. However, it could have been critical at another time when fuel might have been low or the weather bad. It made me pay close attention, and I watched my heading with a critical eye.

We left British Columbia, crossing into the Northwest Territories at 11:55 a.m. This territory has about fifty-two thousand people living in 1,271,438 square miles. Nineteen thousand of the people are Inuit (Eskimo); 13,500 are Indians. It's governed by a commission whose policy is determined by the Governor General in council, or the Ministry of Indian Affairs and Northern Development, and by a twenty-two-member territorial council. Over two-thirds of the mineral wealth consists of zinc, lead, and gold.

"1155 descending. We fly over the west shore of the large body of water called Trout Lake, 85 miles south of Fort Simpson. The height of the hills are 1,000 feet to 2,500 feet or so."

The rugged Mackenzie Mountains join the Rocky Mountains just west of here. The Mackenzie Mountains were the toughest mountains I ever flew or navigated in, and I almost lost my life once eighty miles west of here. I was flying out of Headless Valley (Deadman's Valley) during bad weather in the Red Beaver.

The weather was excellent, with clear skies. I passed a few scattered fair weather cumulus. I loved the feeling of flight, so free, as I soared around the clouds—white, friendly clouds, as opposed to the dark, ugly, angry clouds of yesterday.

"Fort Simpson radio, this is Cessna seven three four uniform whiskey, ten miles south, landing Fort Simpson," I called into the mike.

The familiar long identification reply from the radio operator boomed back, "Cessna November seven three four uniform whiskey. Reported traffic, a Cessna 180, doing touch and goes. Winds from the southeast favoring runway 13. Report on final. What's your ETA?"

"Roger, on the traffic. Estimating the airport in seven minutes," I replied.

I landed at 12:43 p.m. at Fort Simpson. I last flew into this airport with the twin-engine Aztec CH-HIA. Landing here brought back happy memories of another life. I landed near the town some five miles away with the Red Beaver on the mighty Mackenzie River many times while flying for Watson Lake Flying Service.

A young man topped my tanks, and I squared up with him in the lobby of the airport. The warm T-shirt weather felt like the middle of summer on this lazy September day.

I filed a flight plan from Fort Simpson to Inuvik with a stop on the way at Norman Wells for fuel, then climbed once again into the familiar cockpit. The engine started smoothly and reassuringly after a couple of cranks. The elevation here is only 555 feet. In this dense air, we were airborne after a short take-off run from runway 13 at 1343 O/C Norman Wells. My craft climbed rapidly as we made a left climbing turn and picked up our new compass heading of 292 degrees.

My flight journal continued. *"On my heading of 292 degrees, I report my position over Willow Lake River. High Land and Greasy Lakes are a few miles ahead. No sign of man anywhere; wilderness abounds.*

"1432. Passing over Greasy Lake at 8,100 feet. At 1452 we pass over Wrigley which is located on the east bank of the Mackenzie River. I flew the float-equipped Beech 18 CF-NCL in and out of here on a freight haul for an outfitter in the early seventies and know the area well. I can see the beach on this mighty Mackenzie River where I tied up NCL at night."

The leg from Fort Simpson to Wrigley was away from the river, as the Mackenzie made a large bend to the west from my course. The magnitude and the solitude of this enormous empty land penetrated my being, and I felt my size and insignificance in this wilderness that could easily swallow me up without a trace.

My survival gear--food for a month, rifle, fishing pole, tent, downfilled bag, matches, felt-lined boots, knife, eating utensils--didn't seem like much if I were to go down.

"1517; passing over the Red Stone River at 7,200 feet. Lots of smoke, perhaps from the Yukon Territory west of here. There are many forest fires reported burning there. I'm right on course, watching it closely. The Keel River passes underneath, far below near where it enters the Mackenzie." Many years ago, Kathy, Scott and I flew into Norm Simmon's camp on this raging river and spent the night.

Recently I had a welcome encounter with an outfitter who has a camp upstream on the Keel River. At the Spokane Fairgrounds where the Bighorn Sportsman Show was in progress, I noticed a display booth with a sign saying, "Northwest Territory Outfitters." I walked up to the display and caught the eye of the man in the booth. Our eyes locked for several moments.

The bearded man with the cowboy hat spoke first, "You're...Larry...Larry...White."

I replied, "Larry Whitesitt."

He said, "I'm Darrell Nelson; you rescued me and the horses when several of us were trapped on that island in the Nahanni River. When I saw the Beaver fly overhead after being trapped on the island for three days, it was like an angel of deliverance." Emotions swelled as we relived those years on the Nahanni and in the Mackenzie Mountains.

Darrell introduced me to his wife Rose, and we started reminiscing about different people, past experiences and the present. After purchasing Chuck Hayward's outfit at Little Dal Lake, Darrell sold out to his partner. In 1983 he purchased Rex Logan's guiding outfit. The main camp was located on the Keel River, and I knew it well, having landed there several times.

Darrell still flew his own Maule airplane on floats, as he had when I knew him in the early seventies. We had dinner at the Coeur d'Alene Hotel and swapped flying stores before they left Spokane. It was like a breath of fresh air. They invited me to visit their camps on the Keel River and Divide Lakes during the hunting season.

Darell related a story to me. "I took off one day with Chuck Hayward from that rough strip on the side of the mountain south of Little Dal Lake in my Maule. Taking off downhill we hit some bumps and a ditch, bounced in the air and I thought, 'Hey were flying.' but we really weren't yet. We ripped the fabric off the belly and tore the tail wheel off on a tree top. Little Dal Lake was frozen so I landed there. We had some tape, and we wound it around and around the airplane. Chuck and I took off from Little Dal Lake and headed home to Alberta. Later Chuck noticed an airport, 'Should we land there, Darell?' Just then the tape blew off and the roar of the wind was deafening and the belly beneath opened up: I thought we were goners! We were able to land, taped her up again and made it home safe." Darell has a ranch in Alberta and his own landing strip. Watson Lake Flying Service still flies his hunters into the camps in the Mackenzie Mountains, as they have been doing since the '70's.

A couple of weeks later I received a note and a trip ticket that I had made out to the South Nahanni Outfitters, dated July 1, 1975, with the Beaver FLN from Watson Lake to Little Dal Lake, and to the South Nahanni River for Darrell.

Fort Norman was off my starboard wing twenty minutes later. I used to fly into this native village in the early seventies in a float-equipped Beaver. At that time, behind almost every cabin lined along the banks of the river were fifteen or twenty dogs—wild wolf-like sled dogs. They were mangy looking in the hot summer sun, which never does set and can cause temperatures in the nineties.

South and west of Norman Wells I counted twelve forest fires burning.

"Norman Wells radio, this is Cessna seven three four uniform whiskey, fifteen miles southwest landing the airport."

"November seven three four uniform whiskey, roger," a woman's voice replied and gave the wind, "strong out of the east and gusting."

On final, the force of the wind was evident as my ground speed was quite low, and we got a few good jolts. However, the wind blew pretty much down the runway, fairly steady, and I used only a little flap. My reliable bird made an honest, safe landing. The flight from Fort Simpson to here was 2.7 hours.

Taxiing to the pump at midfield, I had the tanks topped and walked to the air radio station, where I learned the latest weather report to Inuvik and Tuktoyaktuk was good. Earlier in the day Tuktoyaktuk was down in fog, but at 2:00 p.m. the fog lifted, and it was now fairly clear.

In 1920, an oil rush occurred near here, and the first bush pilots came into the country, hired by Imperial Oil Company of Canada when the company brought in the first well. Two Junkers (German-built airplanes) named Vic and Rene were piloted by G.W. Gorman and E.G. Fullerton.

On September 6, 1928, a famous early bush pilot named Punch Dickens landed at Fort Simpson after a three-thousand-mile flight from Winnipeg with two American mining men in only twenty-seven hours. That was a trip that, before the airplane, took just about a year.

Walking back to my ship, I looked toward the east and thought of the days when I flew the Red Beaver into a nearby lake close to town. Those were memorable flights for the game biologist Norm Simmons, from here to the Keel River where he had his main camp and was involved in a study of Dal sheep for the federal government.

After take-off I turned left almost 180 degrees to my new heading of 285 degrees--a heading that would take me over Fort Good Hope, as far north as I have flown in the Territories. Once I flew several miles over the Arctic Circle north of Fairbanks in a Cessna 206 on a cold winter day. I was excited to see what the country was like north of Good Hope. The distance there was eighty-two miles, about a forty-five-minute flight.

The Mackenzie River bent to the left, and we passed over several good-sized lakes. Because of increasing dense smoke, visibility below was not very good. It was hazy, not a good day for pictures, I thought, as I continued to click the shutter.

My VOR was tuned to the Fort Good Hope station on 112.3, and the needle stayed close to center on my heading of 285 degrees, which was also plugged into the VOR dial. Even though I hadn't used or relied much on my single VOR, I decided to use it as a backup system to my normal familiar navigation method of map reading.

"My altitude is over 8,000 ft as I fly over Fort Good Hope, and the VOR swings from the TO to the FROM position, indicating it was working properly. My heading changes slightly to 279 degrees which will take me to Inuvik where I plan to refuel before flying on to Tuktoyaktuk."

My journal entry from the air continues....*"Never been this far north in the Northwest or Yukon Territories, seemingly endless lakes. 1805: seems chilly at this high 8,200 ft altitude. Mighty Mackenzie off the starboard wing. Much smoke-- VERY HAPPY."* I thought of Scott and wished he could be here with me.

The constant steady roar of the engines was reassuring. However, just like in the old days as a bush pilot, when there was no sign of man or civilization, I seemed to hear a roughness in the engine from time to time. Some things never change.

We were about 125 miles south of the Beaufort Sea. The weather looked good toward Tuktoyaktuk. "Inuvik radio, this is Cessna seven three four uniform whiskey, thirty miles southeast."

"Cessna November three four uniform whiskey, check you thirty miles southeast," they replied.

"Roger, I'm changing my flight plan to Tuktoyaktuk at this time. Estimate Tuktoyaktuk in about forty-five minutes."

"November seven three four uniform whiskey, your flight plan is changed to

FLIGHT TO THE ARCTIC

Tuktoyaktuk. ETA four-five minutes."

"Roger, thanks, seven three four uniform whiskey," I acknowledged.

"1920: passing Stugi Lake, seventy miles to Tuktoyaktuk. Fantastic...unbelievable."

The Mackenzie River delta spread before me in an unbelievable array of waterways and lakes. Ahead, Eskimo Lake, a saltwater lake, reached to the Arctic Sea.

My camera was getting a good workout...click, click, click, click. I couldn't believe my eyes!

"Tuktoyaktuk radio, this is Cessna seven three four uniform whiskey, twenty miles south. Estimating the airport in ten minutes," I called as my destination neared.

The shining expanse of the Beaufort Sea (Arctic Ocean) stretched as far as I could see to the north and to the west where the Arctic sun hung over the horizon, where the sea disappeared from view. It was just after 8:00 p.m., and my dream of seeing the Arctic Ocean had been fulfilled. I was ecstatic; if I were on the ground, I would be jumping for joy!

FLIGHT OF THE RED BEAVER

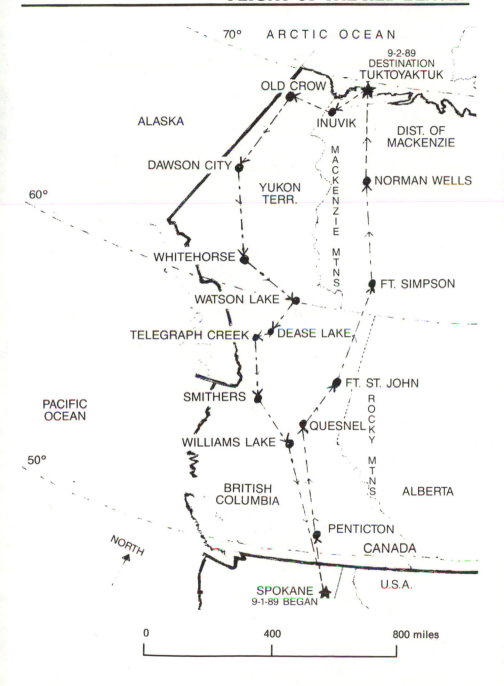

70° A R C T I C   O C E A N

9-2-89
DESTINATION
TUKTOYAKTUK

OLD CROW

ALASKA

INUVIK

DIST. OF
MACKENZIE

DAWSON CITY

60°

YUKON
TERR.

M
A
C
K
E
N
Z
I
E

M
T
N
S

NORMAN WELLS

WHITEHORSE

FT. SIMPSON

WATSON LAKE

TELEGRAPH CREEK

DEASE LAKE

FT. ST. JOHN

PACIFIC
OCEAN

SMITHERS

QUESNEL

R
O
C
K
Y

M
T
N
S

WILLIAMS LAKE

50°

BRITISH
COLUMBIA

ALBERTA

PENTICTON

NORTH

CANADA

U.S.A.

SPOKANE
9-1-89 BEGAN

0   400   800 miles

233

CHAPTER XVII
TUKTOYAKTUK

The small village of Tuktoyaktuk glistened in the late evening Arctic sun. Diamondlike, the shimmering waters of the sea—almost too bright to look at—filled my camera lens as I snapped pictures of this Arctic wonderland. After talking to the air radio operator and getting the wind direction and runway in use, I flew over town and circled wide, passing to the east of the gravel airstrip that extended to the lapping waters of the vast Arctic Ocean. Still I snapped pictures. The wind was strong, about fifteen to twenty knots from the northeast, and blew across runway 09, a strong crosswind, I quickly discovered. We crabbed toward the north, about 45 degrees, on final, and straightened out shortly before touchdown, keeping the port (windward) wing down to keep from drifting sideways and using right rudder to keep the nose headed straight down the runway. We were one, my ship and I, an extension of each other. We touched on first the left wheel, then the right wheel and lastly the nose wheel. My ship handled the crosswind landing well and made a sure, safe, smooth landing. She's a great ship!

Taxiing to the east side of the air radio building, a trailer, I pulled the mixture to full lean, and the engine quit. Master switch off, radio switch off. I sat back and tried to comprehend that I had at last arrived at the Arctic.

The tiedown consisted of two truck tires filled with concrete that I dragged under each wing and tied securely to the metal rings at the top of the wing struts designed for that purpose.

I asked a few questions of the radio operator. "Where's the hotel, and where do I get gas?"

"The hotel is a ten-minute walk down that road; it's an orange building. Didn't anyone tell you, you can't buy fuel at Tuktoyaktuk?"

"Oh! Great," I said to myself, "no gas."

"Well, I was going to stop at Inuvik but changed my mind shortly before landing there and continued on to Tuktoyaktuk after changing my flight plan," I replied. My tanks indicated a bit over one-quarter full, enough to fly to Inuvik, but not much to put in the bank in case of bad weather or disorientation in the maze of waterways that make up the MacKenzie River delta.

As I walked down the dirt road, I gaped in awe at the Arctic setting, like no place I've ever seen or been to in my life. The sun was close to setting over the Arctic Ocean, and the water glistened like fine jewels. The land was mostly flat. A huge log home sat perched on the highest point of land, about one hundred feet above the sea. Because the village is far north of the tree line, it seemed really strange to see a log home, and I wondered who might live there--must be someone who was somebody. Most of the houses were small and had small numbers on them, like a motel. They were owned by the government and rented to the Eskimos, I was told.

Seeing an Eskimo intently working on a snowmobile, I decided to introduce myself and perhaps take some pictures.

"Hi, I'm Larry. What's your name?" I asked.

"I'm George Taylor."

"Say, will you take my picture over there, so I can get the Arctic sun in the background?"

"Sure."

After he snapped my picture, I took a couple of him. George was warm and friendly, and after a short visit I continued down the winding gravel road to the Tuktoyaktuk Inn.

Walking up to the hotel, I noticed the restaurant part has a sign hanging in the window that read, "Sorry, closed." The building was a double-wide trailer, divided into the restaurant, an office and several rooms, some with baths, the others with a common bathroom down the hall.

Walking through the door, I asked a man about forty years old, "Can I get a room?"

"Sure, it's 110 dollars a night," was the quick reply. "You're in luck; it's been filled up."

"Take a Visa card?"

"Sure. Fill out this form."

"Say, could I get a sandwich?"

"Yes, okay, I'm sure the cook can fix you up."

My sandwich consisted of cold Spam. I hate Spam but ate part of it and acted polite. The pie was good, though. I hit the sack at 10:00 p.m. and quickly fell into a deep sleep.

Sunday, September 3, 1989: Slowly, like a dream, the steady patter of rain invaded my sleep world. I just knew with a sinking feeling I was going to be stuck in Tuktoyaktuk for a time. Slowly slipping out of bed and going to the window, I confirmed my suspicion: the clouds and rain and fog were like soup close to the ground.

"Well, Larry," I said to myself, "you might as well go back to bed and finish your deep sleep." Later in the day, after a shower, I ate another good piece of pie. The weather was still bad. Two twin-engine Islanders had tried to fly in from Inuvik but had to turn back. "The weather is right down to the deck," they called to the radio operator at Tuktoyaktuk.

I changed my white, mud-splattered jeans for a dark green pair and ate two delicious jam and honey sandwiches in the airplane, some granola, canned chicken, nuts and water out of the canteen as I sat in the pilot's seat. It was a feast. Food, water, dry, warm clothes and a dry place to sleep are all a person really needs.

Several people told me to see Eddie Gruben, the man who owned the large two-story log home I had seen earlier. He was an interesting Eskimo who reportedly could tell everything about the history of this place.

Walking northeast along the dirt road toward the point of land that joins the Arctic Ocean, I looked at the houses and the institutions. A small wooden ship, beached and set on a platform, had an inscription that read: "Our Lady of Lourdes. Built in Oakland, California, 1930. Supply ship for Catholic Mission. 37 years in the Beaufort Sea. Commanded by Rev. Binameomi OMI. Rev. J. Frenks OMI." A white picket fence in front of the ship stood guard over a Catholic priest's grave. A short distance away lay the graveyard for the community, on a knoll overlooking the Beaufort Sea to the north.

Walking to the east on a low narrow fingerlike spit of land, I reached down and scooped some water for my drink of the Arctic Ocean. It was salty but well worth the trip.

Strips of fish hung to dry in some old wooden cabins on this point, and a few dogs were tied up behind some of the Eskimo wooden frame buildings. I headed toward the towering log home of Eddie Gruben, determined to knock on the door and see if I could find out about this unusual man.

As I approached Eddie's home, I noticed a couple of seaplanes tied up in a little saltwater bay behind the house. The closest one was a Cessna 206 pulled up on the beach for repairs. The other was a Cessna 185 tied to a dock. On the north side of Eddie's home stood a collection of heavy duty cats, trucks and other equipment near a shop building.

I felt like an outsider, an intruder, as I walked up the steps and across the large wooden porch and knocked. Nothing! Finally, a young may opened the door and invited me in.

"Hi, I'm Larry," I said, as I stuck out my hand.

He replied, "I'm Scott. I'm a pilot taking a few flights for the owner of the charter company, James Gruben, Eddie's son, in that Cessna 185 out back."

"Hi, Eddie?" I asked a native man sitting on a nearby couch.

"No, Eddie's upstairs, playing pool," he replied.

The south wall of the living room was covered with various small animals and a large caribou head with an unusual rack. In one corner was a mounted musk ox head. A huge mounted lake trout hung over the doorway into the kitchen.

A handsome Eskimo man, in his sixties, I judged, walked through the doorway by the musk ox and sat down on a couch near me. I was sitting on the floor. "I'm Eddie Gruben."

"I'm Larry," I said and walked over and shook hands. "Eddie, I flew up here yesterday for the first time from Spokane, and I wondered if you would tell me about the early days, what it was like around here."

"Sure," came his open, friendly voice. I sat back on the floor and began to write in my yellow notebook journal.

"I was born near here in 1919 at the mouth of the MacKenzie River, near where it empties into Kugmalit Bay, a place called Kittigazuit. There was a Hudson Bay store there at that time. The village was abandoned, and the people resettled here.

"I trapped and spent my days as a young man in the bush. I didn't take money from the government but earned what I have. Our ways changed forever in 1954 and 1955 when the DEW (Defense Early Warning) line came through.

"We Eskimos would spend maybe one or two weeks out on our trap lines, maybe get a couple of white fox and earn eight to sixteen dollars each. Now we could make a dollar fifty an hour--big money in those days. The Eskimos started coming into Tuktoyaktuk when the DEW line was being constructed and left their old ways forever.

"Prime Minister Trudeau visited me, and we sat out back of the house on that knoll that overlooks the bay. He told me, 'Eddie, there are great changes that will take place in the world, changes coming to the north, and you should get in on the action.' I took his advice, and now I have multimillion-dollar contracts with the oil companies. I own millions of dollars of equipment and earned it myself. I never asked the government for help, but earned my start from trapping. I get one thousand dollars per yard for gravel. I helped my son get started in the flying business. My son James calls his flying company Amaulik Air Service. My son is a good pilot; he's a safe pilot. My wife died a couple of years ago."

"Eddie, what about polar bear hunts?" I asked.

"Oh, the village is allowed twenty-six polar bear permits. The Eskimos can kill them for their own use and sell the hides, or they can take out big game trophy hunters. But they have to use their dog sleds. It gives the bear a better chance, and it's required by the government.

"My father was a German; my mother was an Eskimo. There's not hardly any fullblooded Eskimos, are there?" he asked another man in the room.

"No," replied the other man.

"See these logs for my house? See how even in size each one is? They were cut west of Fort Liard (700 or so miles, maybe twice that by river) in the Mackenzie Mountains and were floated down in a big bundle. They broke loose, and I had to hire a barge to deliver them here. It cost me twenty-seven thousand dollars. The total cost of the logs and construction of my home was about seven hundred thousand dollars. I own it, and I don't owe the government anything."

Eddie was sixty-nine years old but looked and acted much younger. A twinkle came to his eyes as he talked about a young woman he knew--quite well!

"You know we're all alike, you and I and everyone else! Those missionaries here, they're no different. Human nature is the same in all of us."

FLIGHT OF THE RED BEAVER

"I agree, Eddie."

Eddie loved to talk about flying. "I'm thinking about buying my son James a Twin Otter." (An expensive twin-engine STOL plane, it's a terrific performer and works great on floats, as well as wheels.)

We climbed upstairs, where Eddie and a couple of his friends played pool. I excused myself, said goodbye and thanked Eddie for his hospitality before walking to the Tuktoyaktuk Hotel.

"September 3, 1989: Sitting on my $110.00 a night bed, room 110, at the Tuktoyaktuk Inn, weathered in, winds blowing, mostly driving rain, since I arrived.

"2130--seems longer since I arrived, but it's only a bit over 24 hours ago that I landed in a strong crosswind on runway 09."

As a young man I read books by Connie and Bud Hemerlicks about their lives, mostly in Alaska, with the Eskimos right after World War II. They started out with a brand new Cessna two-place 120 on floats and later bought a Cessna 170 four-place airplane when they first came out. I was thrilled to read about their adventures in the Arctic and the wandering life of the nomadic Eskimos of that time. I felt very fortunate to be here and meet some Eskimos and hear stories of their past way of life.

"Monday, September 4, 1989. Tukoyaktuk Hotel: Dogs barking, trucks going by. Only about five miles of road now; however, during winter when it freezes up during January and February they can drive on the river road of ice from here to Inuvik." I was told the winters were much warmer the past several years and it was much later in the winter before the water froze. Perhaps the greenhouse effect? One reason food was so expensive was the freight. Most nonperishable freight was shipped in on the ocean. It cost sixty cents a pound to haul freight to Inuvik by truck, but the cost was $1.80 by the time it was flown from Inuvik to here, which they had to do for milk and other fresh food.

The menu in the tiny restaurant read, "All our burgers are available with your choice of either caribou or beef." Pie was $3.50--$4.50 with ice cream. Cigarettes were $5.00.

I located a sectional chart from Scott, a twenty-six-year-old pilot. It was great to have a detailed map, especially with all the lakes and waterways in the delta, as the only map I had was a WAC chart that covered twice the area and was much less detailed. I had sectional charts for much of the country I flew over, but was unable to purchase sectionals for some areas, as they didn't have any in stock.

After checking out of the hotel I walked toward the airport. Just east of the hotel a new school was under construction. The building sat on pipes driven fifteen feet into the permafrost. Regular foundations would never work. The weather was better than yesterday, with a ceiling of four hundred feet but with good visibility underneath.

I sat by the float dock waiting for Scott to return from a flight so I could get some av gas for my plane. He had gone after a load of caribou some native had shot, flying in the C-185 on floats for James Gruben's Amaulik Air Service. It took two trips to bring in the six caribou. After the last flight, we loaded two six-gallon plastic containers with av gas and drove to the airport. I put six gallons in each wing tank which gave me over half tanks--a good reserve.

"The weather is below VFR minimum at Inuvik, so you'll have to get special VFR when you get close to the airport," the Tuktoyaktuk air radio operator informed me as I get a weather briefing and filed my flight plan from Tuktoyaktuk to Inuvik. I made a walk around and a visual check of the gas tanks. They were close to the top--money in the bank.

Taxiing to the edge of the strip, I did my pre-take-off check, runup and then departed runway zero nine. I had to put my ship in level flight quickly, as I almost climbed into the low four-hundred-foot ceiling.

Flying at about three hundred feet, small bumps in the landscape appeared as mountain peaks. Some clouds extended to the ground, so I had to make some quick turns. Following my heading of 152 degrees as closely as possible, I followed the line drawn on my map, or tried to. The VOR was tuned to the proper frequency as my backup system.

Twenty- to forty-foot protrusions in the tundra appeared as mountains at this low altitude. Looking like round mounds of earth rising up out of the level ground, they were in fact piles of ice camouflaged by debris and tundra growth.

Low level flying, dodging clouds that went to the ground—that kept my juices flowing. I was flying on the edge. Fantastic, exciting, but also scary, this no doubt would contribute to a few more grey hairs, and less hair overall to worry about.

Ah! The west shoreline of Eskimo Lake was below and to the left of my port wing, a few hundred feet east. Right on course. Great! Over one hundred Beluga whales were trapped in this salt water lake, I was told, and couldn't find their way out!

Lakes, lakes, lakes, one after the other in all directions. Noell Lake showed up where it was supposed to be, just a mile or so off my starboard wing.

"Inuvik radio, this is Cessna seven three four uniform whiskey, fifteen miles north of the airport." Air radio checked my position and told me to contact the tower. "Inuvik tower, seven three four uniform whiskey, requests special VFR clearance," I called, relieved to be close to the airport.

"Cessna, November seven three four uniform whiskey, hold northwest of the airport outside the control zone. We have IFR traffic coming in."

"Inuvik tower, this is Cessna seven three four uniform whiskey, I'm flying northeast of the airport to stay clear of the other traffic." A helicopter was holding northwest, and I couldn't see him.

"Cessna November seven three four uniform whiskey, roger, check your holding northeast of the airport."

After some forty-five minutes of holding over a lake that I got to know well, circling some four hundred feet above it, I finally got the tower's permission to land. The long, fat, friendly runway beckoned me, and we touched down, taxied to the pumps and topped the tanks. Pushing the airplane back from the taxiway, I headed to the terminal, hoping for a hamburger and a strong cup of coffee. I was delighted to be on the ground, but looked forward to the next leg of my journey as the blue sky began to appear and the sun burned away the clouds.

TUKTOYAKTUK

Larry standing by his favorite blue 1978 Buick LaSabre, (they have logged some 300,000 miles together) near the beginning of Liberty Creek trail where he hikes year round. Liberty Lake, Washington is about 100 yards left of the car.

A Loon at Twin Lakes, Washington, there is a Loon nest nearby. (Photo by Youngblood)

Larry and his favorite tree, a beautiful Ponderosa Pine on the Liberty Creek Trail.

Felts Field, Spokane, Washington, where my first flying lesson began, three decades ago. Many special memories began here in my early years.

Cessna N734UW and Larry clearing customs at Penticton, British Columbia, Sept. 1, 1989 at the beginning of their flight to the Arctic, and the eskimo village of Tuktoyaktuk.

The ice goddess with outstretched wings and flowing hair, reflected on the wing, passes beneath our starboard wing, as we fly through the Canadian Rockies.

The mighty Mackenzie River and the village of Wrigley N.W. Territories (where I once flew the float equipped Beache 18 out of,) slips beneath my port wing, Sept. 2, 1989.

Magnificient, countless lakes stretched as far as my eyes can see, as my ship and I fly over the Mackenzie River Delta, over 10,000 square miles of lakes and winding river channels of the Mackenzie River as we approach the Arctic Ocean.

The Esk no village of Tuktoyaktuk slips beneath my port wing and the vast Arctic Ocean glistens in the early evening sun, like million of diamonds, almost too bright to look at.

245

TUKTOYAKTUK

Larry on the road to the village and the double wide mobile, TUK Hotel in the distance, top right side of picture.

The village TUKTOYAKTUK. The highest building in the center, is a log home owned by Eddie Gruben an Eskimo. There are no trees this far north.

"The Lady of Lourdes" built in 1930 as a supply ship for the Catholic mission and operated in the Beaufort Sea for 37 years.

Left, Eddie Gruben, the Eskimo with the huge log home and Larry, Sept. 3, 1989. Eddie had the logs cut by Ft. Liard and floated down the Mackenzie River. Eddie was a trapper and hunter in the early days, but now has millions of dollars in heavy equipment, that is used partly for oil exploration, for the oil companies.

247

TUKTOYAKTUK

The fantastic Mackenzie River, and the Delta slips beneath our wings as we head west toward Old Crow, Yukon Territory.

The friendly Yukon skies welcome us as we leave the N.W. Territories behind. I feel like I'm home once again, as we cross the Richardson Mountains, (the farthest northern portion of the Rocky Mountains that extend to the nearby Arctic Ocean and separate the Yukon and N.W. Territories.

CHAPTER XVIII
OLD CROW

Sitting in the Inuvik airport restaurant with my maps strung across the table, I began preparations for my flight out of the Northwest Territories and into the Yukon to a place called Old Crow.

Across the isle a man and woman stared at me. I seemed to detect a familiarity about them. It was Jim and Pat Logan. Jim had been the airport manager at Watson Lake when I flew out of there; now he was the airport manager at Inuvik. We briefly talked about old times. I mentioned that I had been to Watson Lake two years before and had visited with Jim and Stan.

After a delicious lunch of a hamburger, fries and good coffee, I filed a flight plan for Old Crow.

My heading would be 220 degrees direct to Old Crow. The weather report was good. After clearance, we headed down the runway in the low, thick, almost sea level air. At fifty-five knots, I rolled a little nose up trim, and my ship gently lifted skyward at 2:45 p.m. We headed toward the Richardson Mountains just west on the other side of the fantastic Mackenzie River delta, some ten thousand square miles of winding rivers and countless lakes and wetlands.

As I climbed steadily on my westerly course, the sky continued to clear as the warm sun burned off the remaining low clouds. The delta below was an unbelievable sight, and I marvelled at this special place that God had created.

Twenty miles southwest of Inuvik we crossed the Mackenzie River for the last time, near one of its loops around an island. I radioed my position to the Inuvik air radio on 126.7. This leg of my journey would be completely over wilderness, untouched by humans. Exhilarating! The channel of the Mackenzie River and its many adjoining channels looked like serpents crawling across the delta as I recorded the scene with my camera from the starboard window.

Although it had been a fascinating experience seeing the Arctic Ocean, I looked forward longingly to crossing into my favorite northern place, the Yukon. It was like going home. The only planes I had seen airborne since flying out of Fort Saint John had been a Cessna 180 at Fort Simpson doing touch-and-go landings and an airplane that had landed ahead of me at Inuvik. What a refreshing experience to have uncluttered sky and wonderful, clear, clean air and water.

After flying another twenty-five miles, we left the delta behind and entered the foothills of the Richardson Mountains, which are the far northern end of the Rocky Mountains--the end of the range that has its beginnings far south of the United

States. The highest peak on or near my course was 5,750 feet. The weather was good--scattered to broken over the peaks with the cloud base about six thousand feet.

We crossed into the Yukon shortly after 1500. This country looked much like the area farther south that I had flown for many years, and I felt comfortable and at peace in my sky world. I was doing what I loved, flying and experiencing the Yukon. The country felt warm and friendly. I caught a glimpse of some Dall sheep below on a mountain slope.

About eighteen miles north of where it enters the Porcupine River and forty-five miles northeast of Old Crow, we crossed the Driftwood River. An incredible maze of lakes, like a miniature Mackenzie River delta, began northwest of my course. It was about sixty miles long and thirty-five miles wide. The Old Crow River began in this maze and joined the Porcupine River near Old Crow.

Descending through forty-six hundred feet, Porcupine River was below my port wing; Old Crow was dead ahead.

"Old Crow radio, this is Cessna seven three four uniform whiskey fifteen miles northeast landing Old Crow," I called into my black mike.

"Cessna November seven three four uniform whiskey, wilco check you fifteen miles northeast. Winds favoring runway two-one, strip is in good condition, no reported traffic," a native woman's voice replied.

I had the feeling I was really flying into a unique experience, and my senses came alert, wide awake. Old Crow—a place I had wanted to see for many years—was just ahead. I made a straight in approach to runway two-one. I could see Old Crow clearly as I descended through thirty-five hundred feet. Touchdown was at 1835. The 168-mile trip took one hour and thirty-four minutes.

I noticed a tiedown area a couple of hundred feet west of the runway. I taxied up to a fence, shut down and tied up my ship. As I got out of the plane, a pickup truck drove up, and a native man offered me a ride. I introduced myself, and he said, "My name is Steven Frost. I have a trailer over there on the other side of the fence." He pointed to the west. "It's empty, and you can stay there tonight."

We drove over and walked into a large double-wide trailer made into a bunkhouse. It had been used for housing a construction crew at one time. "There's no electricity, but here is a bucket of good water," Steven said.

"Great! Thanks, this will be just fine," I replied. After two nights at 110 dollars a night, this was a great place to stay.

"Maybe you can take me flying later; I would like to find out where all the caribou are," he suggested.

"Sure, Steven, I'll take you up," I replied.

Steven drove me into the village, which ran about the length of the airstrip, some five thousand feet. It sat on a narrow strip between the airfield on the north side and the Porcupine River on the south side. The buildings were made of logs. Until a generator was installed in 1969, the village had had no electricity. There are only a couple miles of road and a few vehicles, but no roads in or out of the village except the river ice road, when it freezes.

My stomach said it was time to eat, so I strolled over to the only restaurant in the village--Charley's Cafe. I walked into a room with several tables, one with two young long-haired men. In our conversation, I learned that they had spent a few months with a native in the bush helping catch and dry salmon. They were from Switzerland and had had a marvelous summer, taking thirty rolls of film. Now they were waiting for a mail plane from Inuvik and a free ride back there. Later they were going to the United States and back to Switzerland. They were handsome young men, and it wasn't long before a cute young Indian girl came in, smiled and began talking to them. They obviously knew each other well.

"What would you like to eat? Our dinner special is spaghetti," a pretty Indian lady asked.

"Oh, I guess I'll try your special. What's your name?"

"Kathy."

"Hi, Kathy, my name is Larry, and I just flew in from Inuvik." We carried on a conversation of sorts between customers. She brought me a heaping bowl of spaghetti, which is not one of my favorites. But this was delicious. Kathy, who was both cook and waitress, made a hit with a very hungry pilot. After supper I finished off the meal with a piece of Kathy's delicious homebaked cherry pie topped with vanilla ice cream.

After dessert, I said goodbye to Kathy and left. I wanted to explore the rest of the town and find out as much as I could about this unique, isolated village surrounded by wilderness that extended north to the Arctic coast and hundreds of miles to the south, east and west.

A young Indian man about twenty years old caught my eye. "Hi, I'm Larry, just flew in for a visit. What's your name?"

"I'm Allen Benjamin. Would you like to see my racing sled dogs?"

"Sure would!" We walked to some houses about half the distance to the airstrip and I saw the healthiest, prettiest and most perfectly matched sled dogs I've ever seen in the North. Allen proudly posed for a few pictures with his matched team of Siberian Huskies. They had the most incredible blue eyes I had ever seen.

"I bred these dogs myself over the years," Allen said proudly. He traveled outside to Whitehorse and other places where they have sled dog team races during the long winter months. Allen was a handsome, quiet, intelligent and industrious man with a kind spirit. The Old Crow Indians I met were very intelligent, handsome people, self-assured and independent. Most of them were born and spent their entire lives here on the banks of the Porcupine River.

The clarity of the air, the beautiful, deep blue skies, super white fair-weather cumulus clouds, crystal clear waters of the Porcupine River--all were bracing. It was a privilege to see an unspoiled land once again and to remember what it was like to see a pristine wilderness on planet earth. I recorded it by snapping many rolls of film for my picture album.

I followed the gravel road east of the village along a sheltered cove away from the swift waters of the river. A dignified old Indian had pulled the stern of his river boat onto the fine sandy beach. The five-foot-wide, flat-bottomed boat was made of wood. Large dried salmon were stacked in the middle of the boat like cordwood, about one hundred fish.

I briefly introduced myself; the old gentleman said hello, but excused himself to begin carrying the dried fish to a pickup that had backed down off the road. Two other natives, somewhat younger, lent a helping hand.

On the opposite side of this peaceful cove were the yellow fall leaves of the willows and poplar trees lining the bank. The image of the trees and their bright yellow were reflected in the waters a few feet east of the bow. The far bank of the river and clouds above and beyond made a pretty wilderness frame for an unforgettable picture.

The Old Crow Indians were busily getting ready for the approach of the long winter. I watched as riverboats lined up on the gravel shore in front of the village and unloaded freshly killed caribou and moose. A white woman walked up the steep bank away from her riverboat while her Indian husband began hauling up their freshly killed moose. It was backbreaking work, as the bank was high and very steep.

These natives were among the most industrious and independent of any I'd met in the North. They have fine-looking river boats, propelled by large outboard motors. The river is their highway into the wilderness during the summer and the winter. Summer transportation is by boat; winter transportation is by snowmobile and a few dog teams.

Walking west, I noticed a tall, well-built young white man in sweatpants and a white T-shirt who was digging in front of a newly constructed building. I stopped to introduce myself.

"I'm Larry Archibald," he said as we shook hands. "I'm in the RCMP, recently transferred here from Watson Lake."

"Oh, I used to live there and fly for Watson Lake Flying Service. You know Jim and Stan, don't you?"

"Sure do." Larry had wanted a tour of duty to this remote outpost before he settled into a big city and finished his career. "I have a private pilot's license and have thought about getting a plane someday."

The government had recently constructed this new RCMP building. One of the Indians from the village was going through RCMP training and would be stationed here permanently when he had completed that training.

We said goodbye, and I walked toward the community center. Darkness was descending as I reached the cabin of Lazarus Charly. Charly was the oldest man in Old Crow, and I had been told he was the person to talk to about village history. The dignified gentleman who introduced himself as Lazarus Charly was sitting on his front porch with his feet on the middle step. He wore a plaid shirt, jeans, white running shoes, a blue striped jacket and a baseball cap. "I'm Larry. I just flew in today in a small plane and was told to see you. I would like to know the history of this village."

A friendly grin came over his face, "I'm sixty-nine years old," he replied.

"That's the same age as Eddie Gruben, the Eskimo I met in Tuktoyaktuk; do you know him?" I asked.

"Yes, I think I know him," Lazarus answered. "The village settlement began here about 1901 as the natives from downriver began to settle here. I was born October 23, 1920. In the fifties I was on the police dog sled patrol in this area and south to Johnson's Crossing (530 air miles). The Old Crow Indians are from the Thyakchick tribe."

I thanked Charly for the information and said goodbye. Outside the Community Center a colorful man about fifty years old joined me. He was wearing a military jacket and sat down to talk. "My father," he said with pride, "was Danish. He was a good trapper and raised our family of six in the bush. My mother was an Indian from near here. We came out once a year to Fort Yukon in Alaska." It's one hundred air miles down river on the Porcupine River near where the Porcupine enters the Yukon. "There we bought all the provisions we would need for one year. Then dad would pay duty when we came back into Canada. My dad was a great trapper; too bad he's gone now," he said with a deep sadness in his eyes.

Night had fallen when we entered the community hall. The room was brightly lit and blaring with music. I spent about three dollars to buy each of us a can of pop. I walked to a wooden bench and sat between Lazarus Charly and an elderly, heavyset Indian with a cane. In the hall's small kitchen a couple of cute Indian girls dispensed pop and candy to the crowd-mostly young teenagers and a few people in their twenties.

The focal point was a rather lively pool game. Being the only white person there, I thought I would get an occasional stare. However, everyone just carried on as though I weren't there or as though my color were no different.

My eyes and body were telling me to take them to bed. It had been an incredible day that began at Tuktoyaktuk and included a somewhat hairy but exciting flight. I had crawled on the plane's belly from Tuktoyaktuk to Inuvik at fifty to four hundred feet, dodged some clouds that extended to the ground, circled for some time before getting special VFR clearance to land at Inuvik and then had the incredible flight over the mighty Mackenzie delta into the friendly skies of the Yukon and this unique Indian village.

As I walked a quiet road back to the trailer, I was thankful for the opportunity that brought me here, for the new friendships that had begun this day, and for a roof covering my head this night. The trailer was dark and empty. I walked to a bunk and crawled into my friendly blue downfilled bag. I was back in the Yukon and snuggled into the familiar bag as I had done hundreds of nights before when I had flown out in the bush. Sleep came quickly; I woke just once to get a drink of water before the morning light woke me up and I began a new day in this log cabin village.

I rolled up my sleeping bag into a small basketball-sized bundle and dropped it and my toothbrush off at the plane before I headed down the now familiar gravel road. I walked toward Charley's Cafe, enjoying the quiet river sliding by and the snug log cabins in the morning light and fresh clean air. I was ready for Kathy's good cooking.

"Hi, Kathy, how are you?"

"Oh, just fine," she replied as I sat down and drank my first cup of good coffee. "Have you decided what you would like yet?" Kathy asked.

"Yes, I think I'll have the bacon and whole wheat toast."

"Okay."

"Kathy you look like a twin to a lady I used to know." "Oh, was she Indian?"

"No Kathy, she was a Philippino lady," I replied.

Breakfast tasted good, and I began planning my day. The weather wasn't very good at Dawson City, and dark clouds were rolling in from the southwest, so I elected to stick around for awhile.

"That was a fine meal," I said, as I walked out the cafe and looked for Steven Frost. He wanted to fly over the surrounding area to look for caribou. Large herds began their migration from Alaska through here at this time of year, but the main herds hadn't been spotted yet by his people. These are the Porcupine herd and number about 180,000.

I took pictures of three Indian children by an old log cabin. Several children were playing on some parallel bars across the road from the school.

I finally located Steven. We took off late in the morning, headed east and made a lazy climbing turn to the south, then flew west downriver over the Porcupine. Many tracks were on the soft beaches of the river, but we saw no game . We flew over Steven's cabin on the north bank. Behind the cabin was a lake. "Are there any fish in that lake, Steven?"

"Sure, good fishing, lots of pike," he replied.

South of his cabin and on the opposite shore at a bend in the river, Steven pointed out his brother's cabin.

"Say, could you take me and some friends up to your cabin next summer for a fishing trip? Could we hire you to do that in your river boat?" I asked.

"Sure, just contact me ahead of time, and I'll make arrangements," he said.

What a relaxing place to come next summer, I thought to myself, as pictures began forming in my mind of spending a lot more time at this place, soaking in this wilderness of clean skies, clear waters, good fishing and a slower way of life. It would be something to look forward to in the coming winter when the days turned gray and cold.

After a twenty-five-mile flight, we landed back at Old Crow on runway two-one. I taxied to the gas pump and asked the air radio operator to call a man from town. Steven had to leave since he was taking some government people downstream to look at old historic buildings at Old Rampart. They were hoping to restore and save the buildings. I later talked to Ethel, Steven's wife, about their life together.

"We met when we were only kids. I was fifteen, and Steven was sixteen. We got married at eighteen and nineteen and had eleven healthy kids. Most of them are married and have families of their own. Steven was born April 5, 1933, in Old Crow, and he has lived here all his life. We have been married thirty-six years. When we first got married, Old Crow had no electricity, no airport, just one small village. Everything has changed since then. I have been working for different airlines for twenty-two years. Steven has worked for the National Health and Welfare for thirty-five years. He also works for an airline and the Yukon Electric Company. He has worked all his life and couldn't live without work."

It took another phone call, but the fuel man from town finally arrived, and we topped both tanks. I made another check on the weather at Dawson City through the radio operator. It revealed a marked improvement, so I quickly filed a flight plan. We were airborne at 2:12 p.m.

I took away pleasant memories of a unique village snuggled along the high banks of the Porcupine River. I remembered bright yellow leaves and the new friendships I made. Old Crow disappeared beneath my wings as we picked up our new heading of 144 degrees, flying direct to Dawson City.

Clear blue skies and crystal pure waters are mine to enjoy along the banks of the Porcupine River at Old Crow, Yukon, Sept. 5, 1989.

Kathy the excellent cook and waitress at Charlie's Cafe, in Old Crow, Sept. 4, 1989. She looked very much like a lady I knew from the Philippine Islands.

An older gentleman, an Old Crow Indian, unloading Salmon, stacked like cordwood. The river is their highway as no roads come into Old Crow. It was a beautiful fall day, the yellow willows in the background reflected beautifully in the clear river.

Allen Benjamin, with the log cabins of Old Crow in the background. Allen has the finest, most perfectly matched sled dogs I've ever seen.

Allen's beautifully matched Siberian Husky's. Note dark one in background.

Old Crow Indians unloading Salmon from one of their river boats. The bright yellow willows in the background reflected like a mirror in the clear waters of the Porcupine River.

Cessna 185 float plane, at rest on Porcupine River as night descends, Sept. 5, 1989, a few hundred yards west of the village of Old Crow.

Steven Frost, looking for the Porcupine Caribou herd that migrate from Alaska through here, some 180,000 strong, as we fly south and west of Old Crow, on the morning of Sept. 6, 1989.

Leaving pleasant memories of Old Crow behind my ship and I fly south toward Dawson City and a new adventure. This is new country for me.

CHAPTER XIX
YUKON SKIES

Overcast skies were all I could see to the south and west. The base of the clouds was fifty-five hundred to six thousand feet. To the east, however, the skies were more open, and sunshine was visible toward the Dempster Highway. I figured we could head over there if the weather deteriorated on our present heading, and I would follow the road on into Dawson City. It was 243 miles over the wilderness in a direct line, unless I elected to fly east to pick up the graveled highway. Most of the peaks along my course were under six thousand feet, although one close to Dawson was 7,250. I felt good about today as I began another leg of this incredible journey and the thrill of a lifetime. I was back in the skies of the Yukon, just my bird and I, taking in this vast wilderness stretching as far as my eyes could see.

The mountains of the Yukon were orange, red and yellow. They had familiar shapes like those south of Dawson I had flown over for many years. This country, however, was new to me since I had flown no farther north than Dawson City.

After flying by Mount Burgess, I passed over Miner River into the Nahanni Range and felt some light turbulence. Forty-five miles farther south I crossed Ogilvie River directly west of Ogilvie, a point near the Dempster Highway, just a circle on my map.

We began to detect moderate turbulence. An uncomfortable feeling entered my cockpit world, as the wings took unseen blows and began to shake. The airplane rolled as an unseen force grasped and played with it as a toy. About sixty miles north of Dawson City, I passed over a rather open, high meadow and flew up a valley with peaks on either side. The turbulence became severe, and I was tipped almost vertically. I thought once we were going over on our backs. I tried to make a gentle 180-degree turn to sneak away from this invisible force but was hammered again and again. Finally, I safely reversed the course and felt the jolts lessen.

I turned due east some thirty miles and picked up the Dempster Highway just south of Chapman Lake. A few miles from there was a visible airstrip. I told myself to follow the gravel highway to Dawson. However, the weather was dropping rapidly. Rain began coming down in sheets, and low fog appeared. I reduced my airspeed, put down twenty degrees of flap and descended rapidly before I lost sight of the ground. I caught glimpses of many goats on an east hillside of the valley. There was a flat, meadowlike plain ahead, and then the road dropped downward as it dipped over a pass. I was able to slip under the rapidly dropping clouds, sneak over the pass and fly close to the road, maybe four or five hundred feet above the surface at about sixty knots. The slow airspeed gave me the ability to turn in a much

YUKON SKIES

smaller radius and the time to maneuver around the scud that was forming fast. With a road under me, I could land in an emergency. I had done it before and began to pick a few spots as potential emergency landing sites. One I chose was near some buildings with a few vehicles close by. I had forty miles to go to Dawson.

However, a short time later I called Dawson. "Dawson City radio, this is Cessna seven three four uniform whiskey, twenty miles northeast of the airport, estimating the airport in 15 minutes.

"Cessna November seven three four uniform whiskey check you twenty miles northeast of the airport," they replied. The nasty weather continued, but I had about one thousand feet of ceiling, enough to continue. I reached the bottom and entered a valley. There was a T in the road. Using my limited knowledge and my map, I figured I needed to turn right and follow that road to the airport.

"Cessna November seven three four uniform whiskey, what's your position now?" Dawson radio boomed.

"Dawson radio, I'm not sure. I think I'm five miles east of the airport...haven't come in this way before," I replied.

As I banked around a mountain at one thousand feet, the airport appeared just ahead. Not wanting to make a go-round in this scud and rain, I put down full forty degree flaps, slowed up to fifty-five knots and made several S turns on my short final. "Cessna November seven three four uniform whiskey, what's your posi...never mind, I see you, Dawson City radio."

I came down steeply in a series of turns, but it worked. We touched down on the gravel strip near the taxiway leading toward the terminal building about one-fourth of the way down the runway. The flight had taken two and one-tenth hours. Mother Earth felt good! The wings were still attached after the severe turbulence that had buffeted them. I was looking forward to a hot meal, a shower, a chance to settle my system down a bit and to get accustomed to the solid ground.

I taxied over to the fuel pump where a young man topped off the tanks. I parked on the grass, shut her down, secured my ship and rode the ten miles into Dawson with the fuel man in his pickup.

The scenery this time didn't look much different from when Scott and I had made a 1975 flight here in the Aztec with those two geologists. The fuel man dropped me off at what he called an inexpensive hotel. I knocked for a long time before a German lady with a heavy accent came to the door and told me they were closed for the season. I carried my luggage five blocks to the Triple J Hotel. Rates there had just dropped from the ninety dollars per night tourist season, to sixty dollars per night for the off season. The Triple J was across the street from the new twelve-million-dollar, two-story, grade and high school combination built as everything else is, in the style of the Klondike Era of 1898-1900, a building code requirement.

After a good steak dinner in the hotel dining room, I called Scott and told him where I was. I gave a brief rundown on my journey so far. "Dad, be careful. Take

262

care of yourself," he advised me.

"I will, Son. I'll talk to you when I get back home. 'Bye, Son, I love you."

"'Bye, Dad, love you, too."

John McDonogh was the first to pilot a plane into the Yukon. August 8, 1925, Bryde and other members of the MacMillin Expedition from the United States were the first to cross the Arctic Circle by air. The territory was separately constituted in 1898. Since 1978, the Yukon has had a legislative assembly consisting of sixteen elected members. In late 1982, the government gave its consent for the Yukon cabinet to call itself the Executive Council and to officially take over some powers that had, before this time, been reserved by the Federal Commission. In 1986, the Yukon population was 23,504, about seventeen percent Indians. One telephone book of about one hundred pages covered the entire territory.

Of course, a visit to the Klondike wouldn't be complete without a visit to Diamond Tooth Gertie's. Games of chance were under way as I walked through the doors. Several blackjack tables were in use. I sat down at the south side of the large room to wait for the can-can girls. I was not disappointed, as four young girls soon came on stage, high kicking and exposing their long shapely legs, black undergarments and rainbow-colored striped petticoats. Their high-pitched screams of delight caught even this tired pilot's attention. However, I was so tired that I left and went back to the hotel in only thirty minutes. In a flash, I was in a deep sleep.

The next morning I awoke feeling fully rested and had a nourishing breakfast of oatmeal. The hotel clerk gave me permission to stow my gear in a corner of the lobby so that I could check out and do some sightseeing before leaving for Whitehorse.

I headed east toward a favorite place of mine--Robert Service's cabin. An older gentleman, dressed in clothes of an era long past, quoted poems of Robert Service. I visited the stately three-story commissioner's house which was built about 1900. Across the backyard stood the old Northwest Mounted Police jail.

I caught a ferry across the river and hiked downstream along the west bank, where I made a discovery. Sitting high and dry above the high water mark was the decaying remains of an old paddle wheeler called *The Seattle III.* Looking at the bridge, you could tell that at one time she was a magnificent, proud river boat with dignity. However, time had taken its toll, and she was slowly disappearing into the earth. The huge steam boilers could be seen through rotted holes in the side.

The trees were in their finest fall coats of bright yellow in the warm afternoon sun. A raven perched on top of a nearby tree. He looked down and watched knowingly, as the spell of the Yukon descended and touched my life. I watched the wide river waters flowing and knew a peace and contentment not found in the outside world.

For a while I sat on a log where the beach was level and sandy and had a light snack. Then I caught the ferry back to the Dawson City waterfront.

I rented a cabin just north of town on the banks of the Yukon River. That night

YUKON SKIES

I watched a play at the Palace Grand where Scott and I had watched a play in 1975, then returned to my river cabin and slept well.

The next morning I caught a lift to the airport and drove to a Shell station to get a sandwich, but the station, which sat where Black Mike's Hotel used to be, was closed. Scott and I had spent one memorable night at Black Mike's. At the age of one hundred, Black Mike had died about twelve years ago in a pioneer rest home. He evidently earned the name "Black Mike" because of his aversion to soap and the way he lived.

At the Dawson City airport I learned the Whitehorse weather was good, so I filed a flight plan. I took a few more pictures for my album, did a walkaround and climbed aboard my ship. A few shots of prime, a couple cranks on the starter, and she caught. Climbing quickly eastward, I made a turn to the southeast to a heading of 120 degrees and the 262-mile distant destination of Whitehorse.

I was over familiar country now. The last time I had flown this route was with my son and two geologists in 1975. We had flown them to the Whitehorse airport so that they could make a connecting flight to the outside world.

My thoughts went back to yesterday when I had met an attractive, dark-haired woman by Robert Service's cabin. We hiked along the western shores of the mighty Yukon River. A raven perched on a nearby tree looked down knowingly when I kissed her for the first time, and I think he winked as the spell of the Yukon decsended and touched our lifes in a most special way by the remains of an old paddle wheeler called the *Seattle III*.

The highest peak along the course I had drawn on the map was 6,338 feet. Thirty miles south, I crossed Dominion Creek. A short time later, about fifty miles out, I crossed the Steward River, just west of a large, heartshaped island. One hundred miles on course, I crossed the Yukon near the site of abandoned Fort Selkirk. Close by, the Pelly River flows into the Yukon. I flew a few miles west of Carmarks, parallel to the Yukon River.

Braeburn Lake approached, and the Braeburn airstrip at the northwestern end of the lake was visible. The weather was lowering dead ahead, so I headed east just before flying over the airstrip. Weather to the east looked better with a higher ceiling. I followed a valley around a ridge of peaks at just over four thousand feet. By the northern edge of the ridge was the beautiful and well-known lake featured in Robert Service's poem, "The Cremation of Sam McGee." Lake Laberge came into view. It is thirty miles long and has a three-mile-long island near the southern end. The waters were quiet as I flew along the west shore, and the rising hills on the east side combined with the puffy clouds reflected on the mirror-like surface under my port wing. The Whitehorse airport is only fifteen miles from the south end of Lake Laberge.

"Whitehorse radio, this is Cessna seven three four uniform whiskey fifteen miles south, landing the airport."

264

FLIGHT OF THE RED BEAVER

"Cessna November seven three four uniform whiskey, roger. Contact the tower ten miles out on one one eight," came the quick reply.

The tower gave me clearance to make a right hand base on runway three one. I flew on a rather wide 747-type downwind leg, and the tower admonished me to tighten up, which I promptly did. They were probably thinking, "One of those dumb Yankee tourist pilots who's a bit on the sloppy side." Turning base, the runway seemed to go on forever--plenty of room to sit down. Concentrating, I made a better approach and landing. My ship did not embarrass me, but touched down smoothly.

The tower closed my flight plan via the radio and gave me the frequency to use to call the fuel truck. I called, pulled off the taxiway to park my bird, and the fuel truck arrived and promptly topped the tanks.

In the terminal cafeteria I had a good four-dollar meal. A tall young lady was talking about flying to a couple near her and moved in my direction. We introduced ourselves and exchanged cards. Hers had a Super Cub on it and read "Ann-Katrin Lehr, Munchon, West Germany."

She was studying to be a doctor, was a trim six feet tall and loved to fly. She owned a white Super Cub, which she proudly pointed out to me where it stood parked on the tarmac in front of the terminal. She flew alone; this was her second trip to Alaska. Ann was twenty-two years old and on her way to do some volunteer work in Alaska hospitals, perhaps flying to Point Barrow.

"Actually, I'm goofing off away from studies for a while. But to keep my parents happy, I told them I was going to do some volunteer work in the hospitals which would help my studies," she said with a wry smile.

We filed our flight plans. Hers was west toward Alaska; mine was to Telegraph Creek. We took photos of each other standing by our respective birds. I climbed aboard, switched to the tower and heard the tower say to Ann as she lifted off runway 31, "Auf wiedersehen," and her light, giggly laugh as she replied, "Auf wiedersehen." She was a special young lady, someone I was priviledged to meet. She was doing her own thing, flying her bird to the far North and new adventures.

After taking off at 1715, shortly behind Ann, I began a climbing right turn and headed south toward Telegraph Creek. However, I had flown only a few miles when I looked longingly toward the east and the familiar mountains near Watson Lake.

"Whitehorse radio, this is Cessna three four uniform whiskey. Change my flight plan to Watson Lake. I want to see some of the people I knew there." I had been able to converse with the air radio operator, and he knew I used to fly out of Watson Lake.

"Roger, we change your flight plan to Watson Lake, Cessna November seven three four uniform whiskey," came the quick reply.

"Thank you and good day, Sir. Seven three four uniform whiskey," I acknowledged.

YUKON SKIES

Turning east to a heading of 071 degrees, I began flying over the country that Scott and I last flew in the Aztec. I had let Scott fly part of the way back on that trip. That was my last Yukon summer as a bush pilot out of Watson Lake. Many flights had been made on this route as I flew critically injured patients from Watson Lake to the hospital at Whitehorse. One trip had been with a body in a bag and the friend of the deceased in the back of the plane. On that occasion it was not an ambulance, but a hearse that met us at the airport. So many memories!

Once Jim Thibaudeau and I had flown to Whitehorse at about three in the morning. Jim had two patients and a nurse in his float-equipped Beech 18; I had one patient and a nurse in the float-equipped Beaver. After we dropped off the patients, we enjoyed breakfast in town. I departed first, and Jim left a little after. Close to where I was now flying, he caught up to me, pulled alongside, wagged his wings and left me behind.

Fifty miles out, I crossed the Teslin River a few miles from the north end of Teslin Lake near Johnson's crossing, and soon the Nisutlin River slipped under my wings. Flying over the Cassiar Mountains, twenty minutes later, the familiar shape of Wolf Lake passed under my port wing. The higher mountain peaks along my course were from six thousand to sixty-seven hundred feet high.

Ice Lakes lay just ahead and a little to the right of my nose. I used to fly hunting parties in here. There was more green in this country, as the fall season is later here than at Dawson and Old Crow. The shapes and the feel of the mountains were both familiar and friendly this day.

Just a few miles after passing Ice Lake, I picked up the Meister River, passing over Caribou Lake, a lake I landed on and operated from almost two decades ago. About ten miles farther north, under my port wing, I took pictures of well-known Meister Lake. It's narrow, bow-shaped and five miles long. Fifteen miles farther east I crossed the Rancheria River where we left the Cassiar Mountains and came into the Liard Valley, almost thirty-five miles across at this point.

Ahead to the north I could see the gap that the Frances River flows through on its journey to meet the Liard River. North of that gap is Frances Lake, where I came close to losing the Beaver and perhaps my life. That night I had landed on a road, almost out of gas, in terrible weather. However, most of my flights were good, happy ones to that lake and the country beyond.

"Watson Lake radio, Cessna seven three four uniform whiskey, ten miles east, landing the airport in five minutes," my happy voice called into the mike.

Cessna November seven three four uniform whiskey. Winds favoring runway two six." Then he gave me the altimeter setting. .

"Runway two six, seven three four uniform whiskey", I acknowledged. I saw the familiar shape of the approaching lake as it took its form before my eyes. My ship touched safely down in the still, smooth air at 1853. I turned off runway two six, closed my flight plan by radio and taxied to some tiedowns hear Watson Lake

Flying Service's hangar. There were no tiedown ropes, so I dug out pieces of rope from under all my baggage in the aft end of the cabin.

At the terminal building I arranged a ride with a man in a tanker truck, who was unloading aviation fuel into an underground tank. We drove to town, where I unloaded by the old log Watson Lake Hotel. It was booked solid, as Archie Lang, one of the owners, found out when he asked the staff at the desk to get me a room. I moved on to find a motel at the southern end of town. Then after a shower and a change of clothes, I headed back to town and the Watson Lake Hotel.

Darkness had fallen as I started my half-mile walk. The stark black, clear night and bright stars glowing across the heavens made me look up in wonder. There was a motion that made me stop and look skyward toward the north. The entire northern sky lit up with a magic curtain that began waving in brilliant multicolored lights. The Northern Lights put on quite a show for this ol' bush pilot. It was a welcome back to the North--a gift! I stood staring in awe, thankful to be here at this moment, witnessing one of the mysteries of the North. It was good to be back!

The Watson Lake Hotel was lit up and shone brightly--a familiar place from times past. This was a place of parties, a meeting place where you picked up clients, often at the bar, and left for flights into the bush. It was a gathering place where we pilots got together often with the outfitters and told tall tales, especially when the phenomenon called a Whiskey Front (bad weather) moved in, and we told tall tales of our exploits in the northern skies! Poose Capays (drinks made with seven liquors) were lit up and delivered to the tables. Those were good times when we were in our youthful prime and when being a bush pilot was the greatest and most exciting occupation in the world. People looked up to bush pilots. You had an important job, and people depended upon you. Sometimes you helped save lives, but mostly you were the lifeline, the link between hunting and mining camps, delivering food and mail and occasionally a bottle of strong spirits. It was a great time, the best of times!

Walking through the outside door into the bar, I sat alone near the door. Archie Lang's wife Karen invited me to their table. With the Langs, on the opposite side of the table, sat a gentleman I did not know. The group bought two rounds of wine for me before they would allow me to buy a round.

To my right was tall Sandy Grunow, a lady I've always liked and respected. Her quick warm smile, warm spirit and love for the North were refreshing. Archie was his usual quick-witted and funny self as he told stories about human nature. After Archie and Karen left, I finished my third glass of wine (I usually don't drink any more) and crashed back at my motel.

The following morning was Friday, September 8. On this bright, clear day I caught up on my washing at the Signpost Laundry and enjoyed a well-rested feeling and the knowledge that I was going to be continuing my flight across the northern skies.

I took a cab to the Watson Lake Flying Service float base. Jim Close was there alone, listening to the radio, taking care of business.

"How's business, Jim?"

"Well, it's really strange. One day we're really busy, and the next day it's very slow." Jim's two sons Bob and Frank were grown now. Scott used to play with them during those summer months when they were all young boys.

I said goodbye and walked out to the float dock, where I had a picture taken with my right hand on the left strut of my favorite airplane of all time—the Red Beaver CF-IBP. She's still flying, with about twenty thousand hours total time. We shared a lot of memories together, some close calls, but mostly enjoyable flights over the spectacular wilderness of this far north country. The Red Beaver never let me down, and it got me out of some dangerous situations when I thought for sure I was a goner!

I left the faithful ship and rode in the cab to the airport. Jimmy had told me that Stan would be there shortly to fuel another plane. I would be able to fuel up then. At the airport I untied my craft and pushed it up behind a Cessna 185 on amphib floats. With the wheels down, this float plane sits quite high off the ground.

Stan arrived later and topped off the 185. We pushed my C-172 to the pumps, and a ladder on wheels to the wing. I topped my tanks while I had a nice conversation wtih Stan. He was his usual happy self. He never seemed to let much get him down. Tanks full, I said goodbye to Stan and taxied away from the pumps, did my runup and pulled up just short of runway two six.

"Watson Lake radio, this is Cessna seven three four uniform whiskey, ready to depart runway two six. Do you have any reported traffic?" I asked.

"No reported traffic, wind calm," and he gave me the altimeter setting

Looking in both directions, I checked for any incoming traffic before pulling onto the center of the runway. The sky looked clear. Full power, and we began moving down the runway, slowly at first but picking up speed quickly. Slight back pressure at fifty-five knots brought up the nose, and then the main gear skyward. I left the runway at 1455, on course to Dease Lake where I would top the tanks. I left the Yukon behind after flying ten miles south, where I entered British Columbia.

Dawson City, once the capital of the Yukon nestled on the banks of the mighty Yukon River. I once flew the Beaver here, and tied up along the banks of the Yukon River by the town.

Robert Services cabin, a famous turn of the century poet, that brought the rip roaring, Klondike Gold Rush alive, in his many poems. I met the attractive dark haired woman about 100 feet to the right of the cabin.

269

Larry standing by the paddle wheeler Keno, along the banks of the Yukon River, Sept. 7, 1989.

Crossing the ferry on the Yukon River from the east, Dawson City side to the west bank. It was a beautiful exciting day and the magic of the Yukon was in the air. Photo by the dark haired woman.

I'm sitting on a log by the decaying wreckage of an old paddle wheeler named the Seattle III on the banks of the Yukon River, where I spent the day with the dark haired woman I met by Robert Services cabin. I kissed her here, the first time, while a raven on a nearby tree top looked down, and winked I think, as the magic of the Yukon descended and touched our lives in a very special way!

The Gaslight Follies where Scott and I watched a play when we stayed overnight there in the summer of 1975, when we flew in with the Aztec. I watched a play while I was here, it was good to be back.

The presence of the past can be felt as you walk by these old buildings from a time long since past, when Dawson City was a rip roaring Klondike gold town that numbered over 25,000; where saloons and gambling casino's kept busy and where the motto was, "Never refuse a man a drink or kick a dog."

Getting ready to climb aboard my ship and head south to Whitehouse, the capital of the Yukon. The strip here at the Dawson City airport is gravel, but in good condition.

My ship and I leave the Dawson City airport behind, on course to Whitehouse. Photo by the dark haired woman.

Following the Yukon River toward Whitehouse. It was a beautiful day and adventure was in the air.

While flying over Lake Labarge, where the cremation of Sam McGee took place in one of Robert Services most famous poems.

My new friend, 6-foot 22 year old Ann Katrin Lehr, from Munchon, West Germany with her Super Cub, on course to Alaska. She was a breath of fresh air. I like people that follow their dreams and take risks!

Between Whitehouse and Watson Lake on a easterly course. The lake in the distance is Wolf Lake.

Beneath our port wing is Meister Lake, in the heart of the Cassiar Mountains, west of Watson Lake.

The Laird River is beneath our wing. Just beyond the gap off our wing tip is Frances Lake, where I often flew, many years ago, and once in bad weather nearly bought the farm, over the east area of the lake.

Approaching Watson Lake airport. Off our nose is the island, I used to canoe to. Watson Lake Flying Service is left of the island.

Flying downwind to runway 26, a familiar friendly feeling, as I prepare to land.

The Watson Lake Hotel where not a few tales were told, about our exploits in the northern skies, as we drank another Poose Capay.

Tall Sandy Grunow with a friend inside the Watson Lake Hotel. I often flew Sandy out in the Red Beaver to Stewart Lake, in the Bush north of Watson Lake.

Before leaving Watson Lake I stopped to see my old friend the Red Beaver. She was a welcome sight after all these years, and she's still my favorite airplane of all times.

CHAPTER XX
SPIRITS OF TELEGRAPH CREEK

About forty miles out a few miles northeast of the Horseranch Range I picked up the Dease River. This was again familiar country and brought back a well of good memories. McDame, Meek Lake, Eagle River passed, and soon the waters of Dease Lake appeared. I flew around the southern end where Dal's summer home used to be. The lake was fairly calm, and I flew several miles west to land at the Dease Lake Airport after a flight of 1.1 hours.

It was quiet at the airport; only natural sounds could be heard. I called a fuel number, and a lady arrived; however, she did not have the correct fuel key so we had to return to her office. I caught a ride with her to Dease Lake. The waters of this pristine lake were so clear that people still used it for drinking water, she said. Dalziel's old summer log home was still standing on the sandy south shoreline, but it was badly deteriorated and boarded up. There were some new log cabins along the southern end--at least they were new since I had last been here in 1975.

We drove back to the airport and topped the tanks, and I was soon airborne for Telegraph Creek, fifty-five miles southwest. I flew over the Tanzilla River most of the way. The road from Dease Lake to Telegraph Creek parallels this river on the west side. The Grand Canyon of the Stikine begins just east of my course, thirty miles below Dease Lake. It is a fantastic, deep, wild-looking canyon I've flown over and appreciated often. I marvelled again at the churning wild waters of the Stikine as it shot through this narrow canyon on its turbulent journey to the sea.

After a flight over some rugged but familiar country, the new airstrip appeared. It bordered the road on the south side and lay between the road and the river a few miles east of Telegraph Creek. There was no noticeable wind as I circled the gravel strip. I elected to land toward the west. I made a short field landing and touched down just past the end of the strip a few feet beyond the bushes bordering the end of the runway. The flight from Dease was thirty minutes. Another airplane was parked nearby—looked like a Cessna 206. Again, as at Dease Lake, the blanket of silence surrounded me.

Walking toward town after securing my plane, I felt good, as if I were in a world where time slowed down, like when I was a boy. The gravel road led me by a helicopter office and then by a log cabin that said "Tahltan Outfitters." Several smaller log cabins were strung out to the west.

I talked to a young man outside the cabin who said this was Fletcher Day's home. "Oh, I know him; I used to fly for Watson Lake Flying Service and flew Fletcher out in the bush for several years."

The young man said, "Fletcher is coming in by seaplane this evening from his hunting camp. One of his guides, Charley Smith, drowned at Victoria Lake, and his funeral is tomorrow at the Tahltan Indian Village."

"Tell Fletcher I'll try to see him while I'm here. Could you tell me the best way to get to town?" I asked.

"Oh, you can take a shortcut on the Indian trail that starts off the road over there. It's a good trail," he assured me.

The trail began under a bluff. On my left towards the river it had sloughed and was almost vertical. One slip, and I figured if I wasn't killed, I'd be so banged up that I would wish I had been. What seemed like forever finally ended at the edge of town, down the steep mountainside close to the river. I wondered to myself if this Indian was trying to get rid of this white man, or just testing his surefootedness. Guess I'll never know.

At about 6:30 in the evening I arrived at the Riversong Cafe. This had been the original Hudson Bay Store when I flew into Telegraph Creek in the late sixties and seventies. A private party owned the other store about a block or so upriver. He's the one I dealt with, and he would drive up to Sawmill Lake on top of the hill when I landed the Beaver and give me a lift to town, bringing me fuel if I needed it. I think he did most of the business at that time in Telegraph Creek.

I obtained a room at the Riversong Cafe and Hotel in one of the adjoining old Hudson Bay buildings. The shower and toilet were in the main building that was also the store and cafe. The room was clean and had cold running water, a stove, refrigerator, couch and bed, all for a very reasonable thirty-five dollars. At least it was reasonable compared to some other places in the North that I had experienced on this trip!

The sun was getting low, and I wanted to get as many pictures as I could before it set. I did not know how long I would be here or what the weather tomorrow would bring. With my camera in hand, I began the steep journey up the road to the Tahltan Indian village. It was near the top of the hill, overlooking the townsite from on high. I knew the graveyard was just behind the village on a knoll, with a wonderful view of the Stikine River and Telegraph Creek below.

A teenaged boy and friend gave me a short lift in an old car. I asked him, "Do you know a retired Tahltan Indian that spends his winters in Seattle?"

"Sure, that's my uncle," he said.

My son Scott works out in Seattle with this retired gentleman, lifting weights. Scott said, "He's in excellent condition—tall, strong, full head of hair and looks much younger than his years. He comes back to Telegraph Creek every summer and hunts here in the fall."

The car barely ran and belched blue smoke up through the floorboard. I walked most of the way; the exercise was good for me since I had been sitting in my flying machine on most of this trip.

As I walked through the Indian village, I was joined by a village dog who became my companion to the graveyard. When Scott and I had flown in here in 1975, there had been spirit houses over most of the graves. I was disappointed to find only one left and was glad to record it on film before it disappeared into the earth. It was constructed of wood and had an iron fence around it. Some of the graves were from the middle of the last century.

After walking around the old part of the cemetery, I sat down with my new companion and took in the view. Downstream toward the west the mighty Stikine River contrasted with the doll-sized houses of Telegraph Creek. I offered two green grapes to my brown furry friend, who spit them on the ground after his first taste. When nothing more was forthcoming, he gingerly picked them up again. Once he decided that they weren't so bad, it took him only fifteen minutes to finish off my sack of grapes.

The sun was setting over the western peaks. I quietly felt the presence of the sacred last resting place of these Tahltan Indians. It was a quiet place, perched on a point of land with an eagle's view of the winding Stikine River below. Its steep hillsides joined the tree-covered banks before disappearing into the swift waters beyond. The scene was framed by rising mountains far to the west and beyond the last bend in the river.

In the Indian village my hiking companion was called home by a native man, and we parted company. He had been a good companion, someone I instantly felt comfortable with.

My journal: *"Friday, September 8, 2230: Think I will leave early and try to get home tomorrow. I think--am tired--time to go home--have accomplished what I set out to do and a little more--It's been a good trip--weather is great here--don't think I would want to be a pilot full time again--no way--even a week of flying is really getting tiring--*

"Saturday, September 9: My sleep was restless--my eyes opened and I looked out the window above my bed. An owl was there in the air--not flapping in the air--but looking at me--perhaps giving me a message, a warning--go back to sleep, delay my departure. The owl floated sideways and disappeared. I was rubbing my eyes. Was it a dream? But I was awake!

"I slept in and felt fit, relaxed. Did the right thing!

"Sitting on a bench in front of the old Hudson Bay store--warm sun feels good. The muddy waters of the Stikine, slipping by quietly, quickly as the current is quite strong--distant chatter of a squirrel--a child's voice, distinctly. A few noises of man--a car starting up--black flies and a few mosquitoes; fall is later here than Dawson City.

"Store doesn't open until 11:00--need film--trying to decide if I should fly to Atlin or straight to Smithers and home."

SPIRITS OF TELEGRAPH CREEK

I wondered about the *Spirit Owl* that had looked so intently into my eyes. It wasn't a threatening stare, but a warning look of concern. I stood up and interrupted my river watching and reflections. An old building upriver that said "River Excursions" sat next to a boat, the "Trina Anne." I introduced myself to the proprietor of the place, Frances Gleason.

"Could you tell me the name of the man who used to run the private store here? I used to fly in here in the sixties and seventies."

"Sure, this building of mine is Doug Blanchard's old store. I bought it from Doug, and he lives downriver now, kind of retired but works some. This is the oldest building in Telegraph Creek. It used to belong to Steel Hyland, and before that it belonged to Steel's father. Doug bought it from Steel Hyland, then later bought the Hudson Bay Store. I was born by that church," and he pointed to a stately looking Anglican Church that looked like the ones in Tuktoyaktuk and Old Crow.

"Well, thanks for the information; I'm going to see Fletcher Day--I used to fly for him when I flew out of Watson Lake."

After getting some film at the Old Hudson Bay Store, I began my walk. Frances picked me up a few minutes later and gave me a lift to Fletcher Day's log home, which was surrounded by cars. The crowd was preparing for the funeral of Fletcher's guide, Charley Smith.

I saw a familiar face and asked, "Are you Fletcher Day?"

"No, he's my dad. I'll get him." Fletcher's son was the image of his father, a handsome, tall, well-built man. I saw Fletcher come out the door, and his warm, friendly grin spread from ear to ear.

"Hi, Larry, how are you?" as we shook hands.

"It's been a long time, Fletcher. It's good to see you."

Fletcher told me the story of Charley's death. "We were camped at Victoria Lake, and I asked Charley to go check on the horses, like he had been doing for several days. Charley took the boat and motor, even though I cautioned him against it. The water was rough and the wind strong. All the weight was in the back of the boat, and the front end was high. I think a gust of wind must have caught the front end and flipped it over. We were fortunate to have found his body on a ledge in shallow water. Just past that ledge there is a dropoff into deep water."

Fletcher had to excuse himself to attend the funeral. This tall, intelligent, warmhearted Tahltan had always been a pleasure to fly for.

Walking east down the gravel road toward the airstrip, I felt at peace with my surroundings. The warm, friendly sun and the complete stillness brought back pleasant memories of times when I had flown into Telegraph Creek, sometimes landing on the Stikine River but more often on nearby Sawmill Lake, usually in a float-equipped Beaver. This town and its people have many stories to tell.

Leaving the spirits of Telegraph Creek behind, my craft and I soared above the glacier that covered nearby Ediziza Peak, almost ten thousand feet high, and we made passing acquaintances of unnamed ice fields beneath rugged peaks.

Pleasant memories of the Yukon and a planned return flight to Old Crow next summer filled my mind as we flew toward another world that lay beneath distant southern skies.

B.C. - YUKON AIR SERVICE LTD.
CHARTER FLYING
SERVING THE YUKON AND NORTHERN B.C.

WATSON LAKE. YUKON

September 30, 1969

TO WHOM IT MAY CONCERN:

    Accept this as a letter of recommendation for Larry Whitesitt.

    During his employment with us Mr. Whitesitt has flown Cessna 180 and Beaver aircraft and I have found him to be very competent on type as well as very accomadating with the customer.

    Mr. Whitesitts seasonal term with us is finished therefore he is leaving our employ with our regards.

    I remain,

        Yours very truly,

        B.C. YUKON AIR SERVICE LTD.

        S.H. Baird
        President

SHB/rb

Watson Lake Flying Services Ltd.

CHARTER FLYING
PHONE 536-2231
TELEX 0498-8511

BOX 7
WATSON LAKE, YUKON

Sept 17/75

TO WHOM IT MAY CONCERN

This letter is to certify that Larry Whitesitt has been employed
by this Company for the past five years and during his employment
here he flew the following Aircraft.

Beech 18S on floats
DeHavilland Beaver on Floats, Wheels & Wheel/Skis
Cessna 185
Piper Azted
Piper Super Cub.

We found Larry to be very competent on all the above mentioned
aircraft and Larry enjoys an excellent customer relationship
and we found him to be a true asset to this Companys overall
operation.

Signed;

Jim Close
Pres.
Watson Lake Flyin Services.

DEPARTMENT OF RECREATION AND CONSERVATION
FISH AND WILDLIFE BRANCH

YOUR FILE No

OUR FILE No

P.O. Box 158
Smithers, B.C.

To Whom It May Concern: January 12, 1969

     This will confirm that Mr. L. L. Whitesitt has been known
to me for a number of years and that I have been a passenger in aircraft
flown by him on numerous occasions while conducting my work for the
a/m Fish and Wildlife Branch. Other members of our staff here have also
flown with Mr. Whitesitt and we have all found him to be an excellent
pilot and a good companion.

L. J. Cox,
Snr. Conservation Officer.

Flying over the clear waters of Dease Lake. It was a beautiful day and exciting as I flew the friendly skies of Northern British Columbia once again.

George Dalziel's old log home, a hundred feet or so from the south end of Dease Lake. I used to stop here when it was alive, now it seems tired, like the old buildings at Dawson City, and is slowly sinking into the earth.

South end of Dease Lake in front of Dal's old home. The water is crystal clear and cold.

Telegraph Creek airstrip, east of Telegraph Creek a mile or so. It's a fairly new strip and it's the first time I used it.

The Stikine River, close to the Old Hudson Bay Store. In the old days they used to run boats from Wrangle, Alaska to Telegraph Creek.

The Old Hudson Bay Store, I slept in the building on the other side of the store, that once was the storeroom. When I flew in here in the 60's and 70's it was still owned and run by the Hudson Bay Company.

My friend the Tahltan Indian dog, who was my companion on the walk to the Indian graveyard. My friend ate my sack full of grapes.

The last old spirit house at the Tahltan Indian cemetary. When my son Scott and I came here in the early 70's there were spirit houses over most of the graves.

Looking down at Telegraph Creek from the Tahltan Indian cemetary, east of town. Note the house in the distance that is tilted toward the river.

Land marks of Telegraph Creek. The Tahltan graveyard towers above the town in the distance. In the foreground is the Anglican Church, a log cabin, Steel Hylands old store, (the oldest building in Telegraph Creek), and the RCMP building.

From left, Frances Gleason, Mrs. Day and Fletcher Day (the outfitter I once flew for) standing in front of Fletcher's home a mile or so east of Telegraph Creek.

My ship and I at 9500' ASL approaching Edizza Peak, south of Telegraph Creek, on a southerly heading. The day was sunny and bright, with glaciers glimmering in the distance.

"Leaving the Spirits of Telegraph Creek behind, my craft and I soared above the Glacier that covered Edizza Peak, almost ten thousand feet high."

"We made passing acquaintances of unnamed ice fields beneath rugged peaks."